ISLAMIC SPIRITUALITY

ISLAMIC SPIRITUALITY

Dr Y A Sabba

MD PUBLICATIONS PVT LTD
NEW DELHI
www.mdppl.com

Published by :

MD Publications Pvt Ltd
"MD House", 11, Darya Ganj,
New Delhi - 110 002
Phone : +91-11-41563325 (Customer Service)
+91-11-41562846 (Editorial)
E-mail (orders): order@mdppl.com
Website: www.mdppl.com

ISBN: 978-81-7533-237-9

Published and Printed by Mr. Pranav Gupta on behalf of **MD Publications Pvt Ltd** at Mohit Enterprises, New Delhi.

PREFACE

It is not possible to discuss Islamic spirituality without dealing with that spiritual reality which is called *futuwwah* in Arabic and *jawân- mardî* in Persian and which can be rendered into English as "mystical youth" or spiritual chivalry. Both the Arabic and Persian terms (*fatâ* in Arabic and *jawân* in Persian) refer to youth or the Latin *juvenis* but have acquired a meaning related much more to the youth associated with the eternal spring of the life of the Spirit than to physical young age. To possess *futuwwah* or *jawânmardî* is to be embellished with the characteristics of courage and generosity associated with a chivalry transposed onto the highest level of meaning from the realm of external action to that of the spiritual life, without, however, excluding the world of external action.

Islamic spirituality is firmly wholistic as illustrated by the Field Model. Islamic spirituality is active in all four aspects of human experience. It thus avoids extremes of interiority and does not portray the physical or the social as being *contra* the spiritual.

Islamic spirituality is based upon the assumption that what appears to us as mystery revealed itself as being God. The Qur'an is this revelation. The Qur'an instructs us in the foundational importance of *awareness of* God and the proper *response to* God. The *sunnah* (lifestyle or practice) of Muhammad expresses and exemplifies this Qur'anic *awareness of*, and *response to* God within actual, historical, phenomenal reality. This is the heart and foundation and *raison d'être* of Islamic spirituality. Muhammad is considered to be a "walking Qur'an".

Islamic spirituality fosters God-consciousness, called *taqwa,* in and through all daily activities in addition to activities we usually identify as "spiritual" such as fasting and prayer. It shuns any extremes.

Islamic spirituality does not gauge its development and growth upon subjective experience, but on the degree to which one imitates the *sunnah.* Evil is that which is *contra* Qur'an and *sunnah-* it has nothing to do with subjective experiences of pleasure or pain, laughter or tears, nor does it have to do with social experiences such as riches or poverty. All of these social and subjective states are somewhat equivalent in Islam. They all originate by the will of God for the purpose of testing the Muslim's use of freedom. The Muslim submits to the will of God with patience. The word "Islam" means "submission to the will of God". It is thus not even a "religion" as we usually think of the term. It is more of an existential way-of-being.

Islamic spirituality encourages science and scholarship in that the Qur'an repeatedly exhorts humanity to observe the signs of God in creation, in history, and in one's self. It also encourages social activism. That is, *jihad-* the struggle of good against evil.

I am very grateful to Mr. Pranav Gupta, Director of MD Publications Pvt Ltd, New Delhi, for his kind cooperation and support for this book.

Dr Y A Sabba

Contents

1

Islamic Spirituality

An Introduction

The World Trade Centre, yesterday's symbol of global finance, has today become a monument to the failure of global Islam to control those who believe that the West can be bullied into changing its wayward ways towards the East. There is no real excuse to hand. It is simply not enough to clamour, as many have done, about 'chickens are coming home to roost', and to protest that Washington's acquiescence in Israeli policies of ethnic cleansing is the inevitable generator of such hate. It is of course true - as Shabbir Akhtar has noted - that powerlessness can corrupt as insistently as does power. But to comprehend is not to sanction or even to empathize. To take innocent life to achieve a goal is the hallmark of the most extreme secular utilitarian ethic, and stands at the opposite pole of the absolute moral constraints required by religion. There was a time, not long ago, when the 'ultras' were few, forming only a tiny wart on the face of the worldwide attempt to revivify Islam.

Sadly, we can no longer enjoy the luxury of ignoring them. The extreme has broadened, and the middle ground, giving way, is everywhere dislocated and confused. And this enfeeblement of the middle ground, was what was enjoined by the Prophetic example, is in turn accelerated by the opprobrium which the extremists bring not simply upon themselves, but upon committed Muslims everywhere. For here, as elsewhere, the preferences of the media work firmly against us. David Koresh could broadcast his fringe Biblical message from Ranch Apocalypse without the image of Christianity, or even its Adventist wing, being in any way besmirched. But when a fringe Islamic group bombs Swedish tourists in Cairo, the muck is instantly spread over 'militant Muslims' everywhere. If these things go on, the Islamic movement will cease to form an authentic summons to cultural and spiritual renewal, and will exist as little more than a splintered array of maniacal factions.

The prospect of such an appalling and humiliating end to the story of a religion which once surpassed all others in its capacity for tolerating debate and dissent is now a real possibility. The entire experience of Islamic work over the past fifteen years has been one of increasing radicalization, driven by the perceived failure of the traditional Islamic institutions and the older Muslim movements to lead the Muslim peoples into the worthy but so far chimerical promised land of the 'Islamic State.' If this final catastrophe is to be averted, the mainstream will have to regain the initiative. But for this to happen, it must begin by confessing that the radical critique of moderation has its force. The Islamic movement has so far been remarkably unsuccessful. We must ask ourselves how it is that a man like Nasser, a butcher, a failed soldier and a cynical demagogue, could have taken over a country as pivotal as Egypt, despite the vacuity of his beliefs, while the Muslim Brotherhood, with its pullulating millions of members, should have failed, and failed continuously, for six decades.

The radical accusation of a failure in methodology cannot fail to strike home in such a context of dismal and prolonged inadequacy. It is in this context - startlingly, perhaps, but inescapably - that we must present our case for the revival of the spiritual life within Islam. If it is ever to prosper, the 'Islamic revival' must be made to see that it is in crisis, and that its mental resources are proving insufficient to meet contemporary needs. The response to this must be grounded in an act of collective muhasaba, of self-examination, in terms that transcend the ideologised neo-Islam of the revivalists, and return to a more classical and indigenously Muslim dialectic. Symptomatic of the disease is the fact that among all the explanations offered for the crisis of the Islamic movement, the only authentically Muslim interpretation, namely, that God should not be lending it His support, is conspicuously absent. It is true that we frequently hear the Quranic verse which states that "God does not change the condition of a people until they change the condition of their own selves." But never, it seems, is this principle intelligently grasped. It is assumed that the sacred text is here doing no more than to enjoin individual moral reform as a precondition for collective societal success.

Nothing could be more hazardous, however, than to measure such moral reform against the yardstick of the fiqh without giving concern to whether the virtues gained have been acquired through conformity (a relatively simple task), or proceed spontaneously from a genuine realignment of the soul. The verse is speaking of a spiritual change, specifically, a transformation of the nafs of the believers - not a moral one. And as the Blessed Prophet never tired of reminding us, there is little value in outward conformity to the rules unless this conformity is mirrored and engendered by an authentically righteous disposition of the heart. 'No-one shall enter the Garden by his works,' as he expressed it. Mean-while, the profoundly judgemental and works - oriented tenor of modern revivalist Islam (we must shun the problematic buzz-word 'fundamentalism'), fixated on visible manifestations of morality, has failed to address the underlying question of what revelation is for. For it is theological nonsense to suggest that God's final concern is with our ability to conform to a complex set of rules. His concern is rather that we should be restored, through our labours and His grace, to that state of purity and equilibrium with which we were born. The rules are a vital means to that end, and are facilitated by it. But they do not take its place.

The Holy Qur'an Sura 13:11.

To make this point, the Holy Quran deploys a striking metaphor. In *Sura Ibrahim*, verses 24 to 26, we read:

> Have you not seen how God coineth a likeness: a goodly word likes a goodly tree, the root whereof is set firm, its branch in the heaven? It bringeth forth its fruit at every time, by the leave of its Lord. Thus doth God coin likenesses for men that perhaps they may reflect? And the likeness of an evil word is that of an evil tree that hath been torn up by the root from upon the earth, possessed of no stability.

According to the scholars of tafsir (exegesis), the reference here is to the 'words' (kalima) of faith and unfaith. The former is illustrated as a natural growth, whose florescence of moral and intellectual achievement is nourished by firm roots, which in turn denote the basis of faith: the quality of the proofs one has received, and the certainty and sound awareness of God which alone signify that one is firmly grounded in the reality of existence. The fruits thus yielded - the palpable benefits of the religious life - are permanent ('at every time'), and are not man's own accomplishment, for they only come 'by the leave of its Lord'. Thus is the sound life of faith. The contrast is then drawn with the only alternative: kufr, which is not grounded in reality but in illusion, and is hence 'possessed of no stability'.

This passage, reminiscent of some of the binary categorisations of human types presented early on in *Surat al-Baqara,* precisely encapsulates the relationship between faith and works, the hierarchy which exists between them, and the sustainable balance between nourishment and fructition, between taking and giving, which true faith must maintain. It is against this criterion that we must judge the quality of contemporary 'activist' styles of faith. Is the young 'ultra', with his intense rage which can sometimes render him liable to nervous disorders, and his fixation on a relatively narrow range of issues and concerns, really firmly rooted, and fruitful, in the sense described by this Quranic image?

Let me point to the answer with an example drawn from my own experience. I used to know, quite well, a leader of the radical 'Islamic' group, the Jama'at Islamiya, at the Egyptian university of Assiut. His name was Hamdi. He grew a luxuriant beard, was constantly scrubbing his teeth with his miswak, and spent his time preaching hatred of the Coptic Christians, a number of whom were actually attacked and beaten up as a result of his khutbas. He had hundreds of followers; in fact, Assiut today remains a citadel of hardline, Wahhabi-style activism. The moral of the story is that some five years after this acquaintance, providence again brought me face to face with Shaikh Hamdi. This time, chancing to see him on a Cairo street, I almost failed to recognise him. The beard was gone. He was in trousers and a sweater. More astonishing still was that he was walking with a young Western girl who turned out to be an Australian, whom, as he sheepishly explained to me, he was intending to marry. What was extraordinary was that his experiences in Islamic activism had made no impression on him - he was once again the same distracted, ordinary Egyptian youth he had been before his conversion to 'radical Islam'.

This phenomenon, which we might label '*salafi burnout*', is a recognised feature of many modern Muslim cultures. An initial enthusiasm, gained usually in one's early twenties, loses steam some seven to ten years later. Prison and torture - the frequent lot of the Islamic radical - may serve to prolong commitment, but ultimately, a majority of these neo-Muslims relapse, seemingly no better or worse for their experience in the cult-like universe of the salafi mindset. This ephemerality of extremist activism should be as suspicious as its content. Authentic Muslim faith is simply not supposed to be this fragile; as the Qur'an says, its root is meant to be 'set firm'. One has to conclude that of the two trees depicted in the Quranic image, salafi extremism resembles the second rather than the first. After all, the Sahaba were not known for a transient commitment: their devotion and piety remained incomparably pure until they died.

What attracts young Muslims to this type of ephemeral but ferocious activism? One does not have to subscribe to determinist social theories to realise the importance of the almost universal condition of insecurity which Muslim societies are now experiencing. The Islamic world is passing through a most devastating period of transition. A history of economic and scientific change which in Europe took five hundred years is, in the Muslim world, being squeezed into a couple of generations. For instance, only thirty-five years ago the capital of Saudi Arabia was a cluster of mud huts, as it had been for thousands of years. Today's Riyadh is a hitech megacity of glass towers, Coke machines, and gliding Cadillacs. This is an extreme case, but to some extent the dislocations of modernity are common to every Muslim society, excepting, perhaps, a handful of the most remote tribal peoples.

Such a transition period, with its centrifugal forces which allow nothing to remain constant, makes human beings very insecure. They look around for something to hold onto, that will give them an identity. In our case, that something is usually Islam. And because they are being propelled into it by this psychic sense of insecurity, rather than by the more normal processes of conversion and faith, they lack some of the natural religious virtues, which are acquired by contact with a continuous tradition, and can never be learnt from a book. One easily visualises how this works. A young Arab, part of an oversized family, competing for scarce jobs, unable to marry because he is poor, perhaps a migrant to a rapidly expanding city, feels like a man lost in a desert without signposts. One morning he picks up a copy of Sayyid Qutb from a newsstand, and is 'born-again' on the spot.

This is what he needed: instant certainty, a framework in which to interpret the landscape before him, to resolve the problems and tensions of his life, and, even more deliciously, a way of feeling superior and in control. He joins a group, and, anxious to retain his newfound certainty, accepts the usual proposition that all the other groups are mistaken. This, of course, is not how Muslim religious conversion is supposed to work. It is meant to be a process of intellectual maturation, triggered by the presence of a very holy person or place. Tawba, in its traditional form, yields an outlook of joy, contentment, and a deep affection for others. The modern type of *tawba,* however, born of insecurity, often makes Muslims narrow, intolerant, and exclusivist. Even more noticeably, it produces people whose faith is, despite its apparent intensity, liable to vanish as suddenly as it came. Deprived of real nourishment, the activist's soul can only grow hungry and emaciated, until at last it dies.

Activism Within

How should we respond to this disorder? We must begin by remembering what Islam is for. As we noted earlier, our din is not, ultimately, a manual of rules which, when meticulously followed, becomes a passport to paradise. Instead, it is a package of social, intellectual and spiritual technology whose purpose is to cleanse the human heart. In the Qur'an, the Lord says that on the Day of Judgement, nothing will be of any use to us, except a sound heart (*qalbun salim*). And in a famous hadith, the Prophet, upon whom be blessings and peace, says that "Verily in the body there is a piece of flesh. If it is sound, the body is all sound. If it is corrupt, the body is all corrupt. Verily, it is the heart. Mindful of this commandment, under which all the other commandments of Islam are subsumed, and which alone gives them meaning, the Islamic scholars have worked out a science, an *ilm* (science), of analysing the 'states' of the heart, and the methods of bringing it into this condition of soundness.

In the fullness of time, this science acquired the name *tasawwuf,* in English 'Sufism' - a traditional label for what we might nowadays more intelligibly call 'Islamic psychology.' At this point, many hackles are raised and well-rehearsed objections voiced. It is vital to understand that mainstream Sufism is not, and never has been, a doctrinal system, or a school of thought - a *madhhab*. It is, instead, a set of insights and practices which operate within the various Islamic *madhhabs*; in other words, it is not a *madhhab*, it is an ilm. And like most of the other Islamic *ulum*, it was not known by name, or in its later developed form, in the age of the Prophet (upon him be blessings and peace) or his Companions. This does not make it less legitimate. There are many Islamic sciences which only took shape many years after the Prophetic age: *usul al-fiqh*, for instance, or the innumerable technical disciplines of hadith.

Now this, of course, leads us into the often misunderstood area of Sunna and *bid'a*, two notions which are wielded as blunt instruments by many contemporary activists, but which are often grossly misunderstood. The classic Orientalist thesis is of course that Islam, as an 'arid Semitic religion', failed to incorporate mechanisms for its own development, and that it petrified upon the death of its founder. This, however, is a nonsense rooted in the ethnic determinism of the nineteenth century historians who had shaped the views of the early Orientalist synthesizers (Muir, Le Bon, Renan, Caetani). Islam, as the religion designed for the end of time, has in fact proved itself eminently adaptable to the rapidly changing conditions which characterise this final and most 'entropic' stage of history.

What is a *bid'a*, according to the classical definitions of Islamic law? We all know the famous hadith:

Beware of matters newly begun, for every matter newly begun is innovation, every innovation is misguidance, and every misguidance is in Hell. Does this mean that everything introduced into Islam that was not known to the first generation of Muslims is to be rejected? The classical ulema do not accept such a literalistic interpretation.

Let us take a definition from Imam al-Shafi'i, an authority universally accepted in Sunni Islam. Imam al-Shafi'i writes:

There are two kinds of introduced matters (*muhdathat*). One is that which contradicts a text of the Qur'an, or the Sunna, or a report from the early Muslims (*athar*), or the consensus (*ijma'*) of the Muslims: this is an 'innovation of misguidance' (*bid'at dalala*). The second kind is that which is in itself good and entails no contradiction of any of these authorities: this is a 'non-reprehensible innovation' (*bid'a ghayr madhmuma*).

This basic distinction between acceptable and unacceptable forms of *bid'a* is recognised by the overwhelming majority of classical ulema. Among some, for instance al-Izz ibn Abd al-Salam (one of the half-dozen or so great mujtahids of Islamic history), innovations fall under the five axiological headings of the Shari'a: the obligatory (*wajib*), the recommended (*mandub*), the permissible (*mubah*), the offensive (*makruh*), and the forbidden (*haram*). Under the category of 'obligatory innovation', Ibn Abd al-Salam gives the following examples: recording the Qur'an and the laws of Islam in writing at a time when it was feared that they would be lost, studying Arabic grammar in order to resolve controversies over the Qur'an, and developing philosophical theology (*kalam*) to refute the claims of the Mu'tazilites.

Category two is 'recommended innovation'. Under this heading the ulema list such activities as building madrasas, writing books on beneficial Islamic subjects, and in-depth studies of Arabic linguistics. Category three is 'permissible', or 'neutral innovation', including worldly activities such as sifting flour, and constructing houses in various styles not known in Medina. Category four is the 'reprehensible innovation'. This includes such misdemeanours as overdecorating mosques or the Qur'an. Category five is the 'forbidden innovation'. This includes unlawful taxes, giving judgeships to those unqualified to hold them, and sectarian beliefs and practices that explicitly contravene the known principles of the Qur'an and the Sunna. The above classification of *bid'a* types is normal in classical Shari'a literature, being accepted by the four schools of orthodox *fiqh*.

There have been only two significant exceptions to this understanding in the history of Islamic thought: the Zahiri school as articulated by Ibn Hazm, and one wing of the Hanbali madhhab, represented by Ibn Taymiya, who goes against the classical *ijma'* on this issue, and claims that all forms of innovation, good or bad, are un-Islamic. Why is it, then, that so many Muslims now believed that innovation in any form is unacceptable in Islam? One factor has already been touched on: the mental complexes thrown up by insecurity, which incline people to find comfort in absolutist and literalist interpretations. Another lies in the influence of the well-financed neo-Hanbali madhhab called Wahhabism, whose leaders are famous for their rejection of all possibility of development.

In any case, armed with this more sophisticated and classical awareness of Islam's ability to acknowledge and assimilate novelty, we can understand how Muslim civilisation was able so quickly to produce novel academic disciplines to deal with new problems as these arose. Islamic psychology is characteristic of the new *ulum* which, although present in latent and implicit form in the Quran, were first systematized in Islamic culture during the early Abbasid period. Given the importance that the Quran attaches to obtaining a 'sound heart', we are not surprised to find that the influence of Islamic psychology has been massive and all-pervasive. In the formative first four centuries of Islam, the time when the great works of tafsir, hadith, grammar, and so forth were laid down, the ulema also applied their minds to this problem of *al-qalb al-salim*.

This was first visible when, following the example of the Tabi'in, many of the early ascetics, such as Sufyan ibn Uyayna, Sufyan al-Thawri, and Abdallah ibn al-Mubarak, had focussed their concerns explicitly on the art of purifying the heart. The methods they recommended were frequent fasting and night prayer, periodic retreats, and a preoccupation with *murabata*: service as volunteer fighters in the border castles of Asia Minor.

This type of pietist orientation was not in the least systematic during this period. It was a loose category embracing all Muslims who sought salvation through the Prophetic virtues of renunciation, sincerity, and deep devotion to the revelation. These men and women were variously referred to as *al-bakka'un*: 'the weepers', because of their fear of the Day of Judgement, or as *zuhhad*, ascetics, or *ubbad*, 'unceasing worshippers'.

By the third century, however, we start to find writings which can be understood as belonging to a distinct devotional school. The increasing luxury and materialism of Abbasid urban society spurred many Muslims to campaign for a restoration of the simplicity of the Prophetic age. Purity of heart, compassion for others, and a constant recollection of God were the defining features of this trend. We find references to the method of *muhasaba*: self-examination to detect impurities of intention. Also stressed was *riyada*: self-discipline. By this time, too, the main outlines of Quranic psychology had been worked out. The human creature, it was realised, was made up of four constituent parts: the body (*jism*), the mind (*aql*), the spirit (*ruh*), and the self (*nafs*). The first two need little comment. Less familiar (at least to people of a modern education) are the third and fourth categories.

The spirit is the *ruh*, that underlying essence of the human individual which survives death. It is hard to comprehend rationally, being in part of Divine inspiration, as the Quran says:

"And they ask you about the spirit; say, the spirit is of the command of my Lord. And you have been given of knowledge only a little."

According to the early Islamic psychologists, the ruh is a non-material reality which pervades the entire human body, but is centred on the heart, the *qalb*. It represents that part of man which is not of this world, and which connects him with his Creator, and which, if he is fortunate, enables him to see God in the next world. When we are born, this *ruh* is intact and pure. As we are initiated into the distractions of the world, however, it is covered over with the 'rust' (*ran*) of which the Quran speaks. This rust is made up of two things: sin and distraction. When, through the process of self-discipline, these are banished, so that the worshipper is preserved from sin and is focussing entirely on the immediate presence and reality of God, the rust is dissolved, and the *ruh* once again is free. The heart is sound; and salvation, and closeness to God, is achieved.

This sounds simple enough. However, the early Muslims taught that such precious things come only at an appropriate price. Cleaning up the Augean stables of the heart is a most excruciating challenge. Outward conformity to the rules of religion is simple enough; but it is only the first step. Much more demanding is the policy known as *mujahada*: the daily combat against the lower self, the *nafs*. As the Quran says:

'As for him that fears the standing before his Lord, and forbids his *nafs* its desires, for him, Heaven shall be his place of resort.'

Hence the Sufi commandment:

'Slaughter your ego with the knives of *mujahada*.'

Once the *nafs* is controlled, then the heart is clear, and the virtues proceed from it easily and naturally. Because its objective is nothing less than salvation, this vital Islamic science has been consistently expounded by the great scholars of classical Islam. While today there are many Muslims, influenced by either Wahhabi or Orientalist agendas, who believe that Sufism has always led a somewhat marginal existence in Islam, the reality is that the overwhelming majority of the classical scholars were actively involved in Sufism.

The early Shafi'i scholars of Khurasan: al-Hakim al-Nisaburi, Ibn Furak, al-Qushayri and al-Bayhaqi, were all Sufis who formed links in the richest academic tradition of

Abbasid Islam, which culminated in the achievement of Imam Hujjat al-Islam al-Ghazali. Ghazali himself, author of some three hundred books, including the definitive rebuttals of Arab philosophy and the Ismailis, three large textbooks of Shafi'i *fiqh*, the best-known tract of *usul al-fiqh*, two works on logic, and several theological treatises, also left us with the classic statement of orthodox Sufism: the *Ihya Ulum al-Din*, a book of which Imam Nawawi remarked:

"Were the books of Islam all to be lost, excepting only the *Ihya'*, it would suffice to replace them all."

Imam Nawawi himself wrote two books which record his debt to Sufism, one called the *Bustan al-Arifin* ('Garden of the Gnostics', and another called the *al-Maqasid*. Among the Malikis, too, Sufism was popular. Al-Sawi, al-Dardir, al-Laqqani and Abd al-Wahhab al-Baghdadi were all exponents of Sufism. The Maliki jurist of Cairo, Abd al-Wahhab al-Sha'rani defines Sufism as follows:

'The path of the Sufis is built on the Quran and the Sunna, and is based on living according to the morals of the prophets and the purified ones. It may not be blamed, unless it violates an explicit statement from the Quran, Sunna, or *ijma*. If it does not contravene any of these sources, then no pretext remains for condemning it, except one's own low opinion of others, or interpreting what they do as ostentation, which is unlawful. No-one denies the states of the Sufis except someone ignorant of the way they are.'

For Hanbali Sufism one has to look no further than the revered figures of Abdallah Ansari, Abd al-Qadir al-Jilani, Ibn al-Jawzi, and Ibn Rajab. In fact, virtually all the great luminaries of medieval Islam: al-Suyuti, Ibn Hajar al-Asqalani, al-Ayni, Ibn Khaldun, al-Subki, Ibn Hajar al-Haytami; tafsir writers like Baydawi, al-Sawi, Abu'l-Su'ud, al-Baghawi, and Ibn Kathir; *aqida* writers such as Taftazani, al-Nasafi, al-Razi: all wrote in support of Sufism. Many, indeed, composed independent works of Sufi inspiration. The ulema of the great dynasties of Islamic history, including the Ottomans and the Moghuls, were deeply infused with the Sufi outlook, regarding it as one of the most central and indispensable of Islamic sciences.Further confirmation of the Islamic legitimacy of Sufism is supplied by the enthusiasm of its exponents for carrying Islam beyond the boundaries of the Islamic world. The Islamization process in India, Black Africa, and South-East Asia was carried out largely at the hands of wandering Sufi teachers. Likewise, the Islamic obligation of jihad has been borne with especial zeal by the Sufi orders. All the great nineteenth century jihadists: Uthman dan Fodio (Hausaland), al-Sanousi (Libya), Abd al-Qadir al-Jaza'iri (Algeria), Imam Shamil (Daghestan) and the leaders of the Padre Rebellion (Sumatra) were active practitioners of Sufism, writing extensively on it while on their campaigns. Nothing is further from reality, in fact, than the claim that Sufism represents a quietist and non-militant form of Islam.

With all this, we confront a paradox. Why is it, if Sufism has been so respected a part of Muslim intellectual and political life throughout our history, that there are, nowadays, angry voices raised against it? There are two fundamental reasons here. Firstly, there is again the pervasive influence of Orientalist scholarship, which, at least before 1922 when Massignon wrote his *Essai sur les origines de la lexique technique,* was of the opinion that something so fertile and profound as Sufism could never have grown from the essentially 'barren and legalistic' soil of Islam. Orientalist works translated into Muslim languages were influential upon key Muslim modernists - such as Muhammad Abduh in his later writings - who began to question the centrality, or even the legitimacy, of Sufi discourse in Islam.

Secondly, there is the emergence of the Wahhabi *da'wa.* When Muhammad ibn Abd al-Wahhab, some two hundred years ago, teamed up with the Saudi tribe and attacked the neighbouring clans, he was doing so under the sign of an essentially neo-Kharijite version of Islam. Although he invoked Ibn Taymiya, he had reservations even about him. Ibn Taymiya himself, although critical of the excesses of certain Sufi groups, had been committed to a branch of mainstream Sufism. This is clear, for instance, in Ibn Taymiya's work *Sharh Futuh al-Ghayb*, a commentary on some technical points in the *Revelations of the Unseen*, a key work by the sixth-century saint of Baghdad, Abd al-Qadir al-Jilani. Throughout the work Ibn Taymiya shows himself to be a loyal disciple of al-Jilani, whom he always refers to as *shaykhuna* ('our teacher'). This Qadiri affiliation is confirmed in the later literature of the Qadiri tariqa, which records Ibn Taymiya as a key link in the *silsila*, the chain of transmission of Qadiri teachings.

Ibn Abd al-Wahhab, however, went far beyond this. Raised in the wastelands of Najd in Central Arabia, he had little access to mainstream Muslim scholarship. In fact, when his da'wa appeared and became notorious, the scholars and muftis of the day applied to it the famous Hadith of Najd:

> Ibn Umar reported the Prophet (upon whom be blessings and peace) as saying: "Oh God, bless us in our Syria; O God, bless us in our Yemen." Those present said: "And in our Najd, O Messenger of God!" but he said, "O God, bless us in our Syria; O God, bless us in our Yemen." Those present said, "And in our Najd, O Messenger of God!" Ibn Umar said that he thought that he said on the third occasion: "Earthquakes and dissensions (*fitna*) are there, and there shall arise the horn of the devil."

And it is significant that almost uniquely among the lands of Islam; Najd has never produced scholars of any repute. The Najd-based *da'wa* of the Wahhabis, however, began to be heard more loudly following the explosion of Saudi oil wealth. Many, even most, Islamic publishing houses in Cairo and Beirut are now subsidised by Wahhabi organisations, which prevent them from publishing traditional works on Sufism, and remove passages in other works considered unacceptable to Wahhabist doctrine. The neo-Kharijite nature of Wahhabism makes it intolerant of all other forms of Islamic expression. However, because it has no coherent *fiqh* of its own - it rejects the orthodox madhhabs - and has only the most basic and primitively anthropomorphic *aqida*, it has a fluid, amoebalike tendency to produce divisions and subdivisions among those who profess it. No longer are the Islamic groups essentially united by a consistent *madhhab* and the Ash'ari [or Maturidi] *aqida*. Instead, they are all trying to derive the *shari'a* and the *aqida* from the Quran and the Sunna by themselves.

The result is the appalling state of division and conflict which disfigures the modern salafi condition. At this critical moment in our history, the umma has only one realistic hope for survival, and that is to restore the 'middle way', defined by that sophisticated classical consensus which was worked out over painful centuries of debate and scholarship. That consensus alone has the demonstrable ability to provide a basis for unity. But it can only be retrieved when we improve the state of our hearts, and fill them with the Islamic virtues of affection, respect, tolerance and reconciliation. This inner reform, which is the traditional competence of Sufism, is a precondition for the restoration of unity in the Islamic movement. The alternative is likely to be continued, and agonising, failure.

Before we can understand Islamic spirituality we must first understand generic human spirituality. We can understand the human spirit as that capacity to be aware of and the ability to respond to the mystery of life and reality. In the words of one author "Mystery is the best name for reality. It indicates not an absence, but an overabundance." What we are calling "mystery" or the "transcendent mystery" is indicated or implied by means of all phenomena: physical, social and psychological. The practice of spirituality would then indicate the disciplined increase of that awareness and a disciplined response to that awareness. In addition we need to make some corrections to how we usually envision human experience from a two-fold "mind & body" model to a four-fold, or "quaternion" model of human experience. Note that this de-centers one's interiority to but one quarter of the total experience that defines us as "human". Hence, there is less emphasis upon feeling states than is often the case when discussing spirituality. We are able to more clearly distinguish between spirituality and psychology.

Islamic spirituality is firmly wholistic as illustrated by the Field Model. Islamic spirituality is active in all four aspects of human experience. It thus avoids extremes of interiority and does not portray the physical or the social as being contra the spiritual.

Islamic spirituality is based upon the assumption that what appears to us as mystery revealed itself as being God. The Qur'an *is* this revelation. The Qur'an instructs us in the foundational importance of *awareness of* God and the proper *response to* God. The *Sunnah* (lifestyle or practice) of Muhammad expresses and exemplifies this Qur'anic *awareness of,* and *response to* God within actual, historical, phenomenal reality. This is the heart and foundation and *raison d'être* of Islamic spirituality. Muhammad is considered to be a "walking Qur'an".

Islamic spirituality fosters God-consciousness, called *taqwa,* in and through all daily activities in addition to activities we usually identify as "spiritual" such as fasting and prayer. It shuns any extremes.

Islamic spirituality does not gauge its development and growth upon subjective experience, but on the degree to which one imitates the *Sunnah.* Evil is that which is *contra* Qur'an and *sunnah*- it has nothing to do with subjective experiences of pleasure or pain, laughter or tears, nor does it have to do with social experiences such as riches or poverty. All of these social and subjective states are somewhat equivalent in Islam. They all originate by the will of God for the purpose of testing the Muslim's use of freedom. The Muslim submits to the will of God with patience. The word "Islam" means "submission to the will of God". It is thus not even a "religion" as we usually think of the term. It is more of an existential way-of-being.

Islamic spirituality encourages science and scholarship in that the Qur'an repeatedly exhorts humanity to observe the signs of God in creation, in history, and in one's self. It also encourages social activism. That is, *jihad*- the struggle of good against evil. Islamic spirituality *is* the "mysticism of the ordinary". Sufism is, in general, not quite what non-Muslims think it is. First, Sufis are *Muslims* and so follow Muslim law. Second, "Sufism" as such is a school of thought that can only be understood in comparison to *other* schools of thought any of which may express extremist trends within Islam. It is more proper to discuss *tasawuuf*, or purification of the self. That is, the bringing of all four aspects of human experience, and especially the subjective interiority, into compliance with the Qur'an and Sunnah.

To divide Islamic practice into "exoteric" and "esoteric" is *prima facie* evidence that one has not understood Islamic spirituality. It is a distinction that is not present in Muslim practice except as a symptom of the poor practice of Islam. What is the spiritual path in Islam and what is its place in the life as a whole? To answer this it is necessary to study carefully the difference between the Islamic concept of spirituality and that of other religions and ideologies. Without a clear understanding of this difference it often happens that, when talking about the spirituality in Islam, many of the vague notions associated with the word 'spiritual' unconsciously come to mind; it then becomes difficult for one to comprehend that this spirituality of Islam not only transcends the dualism of spirit and matter but is the nucleus of its integrated and unified concept of life.

Body-Soul Conflict

The idea which has influenced most the climate of philosophical and religious thought is that body and soul are mutually antagonistic, and can develop only at each other's expense. For the soul, the body is a prison and the activities of daily life are the shackles which keep it in bondage and arrest its growth. This has inevitably led to the universe being divided into the spiritual and the secular. Those who chose the secular path were convinced that they could not meet the demands of spirituality, and thus they led highly material and hedonistic lives. All spheres of worldly activity, whether social, political, economic or cultural, were deprived of the light of spirituality; injustice and tyranny were the result.

Conversely, those who wanted to tread the path of spiritual excellence came to see themselves as 'noble outcasts' from the world. They believed that it was impossible for spiritual growth to be compatible with a 'normal' life. In their view physical self-denial and mortification of the flesh were necessary for the development and perfection of the spirit. They invented spiritual exercises and ascetic practices which killed physical desires and dulled the body's senses. They regarded forests, mountains and other solitary places as ideal for spiritual development because the hustle and bustle of life would not interfere with their meditations. They could not conceive of spiritual development except through withdrawal from the world.

This conflict of body and soul resulted in the evolution of two different ideals for the perfection of man. One was that man should be surrounded by all possible material comforts and regards himself as nothing but an animal. Men learnt to fly like birds, swim like fish, and run like horses and even terrorize and destroy like wolves ¾ but they did not learn how to live like noble human beings. The other was that the senses should be not only subdued and conquered but extra-sensory powers awakened and the limitations of the sensory world done away with. With these new conquests men would be able to hear distant voices like powerful wireless sets, see remote objects as one does with a telescope, and develop powers through which the mere touch of their hand or a passing glance would heal the unhealable. The Islamic viewpoint differs radically from these approaches.

According to Islam, *Allah* has appointed the human soul as His *Khalifah* (vicegerent) in this world. He has invested it with a certain authority, and given it certain responsibilities and obligations for the fulfillment of which He has endowed it with the best and most suitable physical frame. The body has been created with the sole object of allowing the soul to use it in the exercise of its authority and the fulfillment of its duties and responsibilities. The body is not a prison for the soul, but its workshop or factory; and if the soul is to grow and develop, it is only through this workshop. Consequently, this world is not a place of punishment in which the human soul unfortunately finds itself, but a field in which *Allah* has sent it to work and do its duty towards Him.

So the spiritual development should not take the form of a man turning away from this workshop and retreating into a corner. Rather, man should live and work in it, and give the best account of himself that he can. It is in the nature of an examination for him; every aspect and sphere of life is, as it were, a question paper: the home, the family, the neighborhood, the society, the market-place, the office, the factory, the school, the law courts, the police station, the parliament, the peace conference and the battlefield, all represent question papers which man has been called upon to answer. If he leaves most of the answer-book blank, he is bound to fail the examination. Success and development are only possible if man devotes his whole life to this examination and attempts to answer all the question papers he can. Islam rejects and condemns the ascetic view of life, and proposes a set of methods and processes for the spiritual development of man, not outside this world but inside it. The real place for the growth of the spirit is in the midst of life and not in solitary places of spiritual hibernation.

Criterion of Spiritual Development

We shall now discuss how Islam judges the development or decay of the soul. In his capacity as the vicegerent

(*Khalifah*) of God, man is answerable to Him for all his activities. It is his duty to use all the powers which he has been given in accordance with the Divine will. He should utilize to the fullest extent all the faculties and potentialities bestowed upon him for seeking *Allah*'s approval. In his dealings with other people he should behave in such a way as to try to please *Allah*. In brief, all his energies should be directed towards regulating the affairs of this world in the way in which *Allah* wants them to be regulated. The better a man does this, with a sense of responsibility, obedience and humility, and with the object of seeking the pleasure of the Lord, the nearer will he be to *Allah*.

In Islam, spiritual development is synonymous with nearness to *Allah*. Similarly, he will not be able to get near to *Allah* if he is lazy and disobedient. And distance from *Allah* signifies, in Islam, the spiritual fall and decay of man. From the Islamic point of view, therefore, the sphere of activity of the religious man and the secular man is the same. Not only will both work in the same spheres; the religious man will work with greater enthusiasm than the secular man. The man of religion will be as active as the man of the world ¾ indeed, more active ¾ in his domestic and social life, which extends from the confines of the household to the market square, and even to international conferences.

What *will* distinguish their actions will be the nature of their relationship with *Allah* and the aims behind their actions. Whatever a religious man does, will be done with the feeling that he is answerable to *Allah*, that he must try to secure Divine pleasure, that his actions must be in accordance with *Allah*'s laws. A secular person will be indifferent towards *Allah* and will be guided in his actions only by his personal motives. This difference makes the whole of the material life of a man of religion a totally spiritual venture, and the whole of the life of a secular person an existence devoid of the spark of spirituality.

Road to Spirituality

The first necessity for progression along the path of spiritual development is MAN (faith). The mind and heart of a man should always be aware: *Allah* alone is His Master, Sovereign and Deity; seeking His pleasure is the aim of all his endeavors; and His commands alone are the commands that are to be obeyed. This should be a firm conviction, based not merely on the intellect, but also on acceptance by the will. The stronger and deeper this conviction, the more profound a man's faith will be. The second stage is that of obedience (*it~ 'at*), meaning that man gives up his independence and accepts subservience to *Allah*. This subservience is called § slam (submission) in the language of the Qur'~ n. Thus, man should not only acknowledge *Allah* as his Lord and Sovereign but should actually submit before Him and fashion his entire life in obedience to Him.

The third stage is that of *taqw~* (*Allah*-consciousness). It consists in a practical manifestation of one's faith in *Allah* in one's daily life. *Taqw~* also means desisting from everything which *Allah* has forbidden or has disapproved of; man must be in a state of readiness to undertake all that *Allah* has commanded and to observe the distinctions between lawful and unlawful, right and wrong, and good and bad in life. The last and the highest stage is that of *ihs~ n* (godliness) It signifies that man has attained highest excellence in words, deeds and thoughts, identifying his will with the will of *Allah* and harmonizing it, to the best of his knowledge and ability, with the Divine will. He thus begins to like what is liked by the Lord and to dislike what He dislikes.

Man should then not only avoid evil, for it displeases his Lord, but should use all his powers to eradicate it from the face of the earth; he should not be content with adorning himself with the good which *Allah* wants to flourish but should also strive to attain and propagate it in the world, even at the cost of his life. A man who reaches this stage attains the highest pinnacle of spirituality and is nearest to

Allah. This path of spiritual development is not meant for individuals only but for communities and nations as well. Like individuals, a community, after passing through the various stages of spiritual elevation may reach the ultimate stage of *ihs~ n* a state also, through all its administrative machinery, may become *mu'min* (faithful), *muslim* (obedient), *muttaq§* (God-conscious) and *muhsin* (godly). In fact, the ideals aimed at by Islam are fully achieved only when the whole community accepts them and a *muttaq* and *muhsin* state comes into existence. The highest form of civilization, based on goodness, is then reached.

The mechanism of spiritual training which Islam has laid down to prepare individuals and society for this process. The methods that Islam lays down for spiritual development rest, in addition, obviously, to faith (*Im~ n*), on five pillars. The first is the Prayer (Salat), which brings man into communion with *Allah* five times a day, reviving his remembrance, reiterating his fear, developing his love, reminding him of this Divine commands again, and thus preparing him for obedience to *Allah*. It is obligatory to offer some of these Prayers in Congregation as well so that the whole community and society may be prepared to journey on the path of spiritual development. The second is the Fast (Sawm), which for a full month every year trains each man individually, and the Muslim community as a whole, in righteousness and self-restraint,; it enables society, the rich and the poor alike, to experience hunger, and prepares people to undergo any hardships in their search to please *Allah*.

The third is the Almsgiving (Zakat), which develops the sense of monetary sacrifice, sympathy and co-operation among Muslims. There are people who wrongly interpret Zakat as a tax; in fact, the spirit underlying Zakat is entirely different from that of a tax. The real meaning of Zakat is sublimity and purification. By using this word, Islam seeks to impress on man the fact that, inspired by a true love of *Allah*, the monetary help which he renders to his brethren will uplift and purify his soul. The fourth is the Pilgrimage (Hajj), which aims at fostering that universal brotherhood of the faithful which is based on the worship of *Allah*, and which results in a worldwide movement that has been responding to the call of Truth throughout the centuries and will, *Allah* willing, go on answering this call till eternity.

The last is Jihad that is, exerting oneself to the utmost to disseminate the word of *Allah* and to make it supreme, and to remove all the impediments to Islam ¾ through tongue or pen or sword. The aim is to live a life of dedication to the cause of Allah and, if necessary, to sacrifice one's life in the discharge of this mission. This is the highest spirituality, rooted in the real world, which Islam wants to cultivate. Life-affirmation based on goodness and piety, and not life-denial, is what Islam stands for. And this lends a unique character to Islam.

2

The Qadiriyyah Order

The Qadiriyyah has not developed any distinctive doctrines or teachings outside of mainstream Islam. They believe in the fundamental principles of Islam, but interpreted through mystical experience. The movement's founder 'Abd al-Qadir al-Djilani emphasised the importance of humaneness and charity. The order's rituals are chara-cterised by the loud recitation of verses in praise of Muhammad and the singing of sacred hymns. These are sometimes accompanied by various bodily movements designed to induce ecstasy. In some areas local pilgrimages to zawiyas (shrines) of the saints who are believed to be descendants of 'Abd al Qadir and festivals are celebrated in their honour.

Qadiriyyah is one of the oldest tariqhas, and derives its name from 'Abd al-Qadir al-Djilani (1077-1166), a native of the Iranian province of Djilan. In 1134 he was made principal of a Hanbalite school in Baghdad. His most famous work, Sufficiency for the Seekers of the Truth, contains his sermons and gives accounts of various Muslim sects. Contemporary accounts of his life reveal him to have been responsible for the conversion of many Jews and Christians to Islam. Posthumous accounts of his life attribute miraculous powers to him. The early spread of Qadiriyyah was very slow. It was only in the fifteenth century that the order spread significantly beyond Iraq and Syria. At this time it became established in India through the work of Muhammad Ghawth (d.1517).

In the seventeenth century it was established in Istanbul by Isma'il Rumi (d. 1631). In the nineteenth century it reached as far as Malaysia and Indonesia. The order has also played an important role in Islamic religious and political life in North Africa. In the eighteenth century, under the leadership of Usuman dan Fodio (1754-1817) the order moved to enforce Islam over those practising traditional tribal religions in the regions that are now Nigeria and Niger. In nineteenth century Algeria the Qadiriyyah fought at length against the French colonialists. The order continues today in various parts of the Muslim world.

The Qadiriyyah carries no inscriptions, and its founding date has not otherwise been determined. Its founder is equally obscure, for although the building is clearly a funerary madrasah with a tomb chamber and a tomb, the name of its benefactor is nowhere to be found. Vague as its history may be, the Qadiriyyah is a handsome, if simple, medium-size madrasah which is still in fair condition and is still playing a social role. The name "al-Qadiriyyah" indicates the association of the madrasa with the Sufi order named after the Persian Sufi Abd-al-Qadir al-Jilani (1077-1166). It is most likely, therefore, that this madrasah served for some time as a meeting place for that order and was eventually named after it. While the Qadiriyyah order is still active and has several established meeting places in present-day Tripoli, the madrasa is no longer one of them; it has since acquired a different function. Serving as a public kitchen for the poor, it has a sign outside announcing it as a "Restaurant, Free of Charge."

The Qadiriyyah has an organized facade along its entire eastern side; its elements are simple and functional: a doorway, three windows, and three upper openings for ventilation. The domes seen on the elevation are not visible from street level. The windows, a pair and a single, are set on a slightly raised frame of polished stone and topped by a row of flattened-out muqarnas of Tripoli fish-scale motif. The gate is rectangular and raises the entire height of the building. A deep archway with stone mastabahs opens on a back wall containing a high and simple oculus and a rectangular door set three steps above street level. Between the oculus and the door are three plaques, one circular flanked by the other two square ones, which could have had some decoration or even inscriptions, but are now covered by a thick build-up of whitewash.

The gate around this opening has alternate courses of black and white stone, now mostly painted over, and the whole is framed by a band of stone molding ending in a spiral on either side of the mastabahs. This motif of a framing band ending in a spiral, although by no means common, is found on a few Mamluk monuments of the Fertile Crescent, such as the two fountains of Sulayman and Qaytbay (1455) in Jerusalem and the facade of the Qassab mosque (1408) in Damascus. In Tripoli it adorns the gateway of a defense tower in the harbor. The interest of this motif lies in its pre-Islamic Syrian origin, on the whole, a time and style that had very little impact on Islamic architecture. The Muslims preferred to go back to Greek and Roman times for their inspiration rather than borrow from their early Christian predecessors.

In its original form, a sculptured band framing an architectural element such as a small door or window and turning outward in a spiral, this motif was fairly common in Christian Syria of the sixth century. In central Syria it can be seen on religious architecture, such as the facade of the basilica at Qalb-Lawzeh and the chapel of Kokanaya as well as on private dwellings such as the Maison d'Airamis, which the inscription tells us, was built August 13, 510. In northern Syria, it is seen framing round upper-floor windows and rectangular doorways, as on the elevation of the west facade of the Church of Bakirha dated 501, and the Church of Khirbit Tezin dated 585.

While the sixth-century Christian origin of the motif appears to be indisputable, its Mamluk adaptation both in Tripoli and in Jerusalem shows two divergences from the original: the area framed is a tall, vertical span rather than a short, round or square horizontal opening, and in all instances the spiral turns inward rather than outward to include the area framed. The Damascene adaptation is geographically closer to the model and therefore a more exact translation of the motif: it turns outward, and the frame is square rather than oblong even when the door it surrounds is rectangular. The sixth-century Christian motif was adapted by the Mamluks for the framing or enclosing of architectural elements such as doorways and fountains.

A short corridor leads to a long prayer area, a square domed room, and a tomb chamber, the three main parts of the madrasah. The prayer area, a long, rectangular room, runs the width of the building. Its eastern and western walls are both opened by two deeply set windows; its southern side includes the simple mihrab, on the same axis as the square room. The floor is covered by a simple geometric pattern of black, white, and red marble, and the entire hall is covered by a simple cross-vault over the mihrab area. The square room, a step higher than the prayer hall and covered by a well-composed dome, was probably the madrasah's main hali, possibly the room used for teaching and for gatherings other than prayer.

Its western and northern sides extend behind arches beyond the square proper in what looks like shrunken atrophied iwans. The dome is a simple cupola with an octagonal opening resting on an octagonal drum of four opened arches and four corner squinches. The tomb chamber, entered either from the corridor or from the square room, is a small domed room containing a marble tomb. It has no inscription, however, and therefore does not disclose the identity of the person burried there".

The Wahhabiyah Movement

The Muslim World witnessed the appearance of several intellectual and religious movements which emanated from different Islamic territories in the 18th and 19th centuries. A number of social, political and religious causes provided motivation for these multifaced movements. Decline of the Ottoman Empire and diminishing authority of the Caliph, growing political and cultural influence of Western powers throughout the Muslim World, moral laxity and superstitious accretions prevalent among believers for long, rising wave of nationalist trends to establish regional and nation states, all of these aforementioned factors and some others inspired new ideas and orientations that occurred in the Muslim World.

Among these movements, the *Wahhabiyah* is of considerable importance as it has long-lasting influence on the other revivalist and puritan movements. The *Wahhabi* doctrine prompted some of these who had been trying for new reforms which might solve the problems of [the] Muslim World and provide a new understanding of religion.

The Wahhabi Movement

The title *Wahhabi* was given to the followers of Shaykh Muhammad b. 'Abd al-Wahhab by his Muslim opponents. People to whom the *Wahhabi* name was applied have rejected this opprobrious label. Instead, the Wahhabis called themselves *ahl al-tawhid* (People of Unity or *Muwahhidun*), those who profess the doctrine of the Unity of God. [It is not that any section of Islam claims not to be a *Mauwahhid* (i.e., believer in the Unity/Oneness of God), but merely that the *Wahhabis* have appropriated to themselves this title.] The founder, Muhammad b. 'Abd al-Wahhab, was born in Uyayna in Najd in 1703.

His father and grandfather were Hanbalite *qadis,* thus he was brought up and educated in this tradition. He studied in famous learning centres - Medina, Basra, Baghdad, Hamadan, etc. spending many years in travel during which he perused philosophy and Sufism. After having completed his studies, Muhammad b. 'Abd al-Wahhab returned to Uyayna where he publicly preached his doctrines and met both success and opposition. The governor of Uyayna was asked to expel Muhammad b. 'Abd al-Wahhab as a consequence of disputes caused by his teachings.

Implications of Ibn Taymiyyah's Views

Before examining the doctrines of Muhammad b. 'Abd al-Wahhab, I would like to analyse the influence of Ibn Taymiyyah on Wahhabi thought. This analysis will throw light on the development of the Wahhabi movement and its doctrinal relation with the teachings of Ibn Taymiyyah who seems to me as a prototype for Muhammad b. 'Abd al-Wahhab. The originator of the Wahhabiyah movement had been a *Sufi* adept in his youth, but later came under the influence of Ibn Taymiyyah's writings. Ibn Taymiyyah's teachings had three main implications for Wahhabi doctrines:

1. *Concerning State and Religion:* According to Ibn Taymiyyah, the 'ulama' are responsible for the protection of the Divine Law. A government is regarded as Islamic by virtue of the support it gives to Islam and to the 'ulama'. One can accept the rule of anyone who follows the Shariah. This understanding had an important effect on the Wahhabi ideology that accepted al-Sa'ud's dynasty as a legitimate and hereditary Islamic government after taking refuge in Dariyya, a territory controlled by [the] al-Sa'ud family.
2. *Concerning the Sources of True Islam:* Ibn Taymiyyah strives for the pure form of Islam in his enduring pursuit of Divine reality like Ibn Hanbal. Ibn Taymiyyah turns to the Qur'an and the Sunnah as the basis of the Divine law, refusing any accretions of later developments after the initial pristine years of the salaf, the first three generations of Islam. He insists on eliminating all the foreign elements which do not reflect the authentic core of Islam and the purity of Islamic teachings. The idea of going back to the Qur'an and the authentic Sunnah with a puritanical attitude ignoring later fiqhi schools was adopted and applied by Muhammad b. 'Abd al-Wahhab as against the majority of medieval scholars and rejecting ijtihad based on the qiyas (analogy or logical reasoning).
3. *Concerning Sufi Doctrines and Practices*: In the light of recent scholarly works, Ibn Tayymiyyah is said to have

been a Sufi of the Qadiriyyah Order. But he regards the idea of mystical unity with God and ecstatic aspects of Sufism as un-Islamic; therefore he rejects these teachings. It should be noted that he did not reject Sufism itself but denounced intercession, saint veneration and grave cults. Muhammad b. 'Abd al-Wahhab, inspired from the above notion, developed his doctrine to such an extent that the Wahhabis are said to have opened the Prophet's mausoleum and sold or distributed its relics and jewels.

Nature of Wahhabi Doctrines

Muhammad b. 'Abd al-Wahhab wrote on various Islamic subjects such as theology, exegesis, jurisprudence and on the life of Prophet Muhammad (pbuh). His works were collected and published in twelve volumes under the title of *Mu'allafat al-shaykh al-Imam Muhammad 'Abd al-Wahhab* by the Islamic University of Imam Muhammad Ibn Sa'ud. In his works, Muhammad b. 'Abd al-Wahhab denounced a number of beliefs and practices prevailing among the Muslim society. He begins his discourse by stressing the unity of God. He underlines the doctrine of tawhid, God's uniqueness as omnipotent Lord of creation. He stresses the unity of God in deserving worship and absolute devotion of the servants. He regards the associations of persons or things with the Lord as a violation of the doctrine of God's Oneness.

Muhammad b. 'Abd al-Wahhab condemns the intercession, tawassul, which was applied and practised by a large number of Muslims during their prayer to God. He warns the believers against showing excessive devotion to saints and against the use of saints' graves as places of worship for tawassul. He considers these external elements polytheism, shirk. He seeks to purify the Muslim community from any such kind of external elements by returning to the ways of the Prophet (pbuh) and the first generations of pious Muslims. Muhammad b. 'Abd al-Wahhab states that the true Islam is that of the first generations (al-Salaf al-Salih) and protests against all those later innovations as superstitious accretions which brought what he calls 'new gods' into Islam.

As a result of this attitude to Sufi tradition, the Wahhabis felt that it was an obligation upon them to destroy all the existing alien components. Accordingly, they attacked the graves of the Companions of the Prophet (pbuh), tombs of saints, or anything associated with popular veneration like trees or stones. An obvious example of this zealous hatred was seen when the Wahhabis plundered Karbala, a Shi'ia holy city, and destroyed Husayn's tomb. Muhammad b. 'Abd al-Wahhab rejected all kinds of innovations, defined by him as any doctrine or action not based on the Qur'an, Sunnah or on the authority of the Companions. Among the innovations are practices such as celebrating the Prophet's birth, the use of rosary, adding minarets and ornaments to mosques, etc. Following practices may lead the believer to shirk according to the Wahhabis:

1. To visit the tombs of saints to gain God's favour.
2. To introduce a name of a prophet, of a saint or of an angel into prayer.
3. Seeking intercession from any being but God.
4. Interpretation of the Qur'an by ta'wil.

According to Muhammad b. 'Abd al-Wahhab's system, attendance at public prayer is obligatory, smoking of tobacco is forbidden and subject to punishment, shaving the beard and the use of abusive language are also to be punished. With regard to fundamental basis of Islam, Muhammad b. 'Abd al-Wahhab places a great emphasis on the Qur'an and the Sunnah. He attacks the blind acceptance of authority in religious matters in general, thus comes to oppose the earlier 'uluma' who lack independent thinking. He finds it essential to go beyond the medieval authorities to the Sunnah of early generations.

Rejecting qiyas, he recognizes only two major authorities: the Qur'an and the Sunnah of the Prophet Muhammad (pbuh) along with the precedents and the ijma' of the Companions. In Wahhabi mentality, a number of concepts were given a prior importance such as tawhid, shirk and bid'at (innovation) mentioned above. Muhammad b. 'Abd al-Wahhab distinguishes between dar al-Islam and dar al-harb extending the scope of dar al-harb to some other Muslim countries which he regards as having 'unlawful' societies.

Therefore those who live in dar al-harb where there is no freedom have to perform hijrah, emigrating from every country in which shirk and kufr are apparent. Another usage of hijrah appears in Wahhabi texts as a spiritual understanding which necessitates keeping away from all sinful things, forbidden by God and Prophet Muhammad (pbuh). Any kind of political division of the ummah and civil war were regarded as fitnah, social disturbance. The first fitnah appeared under 'Ali's Caliphate when the Kharijites left him. Wherever a fitnah occurs, it must be abolished by declaring a jehad, holy war. The followers of Muhammad b. 'Abd al-Wahhab had been indoctrinated to believe that the opponents of the Wahhabi cause were enemies of Islam who should be fought against.

Religion and State

The modern history of Saudi Arabia began in the eighteenth century with the alliance between Muhammad b. 'Abd al-Wahhab, the founder of the Wahhabi movement, and Muhammad Ibn al-Sa'ud, Amir of Dariyya, son of the founder of the Saudi dynasty. When Muhammad b. 'Abd al-Wahhab was forced to leave Uyayna, he went to Dariyya where he was received by the chieftain, Muhammad Ibn al-Sa'ud, in 1745. Muhammad Ibn Al-Sa'ud accepted Muhammad b. 'Abd al-Wahhab's doctrine and undertook its defence and propagation after having agreed to the conditions that the political sovereignty should rest with Ibn al-Sa'ud, whereas religious authority should belong to Muhammad b. 'Abd al- Wahhab.

The Saudi-Wahhabi alliance was further cemented by intermarriage between the two families. The Saudi-Wahhabi alliance seems to be a turning point through which the Wahhabi movement gained an official acceptance and confirmation from a strong dynasty that used religious authority of the Wahhabi doctrines as a binding force among the Arab tribes. One of the significant aspects of this alliance in the formation of Saudi Arabian history was the fact that it led to an effective union of political-military organization and religious ideology which carried out Saudi-Wahhabi expansion.

As 'Abd al-Aziz b. al-Rahman states, all the desert tribes came under the control of [the] al-Sa'ud family obeying their orders and instructions. The Wahhabi doctrines and socio-political teachings of religion enabled [the] al-Sa'ud dynasty to hold their political authority firmly for ruling the nomad tribes successfully. The Wahhabi 'ulama' gave explicit support and approval to the hereditary rule of the al-Sa'ud family, and the Wahhabi shaykhs utilized the concept of equality as a political tool to control the Bedouin tribes by eliminating tribal particularism.

It was principally through the Wahhabi movement that 'Abd al-'Aziz and the previous Saudi rulers had been able to transcend tribal and urban loyalties while still using their social structure as a basis for political manipulation. Membership of an Islamic community theoretically served to equalize social differentials and as the tribes embraced the Wahhabi doctrine, they came to accept the imamete of al- Sa'ud as leader of a legitimate state validated by Islam (Ibid., p. 113). As a far-reaching effect of this cooperation, the Saudi dynasty firmly established its control in the political arena assuming certain titles indicating temporal power such as amir, haakim and malik, king.

The Ottoman Rule and the Saudi-Wahhabi Dynasty

Muhammad b. 'Abd al-Wahhab declared that Islam protected by the Ottoman Sultan was not the true Islam, implying that the sultan was not the legitimate leader of the *ummah*. The Wahhabis held that the Arabs were worthier than the Turks with regard to *imamete* or leadership. Thus the authority of the Ottoman rule was rejected and challenged.

When the rapid expansion of the Wahhabi movement was reported to Istanbul, the Ottoman Caliph, Sultan Mahmud II, urged Muhammad 'Ali Pasha, the governor of Egypt, to drive the Wahhabis out of the holy cities. Under the Caliphal instruction, Muhammad 'Ali Pasha launched a series of military attacks on Wahhabi-controlled territories. In 1818, he reached Dariyya and captured the capital of the Wahhabi-Saudi alliance.

Although the Wahhabi movement was put down, its expansion did not fade away. After the recovery and restoration of the Saudi dynasty, 'Abd al-'Aziz, Son of 'Abd al-Rahman, entered Riyadh in 1901 and the Saudi dynasty regained authority while regions of Najd, Hijaz, Makkah, Madina, and Jeddah were all also occupied. After an international recognition of hereditary authority or kingship of the Saudi family, new developments in the political arena facilitated the consolidation of the Saudi-Wahhabi alliance as a nation-state.

Later Developments in the Wahhabi World

The Wahhabi world could not remain aloof from the changing nature of world events and patterns of international relations in the modern era. New developments in different spheres of life rapidly occurred. Today the Wahhabi doctrine is supported by the political power of the state as the official form of Islam in the Kingdom of Saudi Arabia, as it has been from the outset of the Wahhabi-Saudi alliance. The members of the royal family seem to be advocates of the Wahhabi ideology. The mufti and the chief qadi come from the House of Shaykhs. The courts are largely Wahhabi in character.

The spread of education and the improvement of communication systems have made it easier to transmit the Wahhabi doctrines to different segments of [the] population. Under the influence of new developments and toleration of less-strict rulers, the Wahhabis of Saudi Arabia have shown a growing openness towards not only non-Wahhabi Muslims, but also non-Muslims. The Shi'ites of the Eastern regions used to be unwelcome residents in the eyes of the governments, but gradually they have seen their situation improve and the Wahhabi King has been an honoured guest at official functions in Shi'ite towns.

The spirit of tolerance has been extended to Christian persons and powers as well. A large number of Christians have been employed in recent years by the government. The armed forces of Arabia have been trained in the past, first by an English military mission and more recently by one from the U.S.A. Until recently illustrations showing human face or form were taboo among the Wahhabis, though the Qur'an itself contains no sweeping prohibition of representational art. The press in Saudi Arabia is now allowed to publish photographs and drawings. The attitude toward tobacco is also changing; smoking is no longer regarded as a moral laxity deserving punishment.

The organization of formal education and introduction of secular subjects into education took place in 1925. When 'Abd al-'Aziz ordered the creation of the Directorate General of Education, the 'ulama' were opposed to the introduction of secular education, fearing that it may damage the fabric of the Wahhabi society. Nevertheless 'Abd al-'Aziz insisted on the establishment of a new educational system and carried out his plan. In the course of time scientific and technical subjects and foreign languages were included in the curriculum. Girls were allowed to have access to public education in 1959.

None of these elements could have been accepted during the early period of the Wahhabi movement. The acquisition of wealth during the past twenty or thirty years posed a serious problem for the Wahhabi society. Particularly under the period of Sa'ud's rules, the extravagance and ostentation of a very un-Wahhabi-like character tainted the atmosphere of the Saudi Court. Those who claimed that the Saudi family departed from Islam with its wealth, occupied the Grand Mosque at Mecca in 1979, but their revolt was put down by the Saudi rule.

3

Rumi and the Mawlawiyyah

The beliefs and practices of the Mawlawiyyah order are generally considered to be consistent with the doctrines of mainstream Sunni Islam. Like other Sufi orders its distinctive identity derives from the particular types of spiritual practices undertaken by its members. Initial entry into the order is made by approaching a Mawlawi shaikh (spiritual guide). The novitiate (known as the murid, which means "seeker") undergoes a long period of trial and training. After completing 1001 days of service, which include intense periods of prayer and the performance of ceremonies, the seeker is considered to be experienced enough to teach the knowledge and the arts which he has acquired to the seekers who have come after him. At this stage the seeker is given the title dada.

Depending upon his ability the dada may become a shaikh. As frequently happens in many orders, the successor of the founder of a tariqa is generally a member of his family. The most characteristic feature of this order, known in Turkish as the Mevleviya, is the celebrated whirling dance. The Mawlawis, the whirling dervishes, are famous for their dancing ritual, a variation of the earlier practice of Sama (the recitation of music and poetry). The Sama ceremony is performed after prayers.

Mawlawiyyah traces its origins to the thirteenth century Turkish mystic and poet Mawlana Jalal al-Din al-Rumi (d. 1273), and owes its name to the fact that the al-Rumi was often referred to as Mawlana (our master). However, it was al-Rumi's son, Sutan Walad, who actually organized an order proper. Mawlawiyyah reached the height of its influence during the Ottoman Empire. During this period the order spread into cities throughout Anatolia, as well as into Istanbul. However, with the emergence of the secular government under Kemal Ataturk in 1925 the order was suppressed and its library in Konya handed over to the town museum. Following the suppression of the Sufi orders in Turkey, the last head of the order, Muhamad Baqir, went to Aleppo, where ritual gatherings were held until the early 1950s when the last active shaikh (Muhammad Shahu) died. Today the Sama is performed for one week annually in Konya between 11 and 17 December.

Other Mawlawi orders had been established in the Islamic world, but they have suffered under the impact of the political and secular pressures that have affected the twentieth century. The Mawlaw community of Damascus, which dates back to the sixteenth century, disappeared in the 1960s when the last shaikh died. The Mawlawiyyah also had centres in Beirut, which were active until May 1982 when the last shaikh lost his life as a result of Israeli bombardment of the city. In the Balkans, the Mawlawiyyah survived into the post-Ottoman era in Greece and Yugoslavia. In Greece it appears to have ceased in the 1920s and in Yugoslavia in about 1959.

The Sama ceremony contains a number of actions which are symbolic in character. During the Sama the right hand of the performer (the samazan) is raised to heaven and is a sign that the dancer is receiving inspiration from God. The left hand is pointed downwards and signifies that the dancer is giving to the people what he has received from God. The dance is performed in four stages, each of which represents a closer experience and manifestation of the presence of God. The order's dress consists of a cap called sikke, a long sleeveless skirt called tennure, a jacket with sleeves called deste-gul, a waist-band called elif-lam-end, and a cloak with sleeves called khirke. The instruments used in the dance are the reed flute, the zither, the rebeck, the drum and the tambourine.

Mawlânâ Jalâl ad-Dîn Muhammad Balkhî, also known as Jalâl ad-Dîn Mu%ammad Rûmî, but known to the English-speaking world simply as Rumi, (30 September 1207 – 17 December 1273), was a 13th-century Persian poet, Islamic jurist, theologian, and mystic. Rûmî is a descriptive name meaning "the Roman" since he lived most of his life in an area called Rûm because it was once ruled by the Byzantine Empire. According to tradition, Rumi was born in Balkh, Bactria, in contemporary Afghanistan, which at that time was part of the Persian Empire, and was the hometown of his father's family. Scholars, however, believe that he was born in Wakhsh, a small town located at the river Wakhsh in what is now Tajikistan. Wakhsh belonged to the larger province of Balkh, and in the year Rumi was born, his father was an appointed scholar there. Both these cities were at the time included in the Greater Persian cultural sphere of Khorasan, the easternmost province of historical Persia, and were part of the Khwarezmian Empire.

His birthplace and native language both indicate a Persian heritage. Due to quarrels between different dynasties in Khorasan, opposition to the Khwarizmid Shahs who were considered devious by Bahâ ud-Dîn Walad (Rumi's father) or fear of the impending Mongol cataclysm, his father decided to migrate westwards. Rumi's family traveled west, first performing the Hajj and eventually settling in the Anatolian city Konya (capital of the Seljuk Sultanate of Rum, now located in Turkey). This was where he lived most of his life, and here he composed one of the crowning glories of Persian literature which profoundly affected the culture of the area. He lived most of his life under the Sultanate of Rum, where he produced his works and died in 1273 CE. He was buried in Konya and his shrine became a place of pilgrimage.

Following his death, his followers and his son Sultan Walad founded the Mawlawîyah Sufi Order, also known as the Order of the Whirling Dervishes, famous for its Sufi dance known as the Sama ceremony. Rumi's works are written in the New Persian language. A Persian literary renaissance (in the 8th/9th century) started in regions of Sistan, Khorâsân and Transoxianaand by the 10th/11th century; it reinforced the Persian language as the preferred literary and cultural language in the Persian Islamic world.

Although Rumi's works were written in Persian, Rumi's importance is considered to transcend national and ethnic borders. His original works are widely read in their original language across the Persian-speaking world. Translations of his works are very popular in other countries. His poetry has influenced Persian literature as well as the literature of the Urdu, Bengali, Arabic and Turkish languages. His poems have been widely translated into many of the world's languages and transposed into various formats; BBC News has described him as the "most popular poet in America".

Life

Rumi was born in Khorâsân, possibly in or near the city of Balkh. His life is described in Shams ud-Din Ahmad Aflâki's *Manâqib ul-Ârifîn* (written between 1318 and 1353). Rumi's father was Bahâ ud-Dîn Walad, a theologian, jurist and a mystic from Balkh, who was also known during his lifetime as Sultan al-Ulama or "Sultan of the Scholars". His mother was Mu'mina Khâṭûn. When the Mongols invaded Central Asia sometime between 1215 and 1220, Baha ud-Din Walad, with his whole family and a group of disciples, set out westwards. On the road to Anatolia, Rumi encountered one of the most famous mystic Persian poets, 'Attar, in the Iranian city of Nishapur, located in the province of Khorâsân. 'Attar immediately recognized Rumi's spiritual eminence.

He saw the father walking ahead of the son and said, "Here comes a sea followed by an ocean." He gave the boy his *Asrârnâma,* a book about the entanglement of the soul in the material world. This meeting had a deep impact on the eighteen-year-old Rumi, and later on became the inspiration for his works. From Nishapur, Walad and his entourage set out for Baghdad, meeting many of the scholars and Sufis of the city. From there they went to Baghdad and Hejaz and performed the pilgrimage at Mecca. The migrating caravan then passed through Damascus, Malatya, Erzincan, Sivas, Kayseri and Nigde. They finally settled in Karaman for seven years; Rumi's mother and brother both died there. In 1225, Rumi married Gowhar Khatun in Karaman. They had two sons: Sultan Walad and Ala-eddin Chalabi. When his wife died, Rumi married again and had a son, Amir Alim Chalabi, and a daughter, Malakeh Khatun.

On 1 May 1228, most likely as a result of the insistent invitation of 'Alâ' ud-Dîn Key-Qobâd, ruler of Anatolia, Baha' ud-Din came and finally settled in Konya in Anatolia within the westernmost territories of the Seljuk Sultanate of Rûm. Baha' ud-Din became the head of a madrassa (religious school) and when he died, Rumi, aged twenty-five, inherited his position. One of Baha' ud-Din's students, Sayyed Burhan ud-Din Muhaqqiq Termazi, continued to train Rumi in the religious and mystical doctrines of Rumi's father. For nine years, Rumi practiced Sufism as a disciple of Burhan ud-Din until the latter died in 1240 or 1241. Rumi's public life then began: he became a teacher who preached in the mosques of Konya and taught his adherents in the madrassa.

During this period, Rumi also travelled to Damascus and is said to have spent four years there. It was his meeting with the dervish Shams-e Tabrizi on 15 November 1244 that completely changed Rumi's life. Shams had traveled throughout the Middle East searching and praying for someone who could "endure my company". A voice said to him, "What will you give in return?" Shams replied, "My head!" The voice then said, "The one you seek is Jalal ud-Din of Konya." On the night of 5 December 1248, as Rumi and Shams were talking, Shams was called to the back door. He went out, never to be seen again.

It is believed that Shams was murdered with the connivance of Rumi's son, 'Ala' ud-Din; if so, Shams indeed gave his head for the privilege of mystical friendship. Rumi's love for, and his bereavement at the death of, Shams found their expression in an outpouring of music, dance, and lyric poems, *Divan-e Shams-e Tabrizi*. He himself went out searching for Shams and journeyed again to Damascus. There, he realized:

> Why should I seek? I am the same as He.
>
> His essence speaks through me.
>
> I have been looking for myself!

For more than ten years after meeting Shams, Mawlana had been spontaneously composing ghazals (Persian poems), and these had been collected in the *Divan-i Kabir* or Diwan Shams Tabrizi. Rumi found another companion in Salah ud-Din-e Zarkub, a goldsmith. After Salah ud-Din's death, Rumi's scribe and favorite student, Hussam-e Chalabi, assumed the role of Rumi's companion. One day, the two of them were wandering through the Meram vineyards outside Konya when Hussam described to Rumi an idea he had had: "If you were to write a book like the *Ilâhînâma* of Sanai or the *Mantiq ut-Tayr* of 'Attar, it would become the companion of many troubadours. They would fill their hearts from your work and compose music to accompany it." Rumi smiled and took out a piece of paper on which were written the opening eighteen lines of his *Masnavi*, beginning with:

> Listen to the reed and the tale it tells,
>
> How it sings of separation...

Hussam implored Rumi to write more. Rumi spent the next twelve years of his life in Anatolia dictating the six volumes of this masterwork, the Masnavi, to Hussam. In December 1273, Rumi fell ill; he predicted his own death and composed the well-known ghazal, which begins with the verse:

How doest thou know what sort of king I have within me as companion?

Do not cast thy glance upon my golden face, for I have iron legs.

Rumi died on 17 December 1273 in Konya; his body was interred beside that of his father, and a splendid shrine, the *Yeºil Türbe,* was erected over his place of burial. His epitaph reads:

When we are dead, seek not our tomb in the earth, but find it in the hearts of men.

Teachings

The general theme of Rumi's thought, like that of other mystic and Sufi poets of Persian literature, is essentially that of the concept of tawhîd– union with his beloved (the primal root) from which/whom he has been cut off and become aloof– and his longing and desire to restore it. The Masnavi weaves fables, scenes from everyday life, Qur'anic revelations and exegesis, and metaphysics into a vast and intricate tapestry. Rumi is considered an example of Insan-e Kamil— Perfect Man, the perfected or completed human being. In the East, it is said of him that he was "not a prophet— but surely, he has brought a scripture".

Rumi believed passionately in the use of music, poetry, and dance as a path for reaching God. For Rumi, music helped devotees to focus their whole being on the divine, and to do this so intensely that the soul was both destroyed and resurrected. It was from these ideas that the practice of "whirling" dervishes developed into a ritual form. His teachings became the base for the order of the Mevlevi which his son Sultan Walad organized. Rumi encouraged *Sama,* listening to music and turning or doing the sacred dance. In the Mevlevi tradition, *Sama* represents a mystical journey of spiritual ascent through mind and love to the Perfect One. In this journey, the seeker symbolically turns towards the truth, grows through love, abandons the ego, finds the truth, and arrives at the Perfect.

The seeker then returns from this spiritual journey, with greater maturity, to love and to be of service to the whole of creation without discrimination with regard to beliefs, races, classes, and nations. According to Shahram Shiva, one reason for Rumi's popularity is that Rumi is able to verbalize the highly personal and often confusing world of personal/spiritual growth and mysticism in a very forward and direct fashion. He does not offend anyone, and he includes everyone. The world of Rumi is neither exclusively the world of a Sufi, nor the world of a Hindu, nor a Jew, nor a Christian; it is the highest state of a human being— a fully evolved human.

A complete human is not bound by cultural limitations; he touches every one of us. Today, Rumi's poems can be heard in churches, synagogues, Zen monasteries, as well as in the downtown New York art/performance/music scene. According to Professor Majid M. Naini, Rumi's life and transformation provide true testimony and proof that people of all religions and backgrounds can live together in peace and harmony. Rumi's visions, words, and life teach us how to reach inner peace and happiness so we can finally stop the continual stream of hostility and hatred and achieve true, global peace and harmony.

In other verses in the *Masnavi*, Rumi describes in detail the universal message of love:

Lover's nationality is separate from all other religions,
The lover's religion and nationality is the Beloved (God).
The lover's cause is separate from all other causes
Love is the astrolabe of God's mysteries.

Major Works

Rumi's poetry is often divided into various categories: the quatrains (rubayât) and odes (ghazal) of the *Divan*, the six books of the *Masnavi*, The Discourses, The Letters, and the almost unknown *Six Sermons*.

Poetic works:

- Rumi's major work is the *Mahnawîye Ma'nawî*, a six-volume poem regarded by some Sufis as the Persian-language Qur'an. It is considered by many to be one of the greatest works of mystical poetry.
- Rumi's other major work is the *Dîwân-e Kabîr* (*Great Work*) or *Dîwân-e Shams-e Tabrîzî* (*The Works of Shams of Tabriz*; named in honor of Rumi's great friend and inspiration, the dervish Shams) and comprising some forty thousand verses. Several reasons have been offered for Rumi's decision to name his masterpiece after Shams; some argue that since Rumi would not have been a poet without Shams, it is apt that the collection be named after him.

Prose works:

- *Fihi Ma Fihi* (*In It What's in It*, Persian) provides a record of seventy-one talks and lectures given by Rumi on various occasions to his disciples. It was compiled from the notes of his various disciples, so Rumi did not author the work directly. An English translation from the Persian was first published by A.J. Arberry as *Discourses of Rumi* (New York: Samuel Weiser, 1972), and a translation of the second book by Wheeler Thackston, *Sign of the Unseen* (Putney, VT: Threshold Books, 1994).
- *Majâles-e Sab'a* (*Seven Sessions*, Persian) contains seven Persian sermons (as the name implies) or lectures given in seven different assemblies. The sermons themselves give a commentary on the deeper meaning of Qur'an and Hadeeth. The sermons also include quotations from poems of Sana'i, 'Attar, and other poets, including Rumi himself. As Aflakî relates, after Shams-e Tabrîzî, Rumi gave sermons at the request of notables, especially Salâh al-Dîn Zarkûb.
- *Makatib* (*The Letters*, Persian) is the book containing Rumi's letters in Persian to his disciples, family

members, and men of state and of influence. The letters testify that Rumi kept very busy helping family members and administering a community of disciples that had grown up around them.

Philosophical Outlook

Rumi was an evolutionary thinker in the sense that he believed that the spirit after devolution from the divine Ego undergoes an evolutionary process by which it comes nearer and nearer to the same divine Ego. All matter in the universe obeys this law and this movement is due to an inbuilt urge (which Rumi calls "love") to evolve and seek enjoinment with the divinity from which it has emerged. Evolution into a human being from an animal is only one stage in this process. The doctrine of the Fall of Adam is reinterpreted as the devolution of the Ego from the universal ground of divinity and is a universal, cosmic phenomenon. This synthesis of evolution and creationism is a culmination of the ideas of Plotinus and of previous Muslim philosophers like Al Farabi. The French philosopher Henri Bergson's idea of life being creative and evolutionary is similar, though unlike Bergson, Rumi believes that there is a specific *goal* to the process: the attainment of God.

Rumi's Universality

It is often said that the teachings of Rumi are universal in nature. For Rumi, religion was mostly a personal experience and not limited to logical arguments or perceptions of the senses. Creative love, or the urge to rejoin the spirit to divinity, was the goal towards which every thing moves. The dignity of life, in particular human life (which is conscious of its divine origin and goal), was important.

I searched for God among the Christians and on the Cross and therein I found Him not.

I went into the ancient temples of idolatry; no trace of Him was there.

I entered the mountain cave of Hira and then went as far as Qandhar but God I found not.

With set purpose I fared to the summit of Mount Caucasus and found there only 'anqa's habitation.

Then I directed my search to the Kaaba, the resort of old and young; God was not there even.

Turning to philosophy I inquired about him from ibn Sina but found Him not within his range.

I fared then to the scene of the Prophet's experience of a great divine manifestation only a "two bow-lengths' distance from him" but God was not there even in that exalted court.

Finally, I looked into my own heart and there I saw Him; He was nowhere else.

Legacy

Rumi's Universality

What can I do, Submitters to God? I do not know myself.

I am neither Christian nor Jew, neither Zoroastrian nor Muslim,

I am not from east or west, not from land or sea,

not from the shafts of nature nor from the spheres of the firmament,

not of the earth, not of water, not of air, not of fire.

I am not from the highest heaven, not from this world,

not from existence, not from being.

I am not from India, not from China, not from Bulgar, not from Saqsin,

not from the realm of the two Iraqs, not from the land of Khurasan

I am not from the world, not from beyond,

not from heaven and not from hell.

I am not from Adam, not from Eve, not from paradise and not from Ridwan.

My place is placeless, my trace is traceless,
no body, no soul, I am from the soul of souls.
I have chased out duality, lived the two worlds as one.
One I seek, one I know, one I see, and one I call.
He is the first, he is the last, he is the outer, he is the inner.
Beyond "He" and "He is" I know no other.
I am drunk from the cup of love; the two worlds have escaped me.
I have no concern but carouse and rapture.
If one day in my life I spend a moment without you
from that hour and that time I would repent my life.
If one day I am given a moment in solitude with you
I will trample the two worlds underfoot and dance forever.
O Sun of Tabriz (Shams Tabrizi), I am so tipsy here in this world,
I have no tale to tell but tipsiness and rapture.

Rumi's importance transcends national and ethnic borders. Readers of the Persian language in Afghanistan, Iran, Tajikistan and Uzbekistan see him as one of their most significant classical poets and an influence on many poets through history. Rumi has also had a great influence on Turkish literature through the centuries. Rumi's poetry forms the basis of much classical Iranian and Afghan music. Contemporary classical interpretations of his poetry are made by Muhammad Reza Shajarian, Shahram Nazeri, Davood Azad (the three from Iran) and Ustad Mohammad Hashem Cheshti (Afghanistan). To many modern Westerners, his teachings are one of the best introductions to the philosophy and practice of Sufism. Pakistan's National Poet, Muhammad Iqbal, was also inspired by Rumi's works and considered him to be his spiritual leader, addressing him as "Pir Rumi" in his poems (the honorific Pir literally means "old man", but in the sufi/mystic context it means founder, master, or guide).

Rumi's work has been translated into many of the world's languages, including Russian, German, Urdu, Turkish, Arabic, French, Italian, and Spanish, and is being presented in a growing number of formats, including concerts, workshops, readings, dance performances, and other artistic creations. The English interpretations of Rumi's poetry by Coleman Barks have sold more than half a million copies worldwide, and Rumi is one of the most widely read poets in the United States. Recordings of Rumi poems have made it to Billboard's Top 20 list.

Rumi and the Persian World

Say all in Persian even if Arabic is better– Love will find its way through all languages on its own. Rumi's poetry reflects the richness of Iranian culture and represents the literary environment of Khorasan, the medieval center of the Persian world. These cultural, historical and linguistic ties between Rumi and the Iranian world have made Rumi an iconic Persian and Iranian poet. Rumi's poetry is displayed on the walls of many cities across the Persian-speaking world, sung in Persian music, and read in school books. Persian speakers literally live Rumi's poetry.

The Mawlawî Sufi Order

The Mawlawî Sufi order (Mawlawîyah or Mevlevi, as it is known in Turkey) was founded in 1273 by Rumi's followers after his death. His first successor in the rectorship of the order was Husam Chalabi himself, after whose death in 1284 Rumi's younger and only surviving son, Sultan Walad (died 1312), favorably known as author of the mystical *Matnawî Rabâbnâma*, or the *Book of the Rabab*, was installed as grand master of the order. The leadership of the order has been kept within Rumi's family in Konya uninterruptedly since then. The Mawlawî Sufis, also known as Whirling Dervishes, believe in performing their dhikr in the form of Sama. During the time of Rumi (as attested in the *Manâqib ul-Ârefin* of Aflâkî), his followers gathered for musical and "turning" practices.

Rumi was himself a notable musician who played the robâb, although his favorite instrument was the Ney or reed flute. The music accompanying the Sama consists of settings of poems from the *Matnawî* and *Dîwân-e Kabîr*, or of Sultan Walad's poems. The Mawlawîyah was a well-established Sufi order in the Ottoman Empire, and many of the members of the order served in various official positions of the Caliphate. The center for the Mawlawiyyah was in Konya. There is also a Mawlawî monastery (dargâh) in Istanbul near the Galata Tower in which the Sama is performed and accessible to the public.

During Ottoman times, the Mawlawîyah produced a number of notable poets and musicians, including Sheikh Ghalib, Ismail Rusuhi Dede of Ankara, Esrar Dede, Halet Efendi, and Gavsi Dede, who are all buried at the Galata Mawlawî Khâna (Turkish: Mevlevi-Hane) in Istanbul. Music especially that of the Ney plays an important part in the Mawlawiyyah, and thus much of the traditional, oriental music that Westerners associate with Turkey originates from the Mawlawî order.

With the foundation of the modern, secular Republic of Turkey, Mustafa Kemal Atatürk removed religion from the sphere of public policy and restricted it exclusively to that of personal morals, behavior, and faith. On 13 December 1925, a law was passed closing all the tekkes (or tekeyh) (dervish lodges) and zâwiyas (chief dervish lodges), and also the centers of veneration to which pilgrimages (ziyârat) were made. Istanbul alone had more than 250 tekkes as well as small centers for gatherings of various fraternities; this law dissolved the Sufi Orders, prohibited the use of mystical names, titles and costumes pertaining to their titles, impounded the Orders' assets, and banned their ceremonies and meetings.

The law also provided penalties for those who tried to re-establish the Orders. Two years later, in 1927, the Mausoleum of Mevlana in Konya was allowed to reopen as a Museum. In the 1950s, the Turkish government began allowing the Whirling Dervishes to perform once a year in Konya. The Mawlânâ festival is held over two weeks in December; its culmination is on 17 December, the Urs of Mawlânâ (anniversary of Rumi's death), called *Đabe Arûs* (Persian meaning "nuptial night"), the night of Rumi's union with God. In 1974, the Whirling Dervishes were permitted to travel to the West for the first time.

Rumi's Religious Denomination

According to Edward G. Browne, the three most prominent mystical Persian poets Rumi, Sana'i and Attar were all Sunni muslims and their poetry abound with praise for the first two caliphs Abu Bakr and Umar ibn al-Khattâb. According to Annemarie Schimmel, the tendency among Shia authors to include leading mystical poets such as Rumi and Attar among their own ranks became stronger after the introduction of Twelver Shia as the state religion in the Safavid Empire in 1501.

Rumi and Islam

According to the great authority on Sufism, Seyyed Hossein Nasr, in Sufism: Paradoxically, however to become someone spiritually means also ultimately to become no one".

A poem attributed to Rumi states, which according to Nasr there is no proof that it is not by him and is one of the most famous poems associated with the name Rumi over the centuries states:

"What is to be done, O Muslims, for I know myself not,

Neither a Christian am I, nor Jew, nor Magian nor Muslim

Neither of the East am I nor West, nor of the land, nor sea;

Nor of nature's quarry, nor of heavens circling above.

I am not made of earth or water, not of wind or fire;

Nor am I of the Divine Throne nor of floor carpeting,

Nor of the realm of the cosmos, nor of minerals.

I am not from India, nor China, nor Bulgaria, nor Turkistan;

I am not from kingdom of the two Iraqs, nor from the earth of Khorasan.

Neither of this world am I nor the next; nor of heaven nor hell;

Nor from Adam nor Eve nor of Eden, nor paradise or its porter.

My place is the placeless, my mark the markless;

Not either body or soul for I am myself the Beloved."

Rumi's approach to Islam is clarified his quatrain:

Man banda-ye qur'ânam, agar jân dâram

man khâk-e rah-e muhammad-e mukhtâram

gar naql konad joz în kas az goftâram

bçzâram azô waz-în sokhan bçzâram.

I am the servant of the Qur'an as long as I have life.

I am the dust on the path of Muhammad, the Chosen One.

If anyone quotes anything except this from my sayings,

I am quit of him and outraged by these words.

Seyyed Hossein Nasr states:

One of the greatest living authorities on Rûmî in Persia today, Hâdî Hâ'irî has shown in an unpublished work that some 6,000 verses of the Dîwân and the Mathnawî are practically direct translations of Qur'ânic verses into Persian poetry.

Rumi states in his Dîwân:

The Sufi is hanging on to Muhammad, like Abu Bakr.

Make your intellect a sacrifice in the presence of Muhammad, and say, "God is sufficient for me, since God is enough for satisfying me.

Eight Hundredth Anniversary Celebrations

Mawlana Jalal-ud-Dine Balkhi-Rumi is one of the greatest spiritual masters and mystic poets of Islamic civilization. In Afghanistan, he is known as "Mawlana" and in Iran as "Mawlawi". At the proposal of the Permanent Delegations of Afghanistan, Egypt, and Turkey, and as approved by its Executive Board and General Conference in conformity with its mission of "constructing in the minds of men the defences of peace", UNESCO was associated with the celebration, in 2007, of the eight hundredth anniversary of Rumi's birth. The commemoration at UNESCO itself took place on 6 September 2007; UNESCO issued a medal in Rumi's name in the hope that it would prove an encouragement to those who are engaged in research on and dissemination of Rumi's ideas and ideals, which would, in turn, enhance the diffusion of the ideals of UNESCO.

The Afghan Ministry of Culture and Youth established a national committee which organized an international seminar to celebrate the birth and life of the great ethical philosopher and world-renowned poet. This grand gathering of the intellectuals, diplomats, and followers of Maulana was held in Kabul and in Balkh. On 30 September 2007, Iranian school bells were rung throughout the country in honor of Mowlana. Also in that year, Iran held a Rumi Week from 26 October to 2 November. An international ceremony and conference were held in Tehran; the event was opened by the Iranian president and the chairman of the Iranian parliament. Scholars from twenty-nine countries attended the events, and 450 articles were presented at the conference. Iranian musician Shahram Nazeri was awarded the Légion d'honneur and Iran's House of Music Award in 2007 for his renowned works on Rumi masterpieces. 2007 was declared as the "International Rumi Year" by UNESCO.

Also on 30 September 2007, Turkey celebrated Rumi's eight-hundredth birthday with a giant Whirling Dervish ritual performance of the Sama, which was televised using forty-eight cameras and broadcast live in eight countries. Ertugrul Gunay of the Ministry of Culture and Tourism of Turkey, stated, "Three hundred dervishes are scheduled to take part in this ritual, making it the largest performance of Sama in history."

The term "Sufi" derives from the Arabic word "suf" (meaning "wool") and was applied to Muslim ascetics and mystics because they wore garments made out of wool. Sufism represents a dimension of Islamic religious life that has frequently been viewed by Muslim theologians and lawyers with suspicion. The ecstatic state of the mystic can sometimes produce extreme behaviour or statements that on occasion appear to border on the blasphemous. The cause of this is that the Sufis can sometimes feel so close to God that they lose a sense of their own self identity and feel themselves to be completely absorbed into God. This in fact is the goal of the Sufi. Through following a series of devotional practices, which lead to higher levels of ecstatic state, Sufis aspire to realise a condition in which they are in direct communion with God. Ultimately the individual human personality passes away and the Sufi feels his soul absorbed into God.

The origins of Islamic mysticism can be traced back to the 8th century. A consequence of the rapid spread of Islam under the Ummayad dynasty was the exposure of Muslims to a large number of different ethnic groups and the acquisition of considerable wealth that was the fruit of military conquest. The growing opulence of Islam was symbolised by the relocation of the capital of the empire from Medina to the more cosmopolitan city of Damascus. In reaction to the worldlier outlook of the Ummayads various groups and figures emerged who encouraged a return to the pure values of the Prophet and the Qur'an.

One such figure, Hasan al-Basri (642-728), preached a rejection of the world and courageously criticised those in power when he felt that they were not conducting themselves according to the ethical standards of Islam. A second figure,

Rabi'ah al-Adawiyah (d.801), cultivated the attainment of mystical union with God through the love of God. A third, and controversial, mystic, al-Hallaj (857-922), lived as a wandering preacher who gathered around him a large number of disciples. Such was al-Hallaj's sense of the intimate presence of God that he sometimes appeared to be identifying himself with God. He is reported to have made one statement - "I am the Truth!" - which caused such outrage that he was imprisoned for eight years and in 922 executed by crucifixion. Al-Hallaj's death illustrates in an extreme way the tensions that would characterise the relationship between Sufi mysticism and the Islamic legal authorities.

The kind of loose master-disciple relationship characteristic of 9th century mystical Islam gradually evolved into organised establishments. By the 11th century there were distinctive groups associated with a particular master. These groups, however, were often not cohesive enough to survive the death of the master. It was only in the 12th and 13th centuries that orders emerged which were stable enough to continue after the death of the founder. This continuity was achieved through the current master nominating a successor who would lead the order following the current master's death. Thus, these orders were able to trace their origins through a chain of masters. Such orders were called tariqahs.

The three regions principally associated with Sufism are Mesopotamia (Iran and Iraq), Central Asia and North Africa. The most important orders to emerge out of Mesopotamia are Rifa'iyyah, Suhrawardiyyah, Kubrawiyyah and Qadiriyyah. These are all among the earliest of the Sufi orders. Rifa'iyyah was founded in Basra, Iraq in the 12th century, soon spreading from Iraq into Syria and Egypt. Suhrawardiyyah also founded in 12th century Iraq spread westwards into India. Qadiriyyah and Kubrawiyyah are both Iranian orders. Qadiriyyah, the earlier of the two orders, emerged in the 12th century, and spread both eastwards and westwards into India and North Africa. Kubrawiyyah is historically linked to Suhrawardiyyah in that its founder,

Nayim al-din Kubra (1145-1221), was a disciple of the founder of Suhrawardiyyah, Abu Najib as—Suhrawardi (1097-1168).

Sufism was transplanted into North Africa as a result of the expansion of the Rifa'i order into Syria and then Egypt. The presence of Rifa'iyyah inspired the founding of other orders. In the 13th century Badawiyyah was founded in Egypt by Ahmad al-Badawi (1199-1276), who acquired a reputation for mysticism and the performance of miracles. This order continues today and thousands of visitors attend its annual festival in Tanta, Egypt. At about the same time that Sufism was developing in Egypt, it was gaining in strength in North-West Africa through the support of the ruling Almohad dynasty (1130-1269), who ruled over Morocco, Algeria, Tunisia and Muslim Spain. In 13th century Tunisia a certain al-Shadhili acquired a group of disciples and formed who formed the basis of an order that came to be known as Shadhiliyyah. This order continues to flourish in Algeria, Tunisia and Morocco.

In the 18th century the Islamic world fell under the influence of a reform movement called Wahabiyyah. This movement sought to rid Islam of what it regarded as illegitimate innovations such as the worship of saints and to encourage strict adherence to the shari'ah. The spirit of reform spread into North Africa, leading to the establishment of new orders which rejected the more extreme forms of behaviour characteristic of some Sufi orders. An important order that came out of this context is Tidjaniyyah, which was founded in the 1780s by Ahmad al-Tidjani (d.1815) and which rejected many popular Sufi practices such as the adoration of saints. This order continues to exist today and has spread throughout North Africa and western Sub-Saharan Africa.

Another order of this type is Sanusiyyah, which was founded in Cyrenaica (in eastern Libya) in the 1840s by Muhammad b. ali Sanusi (1787-1859). This order was characterised by the rejection of all forms of luxury and a strong sense of veneration for the Prophet. Following the departure of European colonialists from North Africa in the 1940s and 1950s the Sanusis established the state of Libya. The Sanusis were overthrown in 1969 by Colonel Muammar al-Qadafi. Since then the Sanusis have provided an important source of opposition to the Qadafi regime and survive to the present day in spite of the Qadafi regimes attempt to curtail their activities.

In Central Asia and Anatolia (equivalent to modern day Turkey) a number of major Sufi orders emerged between the 12th and 17th centuries. The earliest of these, Yasawiyyah, was founded in the region now known as Turkestan and played a major role in spreading Islam among the Turkish tribes of Central Asia. Possibly deriving from Yasawiyyah is the Bektashiyyah order. According to tradition, Hajj Bektash, the putative founder of Bektashiyyah, originally belonged to the Yasawiyyah order. Bektashiyyah continues to survive in the Balkan region to the present day.

Another Central Asian order is Chishtiyyah. The origins of this order are uncertain, although the founder is generally believed to be Mu'in al-Din Chishti (c.1142-1236), a native of Sijistan. The order gradually spread into India where it remains today as the largest and most important Sufi order. Mawalwiyyah traces its origins to the famous Turkish mystic and poet al-Rumi (1207-1273). The order's name derives from the Arabic word Mawlana (our master), a title given to al-Rumi by the order. Mawlawiyyah is based in the Turkish town of Konya. Like many Turkish orders it was effectively suppressed when Turkey became a secular state in 1925. In other parts of the Islamic world the once important order has seriously declined or disappeared altogether.

The Naqshbandis, however, have enjoyed more success. Founded by Baha al-din Naqshband (d.1389) in a village near Bukhara in Central Asia, the order gradually spread eastwards into India and westwards into Turkey. Supported by the Ottomans, Naqshbandiyyah flourished until the demise of the Ottoman Empire and the establishment of a secular state under Kemal Ataturk in Turkey. Ataturk regarded the Sufi orders as decadent, reactionary and an obstruction to the modernisation of Turkey. In order to reform the state in 1925 he ordered the abolition of all mystical orders in Turkey. The Khalwatiyyah order was founded in Persia but spread quickly into Anatolia. Out of Khalwatiyyah two other important orders emerged: Bayramiyyah and Jalwatiyyah.

Bayramiyyah was founded at Ankara in the 14th century and continued until its dissolution in 1925. Jalwatiyyah was founded in the 17th century by Aziz Mahmud Huda'i (d.1628) who was previously a member of the Khalwati order. Like the other Turkish orders it was banned in 1925 by the Ataturk government; the last master of the order died in 1946. The abolition of these orders in Turkey demonstrates the kinds of pressures they have encountered as a result of the growing strength of secularism in the world during the modern period. In many parts of the Arab world the orders have all but disappeared. In other parts of the Islamic world, however, they have continued. In North Africa and India Sufism has lost the influence they once had but nevertheless remain a part of the religious identity of the area. The continued existence of such orders suggests the inseparability of religion and its mystical dimension.

4

The Chrishtiyyah

Hazrat Khwaja Abu Ishaq Shami ("the Syrian") (d. 941 C.E.) brought Sufism to the town of Chisht, some 95 miles east of Herat in present-day Afghanistan. Before returning to the Levant, Shami initiated, trained, and deputized the son of the local Amir, Khwaja Abu Ahmad Abdal (d. 966). Under the leadership of Khwaja Abu Ahmad's descendants, the Chishtiyya flourished as a regional mystical order specializing in *Sama'*, ritual music and moving meditation. Early in the 13th century, Hazrat Khwaja Mu'inuddin Hasan Sanjari (d. 1229) and his disciples introduced a branch of the Chishtiyya in the Indian Subcontinent. Khwaja Mu'inuddin's ethos was: "Generosity like a river, affection like the sun, humility like the earth." Remembered as "Gharib-nawaz," "the Helper of the Poor,"' his legacy is such that today hundreds of thousands of pilgrims, of all castes and creeds, flock to his tomb in Ajmer for the annual *'urs* festival.

Khwaja Mu'inuddin's successor, Khwaja Qutbuddin Bakhtiyar Kaki (d. 1235) expired after a mystical couplet sent him into a swoon of ecstasy. He was succeeded by Khwaja Fariduddin Mas'ud (d. 1265), whose elegant verses grace the pages of the Sikh holy book, the Guru Granth Sahib. Khwaja Fariduddin's successor, Khwaja Nizamuddin Awliya'(d. 1325)—remembered as "Mahbub-i Ilahi," "Beloved of God"—presided over an era of florescence, when the Chishti message spread throughout the Subcontinent. The death of his successor, Khwaja Nasiruddin Mahmud, the "Lamp of Delhi" (d. 1356), who was buried with the sacred relics of office, closed a glorious chapter. The initiatic tree of the Chishtiyya sprouted many branches and shoots. The lineage of Khwaja Nizam al-Din (the Nizamiyya) was paralleled by the lineage of Khwaja 'Ala al-Din 'Ali Sabir (the Sabiriyya). Our lineage is traced to Khwaja Nasir al-Din through his nephew Shaykh Kamal al-Din 'Allama (d. 1355), whose descendants established a mystical institution in Gujarat that continues to this day.

Among these descendants was Shaykh Muhammad Chishti (d. 1630), who attained the cosmic initiations of *Qutb* (Axis) and *Mahbub* (Beloved) at the dawn of the second *Hijri* millennium. In Medina, Shaykh Muhammad's grandson Shaykh Yahya Madani (d. 1689) deputized Shah Kalim Allah (d. 1729), who came from the family of architects that designed the Taj Mahal. Shah Kalim Allah later composed the meditation manual *Kashkul-i Kalimi,* which documents the technical repertory of the Chishtiyya, a sophisticated combination of Arabic ritual formulae, Central Asian subtle physiology theory, and hathayogic body techniques. Shah Kalim Allah established a school in Delhi that flourished under the leadership of the descendants of his successor Shah Nizam al-Din (d. 1730), until it was displaced in the aftermath of the ill-fated Revolt of 1857, when the Mughal Emperor Bahadur Shah Zafar—a disciple of Shah Nizam al-Din's great grandson Kale Miyan—was exiled to Rangoon.

Just before the Revolt, a premonition prompted Kale Miyan's successor Shaykh Muhammad Hasan Jili Kalimi to take his family to Hyderabad. There he deputized Sayyid Abu Hashim Madani, who became the Murshid (teacher) of Hazrat Inayat Khan. Hazrat Inayat Khan's own memories of his Murshid, beginning with the first encounter, are recorded in his *Confessions*:

After a time of suspense the Pir-o-Murshid entered, bringing with him a very great sense of light. As all those present greeted him, bowing down in their humility, it seemed to me all at once that I had seen him before, but where I could not recall. At last, after gazing at him earnestly, I remembered that his was the face which so persistently haunted me during my silence. The proof of this was manifested as soon as his eyes fell on me.

He turned to his host, saying, "O Mawlana, tell me who this young man may be? He appeals intensely to my spirit." Mawlana Khayr al-Mubin answered, "Your holiness, this young man is a genius in music, and he desires greatly to submit himself to your inspiring guidance." Then the Master smiled and granted the request, initiating me into Sufism there and then. Muhammad Abu Hashim Madani belonged to a distinguished family of Medina, and was a direct descendant of the Holy Prophet. My joy in him was so great that it found its expression in poetry and music. I had at last found my pearl among men, my guide, my treasure, and beacon of hope. I composed a song and sang it to him and this; has brought me all my success and will aid me in my future life.

And thus was my song:

Thou art my salvation and freedom is mine,

I am not, I melt as a pearl in sweet wine!

My heart, soul, and self, yea, all these are thine;

O Lord I have no more to offer!

I drink of the nectar of truth the divine,

As Moses thy word, as Yusuf they shine

who walk in thy ways; and Christ is thy sign:

Thou raisest to life everlasting!

Thou art as Muhammad to them that repine,

My spirit is purged as the gold from a mine!

I only know that my heart beats with thine,

And joys in boundless freedom!

My Murshid greatly appreciated this outburst of love on my part and exclaimed in deep emotion, "Be thou blessed with Divine Light and illuminate the beloved ones of Allah!" From this time a spiritual attachment between myself and my Murshid was firmly established, and as it grew more and more it opened up in me the ways of light through my attachment to that Inner Radiance, which can never be gained through discussion or argument, reading, writing, nor mystical exercises. I visited him at the expense of all my affairs whenever I felt his call, receiving rays of his ecstasy with bent head, and listening to all he said without doubt or fear. Thus the firm faith and confidence I brought to bear upon my meditations prepared me to absorb the Light of the World Unseen. I studied the Qur'an, Hadith, and the literature of the Persian mystics. I cultivated my inner senses, and underwent periods of clairvoyance, clairaudience, intuition, inspiration, impressions, dreams, and visions. I also made experiments in communicating with the living and the dead. I delved into the occult and psychic sides of mysticism, as well as realizing the benefits of piety, morality, and *bhakti* (or devotion).

The more progressed in their pursuit, the more unlearned I seemed, as there was always more and more to understand and acquire. Of all that I comprehended and experienced I valued most that Divine Wisdom which alone is the essence of all that is best and attainable, and which leads us on from the Finite World unto Infinitudes of Bliss. After receiving instruction in the five different grades of Sufism, the physical, intellectual, mental, moral, and spiritual, I went through a course of training in the four schools: the Chishtiyya, Naqshibandiyya, Qadiriyya, and Suhrwardiyya. I still recall this period, under the guidance of so great and merciful a Murshid, as the most beautiful time of my life. In him I saw every rare quality, while his unassuming nature and his fine modesty could hardly be equaled even among the highest mystics of the world. He combined within himself the intense spell of ecstasy and constant flow of inspiration with the very soul of spiritual independence.

Although I had found most wonderful attributes among the mystics I had met, some in greater and some in lesser degrees, I had never until then beheld the balance of all that was good and desirable in one man. His death was as saintly as his mortal life had been. Six months before his end he predicted its coming and wound up all his worldly affairs in order to be freed for his future journey. "Death is a chain which unites friend with friend unto the Beyond." He apologized not only to his relatives, friends, and mureeds, but even to his servants, lest there might be aught that he had done to their displeasure and hurt. Ere the soul departed from his body, he bade farewell to all his people with loving words. And then, sitting upright and unwavering, he continued *zikr*, and lost in his contemplation of Allah, he, by his own accord, freed his soul from the imprisonment of this mortal frame forever. "Fare forth into the world, my child, and harmonize the East and the West with the harmony of thy music. Spread the wisdom of Sufism abroad, for to this end art thou gifted by Allah, the most Merciful and Compassionate."

The Chishtî Order is a Sufi order within the mystic branches of Islam which was founded in Chisht, a small town near Herat, about 930 C.E. and continues to this day (2008). The Chishti Order is known for its emphasis on love, tolerance, and openness. The order was founded by Abu Ishaq Shami ("the Syrian") who brought Sufism (Tasawwuf) to the town of Chisht, some 95 miles east of Herat in present-day western Afghanistan. Before returning to the Levant, Shami initiated, trained and deputized the son of the local Amir, (Khwaja) Abu Ahmad Abdal (d. 966). Under the leadership of Abu Ahmad's descendants, the *Chishtiyya* as they are also known flourished as a regional mystical order.

The most famous of the Chishti saints is Moinuddin Chishti (popularly known as *Gharib Nawaz* 'Benefactor of the Poor') who settled in Ajmer, India. He oversaw the growth of the order in the 13th century as religious laws were canonized. He saw Hazrat Muhammad in a dream and then set off on a journey of discovery. Other famous saints of the Chishti Order are Qutbuddin Bakhtiar Kaki, Fariduddin Ganjshakar of Pak Pattan, Nizamuddin Auliya of Delhi, Alauddin Ali Ahmed Sabir Kalyari, Mohammed Badesha Qadri of Wadi, Shah Waliyullah of Delhi, and Hazrat Ashraf Jahangir Semnani of Kicchocha Sharif, Uttar Pradesh.

The Chishti Order is famous for its emphasis on love, tolerance, and openness. The Order traces its origins through various saints all the way to Hazrat Ali and Hazrat Muhammad himself. Sema or Qawwali is a type of devotional music to enhance the remembrance of Allah Taalah and is not a part of worship or prayer. Followers of Pir Zada Masood Ali Chishty son of the famous Sufi saint Imamuddin Chishty of Lahore claim he was the first to bring the Chishti order to the UK. Also he is a direct descendant of Khwaja Moinuddin Hasan Chishty as is his sons Mohammed Ahsan Ali, Mohammed Mohsin Ali and his Grandson Mohammed Mahdi Chishty.

Chishti master Hazrat Inayat Khan (1882—1927) was the first to bring the Sufi path to the West, arriving in America in 1910 and later settling near Paris, France. His approach exemplified the tolerance and openness of the Chishti Order, following a custom began by Moinuddin Chishti of initiating and training disciples regardless of religious affiliation and which continued through Nizamuddin Auliya and Shaykh ul-Masha'ikh Kalimullah Jehanabadi (d. 1720). All his teaching was given in English, and 12 volumes of his discourses on topics related to the spiritual path are still available from American, European, and Indian sources. Initiates of his form of Sufi practice now number in the several thousands all over the world.

A number of Chishti family members are now living in Pakpatan and Bahawal Nagar, North of Punjab, Pakistan. Hazrat Baba Faridudeen Gang Shakar (rahmatullahi alaihi) was one of the most influential and pivotal figures in the Chishtiyya silsila, and is widely renowned for his intensely rigorous mujahedas in Allah's path. After the premature death of Khwaja Qutubuddin Kaki (rahmatullahi alaihi), only a year after the demise of Khwaja Moinudeen Chishti (rahmatullahi alaihi), the bulk of the work begun by the latter fell upon his shoulders. It was he who, in his 37 years as head of the silsila, ensured the propagation of Islam throughout India and the lands beyond.

Miraculous events surrounded Baba Faridudeen's (rahmatullahi alaihi) birth. He was born on the 29th Shabaan in 569 AH, the son of a pious alim and a waliah (female saint). As the night was cloudy, people did not know whether Ramadaan had begun or not. But a dervish told them that a wali had been born who would be the Qutb (spiritual monarch) of his time, and that they must look to the child for their answer. Sure enough, the one-day old Baba Faridudeen (rahmatullahi alaihi) did not touch his mother's milk after sehri, indicating to all that Ramadaan had in fact begun. Baba Faridudeen (rahmatullahi alaihi) was a direct descendent of Hazrat Umar Farooq (rahmatullahi alaihi). At the age of 7 he memorised the Qur'an and later became an alim. When Khwaja Qutbudeen Kaki (rahmatullahi alaihi) visited the city of Multan, where he was studying, he was so impressed by the child's spiritual prowess that he immediately accepted him as a mureed.

After his education finished, Baba Faridudeen (rahmatullahi alaihi) was ordered by his Pir-o-murshid to begin a tour of all the Islamic countries in order to meet the leading mystics of his time. On this journey, he came into contact with many great sufis. Whilst in Madinah performing Hajj, he was spiritually directed by the Holy Prophet (saw) to go to Baghdad. Doing so, he was welcomed by the son of Hazrat Shaykh Abdul Qadir Jilani (rahmatullahi alaihi) and given khilafah in the Qadriyya silsila, as well as receiving from him various sacred relics such as a turban and wooden food bowl of Rasulallah (sallalahu alaihi wasallam). After eighteen years of travelling, he returned to Delhi and his

Pir-o-murshid, and was given khilafah by Khwaja Qutbudeen Kaki (rahmatullahi alaihi) in the presence of many great sufis. Baba Faridudeen (rahmatullahi alaihi) was then ordered to go to Hansi and begin preaching Islam there. But before he had even settled down, he received the sad news of Khwaja Qutbudeen Kaki (rahmatullahi alaihi)'s death, and rushed back to Delhi arriving, as Khwaja Qutbudeen Kaki (rahmatullahi alaihi) had prophesied, three days after his death.

There he was given the khilafa-e-azam of Khwaja Qutbudeen Kaki (rahmatullahi alaihi) and decided, because of the political upheavals occuring in Dehli, to move the Chishtiyya headquarters to Ajodhan, the city renamed Pak Pattan in honour of him. Ajodhan was a small, isolated town surrounded by jungles and wild animals, but with the spiritual blessings of Baba Faridudeen (rahmatullahi alaihi), it soon became a bustling centre of Islam. Scholars and sufis flocked from all over India and the lands around to study under the great wali, who built up a veritable university of Islamic education along with a great khanqah. From Ajodhan would leave many missionaries who spread out over the whole of India to propagate Islam and Sufism. His great popularity aroused the ire and jealousy of Ajodhan's qadhi, who out of his envy wrote a letter to the leading ulema of the time complaining about Baba Faridudeen's (rahmatullahi alaihi) love of Sama. But the ulema rebuffed him, saying, "Baba Farid is the Qutb of our time, and the highest authority on Shariah among all of us. If he says Sama is permissible, then it is."

The above incident bears ample testimony to the universal awe in which Hazrat Baba Faridudeen (rahmatullahi alaihi) was held. His mujahedas were of such rigour that few in the history of Sufism have managed to surpass them. Once he was ordered by Khwaja Qutbudeen Kaki (rahmatullahi alaihi) to perform forty night seclusion whilst suspended upside down in a well, being pulled up only for salaah and to perform more ordinary devotions. On another occasion, he was so exhausted by his mujahedas that he could not stand up to greet Khwaja Moinudeen Chisti (rahmatullahi alaihi) when he came to visit. At that, Khwaja Moinudeen Chisti (rahmatullahi alaihi) remarked to Khwaja Qutbudeen Kaki (rahmatullahi alaihi), "You have captured a hawk whose nest is no lower than the 7th heaven", and a divine voice proclaimed, "We have accepted Farid." Baba Faridudeen (rahmatullahi alaihi)'s kindness and forbearance were legendary. Once a soldier came with the intention of killing him, but the great saint merely told him, "Dear brother, I have done you no harm.

Why would you kill a dervish and earn the curse of God?" When the man relented, he immediately embraced and forgave him. He was the most humble of men; despite all the vast knowledge he had at his disposal, he would refrain from even correcting those who came to him arrogantly for fear of puncturing their egos. Baba Faridudeen (rahmatullahi alaihi) enjoined the strict adherence to Shari'ah and the necessity of renouncing the pleasures of the world as pre-requisites for embarking on the journey towards Allah. His love for the Prophet (sallalahu alaihi wasallam) was so intense that he would sometimes break down and cry whilst lecturing on him, realising his own worthlessness as compared to that of our beloved Prophet (sallalahu alaihi wasallam). As with all the great sufis, the object of his life was devotion to Allah and service of mankind. His miracles or karamaat are too numerous to mention, but the greatest stretched over years before they came to fulfilment. One of his descendants, Hazrat Ibrahim Farid Saani (rahmatullahi alaihi), was visited and held in awe by Guru Nanak, founder of the Sikh religion. Hazrat Baba Faridudeen (rahmatullahi alaihi) left 14 khulafa behind him, principal of whom was Hazrat Sabir Paak (rahmatullahi alaihi), the founder of the Sabriyya silsila and Hazrat Nizamudeen Auliya Mehboobe Elahi (rahmatullahi alaihi), and founder of the Nizamiyya order.

Hazrat Nizamudeen (rahmatullahi alaihi) was his principal khilafa, and was located in Dehli. Under him, the Chishtiyya silsila achieved the zenith of its glory and influence. He collected the gathered teachings of his master as Baba Farid had collected those of his murshid Khwaja Qutbudeen Kaki (rahmatullahi alaihi). Death comes to all, even the greatest of saints, but the manner in which we receive it is not the same for all. As Baba Faridudeen (rahmatullahi alaihi) was born in a state of devotion, so too he died in that state. For days before his death he maintained complete silence within his cell, only speaking for salaat and to recite the Holy Qur'an. Eventually, his illness grew so severe that after Isha salaat he became unconscious. Upon waking, he decided to perform his Isha again, but once more he passed out. In sajdah on his third Isha salaat, he breathed his last. His last words were, "Ya Hayyo ya Qayyum."

Hazrat Baba Fariduddin Ganj-e-Shakar R.A. was born on the 29th Sha'ban in 569 A.H. [April 4, 1179 C.E.] in Khotwal, a village near Lahore [Pakistan]. He was a direct descendant of Hazrat Umar Farooq R.A., the second Caliph of Islam. It is narrated that a miracle occurred before his birth proving his Saintship. One day, during the pregnancy of his mother, she wanted to pluck some plums from her neighbour's tree without his permission, but the child in her womb (Hazrat Baba Farid) created a severe pain in her stomach that forced her to abandon the idea of plucking. After a few years after Hazrat Baba Farid's R.A. birth, his mother lovingly expressed: "My dear son, during your confinement I never ate anything which was unlawful." Hazrat Baba Farid R.A., however, smiled and said, "But, my dear mother, you wanted to pluck some plums from our neighbour's tree without his permission when I had created a severe pain in your stomach which saved you from this unlawful act."

After he had completed his early religious education at the age of 7 in Khotwal, his mother sent him for higher education to Multan. Here he stayed in a *masjid* [mosque] where he learnt the Holy Qur'an by heart and studied Hadith, Fiqh, Philosophy and Logic under the tutorship of Maulana Minhajuddin. During his studies, Hazrat Khwaja Qutbuddin Baktiar Kaki r.a. of Delhi visited Multan where Hazrat Baba Farid r.a. became his Murid (disciple) in the Chishtiyya Silsila. Upon the instructions of his *Pir-o-Murshid,* he undertook a tour of Islamic countries, for about 18 years from 593 A.H. to 611 A.H. [1196 C.E. to 1214 C.E.] he travelled to Ghazni, Baghdad Sharif, Jerusalem, Afghanistan, Syria, Iran, Mecca and Medina meeting many great saints and Sufis. After the demise of Hazrat Khwaja Qutbuddin r.a. the mantle of spiritual leadership in the Chishtiyya Silsila fell on the shoulders of Hazrat Baba Farid *r.a.* when Khwaja Qutbuddin *r.a.*nominated him to be his *Khalifa* or spiritual successor.

It is narrated that when Hazrat Baba Farid r.a.visited Medina Sharif he was spiritually commanded by the Holy Prophet s.a.w.s. to visit Baghdad Sharif and meet Hazrat Abdul Wahab, son of Hazrat Ghaus-al-Azam Sheikh Abdul Qadir Gilani r.a. He was to receive some sacred relics from him. Accordingly, when he reached Baghdad Sharif, he received a box from Hazrat Abdul Wahab r.a. which contained the following holy relics: Two flag-poles which were used by the Holy Prophet s.a.w.s. in some of the battles fought by him; one wooden bowl in which the Prophet s.a.w.s. used to eat from; one pair of scissors and one turban which was used by the holy Prophet s.a.w.s.

Because of political upheavals in Delhi, he was obliged to shift the centre of the Chishtiyya mission from Delhi to Ajodhan now known as "Pak Patan". The *Khanqah* of Baba Farid R.A., with his patronage, became a great university of "moral and spiritual training." Thousands of aspirants, scholars, dervishes and Sufis reaped benefit from this spiritual university. Hazrat Baba Farid *R.A.* reached the pinnacle of spiritual glory through extremely hard *Mujahidas* (spiritual striving) to gain mastery over the *Nafs.*

Once Hazrat Khwaja Qutbuddin R.A. ordered Hazrat Baba Farid R.A. to perform the *"Chilla-e-Maakoos"* for 40 days and this chilla was seldom undertaken by Sufis and was one of the most difficult tests of Hazrat Khwaja Baba Farid's R.A. faith and courage. It was to be performed in a well by hanging himself in a reverse or headlong position with his feet tied up by a rope to a sturdy branch of a treetop.

Once, due to utter weakness, Hazrat Baba Farid R.A. helped himself to walk with the aid of a staff. But after a few steps, the colour of his face suddenly became purple, as if he was under heavy punishment. He threw away the staff. When Hazrat Khwaja Nizamuddin *R.A.*, who was escorting him, enquired the reason for this, Hazrat Baba Farid R.A. replied, "I wanted to take help of the staff, but Allah's Displeasure frowned upon me for depending on other's help instead of His. I, therefore, threw away the staff and felt highly ashamed of this weakness in my faith in Rabb, the Almighty." It is also narrated that once a trader was taking a caravan of camels laden with sugar from Multan to Delhi. When he was passing through Ajodhan (now Pakistan), Hazrat Baba Fariduddin R.A. enquired casually as to what he was carrying on his camels. The trader sarcastically replied, "It is salt." Hazrat Baba Fariduddin R.A. also affirmed, "Yes, it may be salt." When the trader reached Delhi, he was awfully perturbed to find that all his bags of sugar had turned to salt. He immediately returned to Ajodhan and apologized before Hazrat Baba Farid R.A. Hazrat Baba Farid R.A. said: "If it is sugar then it shall be sugar." The trader returned to Delhi and was pleased to find that the salt had turned back to sugar by the Grace of Almighty Allah. This is how Hazrat Baba Sahib R.A. received the title of "Ganj-e- Shakar."

One of the devotees of Hazrat Baba Farid R.A. named Mohammed Nishapuri lived in Gujerat and was going to Delhi with three other companions. On their way through the jungle, robbers encountered them. Mohammed Nishapuri and his companions had no wepons to defend themselves. In such a helpless state, Mohammed Nishapuri remembered his *Pir,* Hazrat Baba Farid R.A., and also offered prayers seeking Allah's help in their predicament. Surpassingly, the robbers threw away their weapons and offered an apology to the party and went away. One day some poor people came from Arabia to see Hazrat Baba Farid R.A. and said that they were strangers to the land and that all their money was spent before the end of the journey. Hazrat Baba Farid R.A. gave them some dried dates which were lying in front of him at the moment and said, "Take them and go. Your journey shall be completed by the Grace of Allah." Apparently, these persons were very disappointed with such a "cheap gift". After leaving the *Khanqah,* they wanted to throw away the dates, but just as they were about to do so, to their amazement, the dates turned into gold. Regretting their thoughts, these people left happily uttering their heartfelt gratitude and prayers for Hazrat Baba Farid R.A.

He fasted throughout his life and maintained his nightly prayers and devotions. Fear of Allah always dominated him. He was a staunch devotee of Prophet Muhammad s.a.w.s. and dedicated his entire life to the veneration of the beloved Prophet's s.a.w.s. immortal glory. At the mention of the Holy Prophet's s.a.w.s. character he would often weep out of his love and devotion. Hazrat Baba Farid R.A. avoided kings, government officials and the rich. He also warned his *Khalifas,* devotees and *Murids* to avoid their company. He was a living picture of humility. Whatever he received was spent in the name of Allah and his chest overwhelmed with mercy and forgiveness. Many miracles are attributed to him during his lifetime and after his passing away. On the 5th of Muharram, during the Isha prayer [evening prayer] while in the act of *Sajdah,* [prostration during prayer] he uttered *"Ya Hayo Ya Qayum"* [O Self-Subsisting, O Eternal — two names of God] and with these words on his lips his soul disappeared into the eternal bliss of his beloved Allah. Immediately a *"Nida"* or Divine Voice declared: *"Dost ba Dost Pewast"* - Friend has merged into the unity of "Friend" (Allah).

An old woman that was one of the devotees of the Saint presented a piece of cloth for the *kaffan* [shroud] of Hazrat Baba Farid r.a.. She implored: "I have not spun even a single thread of this cloth without having *Wudu* [purification]. I had prepared it for my own coffin but if it is accepted for the *kaffan* of this great Saint, I feel confident, Allah would be pleased with to pardon my sins and grant me salvation." Hazrat Baba Farid's R.A. son accepted this cloth as the *Kaffan.* His *Mazar Sharif* [noble shrine] is in Pak Patan, Pakistan. Hazrat Sabir Pak, Hazrat Nizamuddin Auliya and Hazrat Jamaluddin Hansi *rehmatulla alaihim* [may Allah have mercy upon them] are among his favourite *Murids* and *Khalifas.* It is generally recognized that he had three wives and many children. Hazrat Baba Farid R.A. was indeed one of the most brilliant stars of the Chishtiyya Silsila and is held in high esteem by one and all.

5

The Nimatullahi

The Ni'matullâhî or Ne'matollâhî (also spelled as "Nimatollahi", "Nematollahi" or "Ni'matallahi) is a Sufi Order or Tariqa originating in Iran. The Nimatullahi sufis are one of the genuine orders still in existence, with an initiatic chain of succession (*silsilah*) that extends through Ma'ruf al-Kharkhi. It is one of the few Sufi orders to have derived from Shi'i traditions. Historically, it has had a close relationship with the Nizari Ismaili community, particularly with the Nizari Imams and the Persian and Arabic-speaking Ismailis. It is named after its 14th century founder Nur ad-Din Ni'matullah *Wali,* known as Shah Nimatullah, who settled in and is buried in Mahan, Kerman Province, Iran.

Until the 1970s, the majority of members resided in Iran. However, through the charisma and influence of its Master for 55 years, Dr. Javad Nurbakhsh, as well as the emigration of dervishes after the Iranian Revolution, the tariqa has attracted numerous followers outside of Iran, mostly in Europe, West Africa and North America. The numerous publications of the order include the bi-annual SUFI journal. The Khaniqahi Nimatullahi also publish in Persian, English and other languages, Dr. Nurbakhsh's seven-volume treatment of the states and stations of traversing the Sufi path, his comprehensive, twelve-volume explanation of the meanings of Sufi mystical terminology and his many annotated biographies of the great, historic masters of the path. Social activities of the present-day order include the establishment of clinics and medical centers in impoverished regions of West Africa, where the order has attracted numerous adherents.

There are other offshoots of the original Nimatullahi Order still active in Iran and elsewhere, including the Bonyad Erfan Gonabadi Order. Dr. Javad Nurbakhsh (10 December 1926 - 10 October 2008) was the Master (*pir*) of the Nimatullahi Sufi Order from 1953 until he died. Dr. Nurbakhsh was born in Kerman, Iran on the 10th of December 1926, in a city affectionately referred to by Sufis as the 'capital of spiritual poverty'. Shah Nimatullah, the founder of the order bearing his name, called it the 'heart of the universe'. Nurbakhsh was descended from Sheykh Kamal ad-Din Nurbakhsh, one of the distinguished Sheykhs of the Nurbakhshi Sufi Order, over whose tomb the present Sufi centre in Kerman was built. After a prodigious early life, he began his professional career as a medical doctor at the age of 26 when he became head of a local hospital in the southeastern town of Bam, Iran. The following year, 1953, he succeeded his master, Mo'nes 'Ali Shah Zo'r-Riyasateyn, as master of the Nimatullahi Sufi Order, with the Sufi sobriquet of Nur 'Ali Shah.

Following a term serving the people of Bam, he was transferred to Tehran, where he took up residence in the small Sufi centre in the downtown district of Shahpur Square. This became the centre of a Sufi revival in Iran as well as attracting western seekers and scholars from around the world. Through his tireless energy Dr. Nurbakhsh initiated the greatest renaissance of the Nimatullahi Sufi order since the work of the founder, Shah Nimatullah Vali in the 15th century. His teachings have attracted a massive following from every race, ethos, creed and national origin, inspiring a way of loving-kindness and service to humankind according to the tenets of Sufism. Dr Nurbakhsh never distinguished people in terms of their worldly position or rank, treating all as equal in love and he attracted a wide association of eminent figures from around the world, who became his friends, remaining in regular communication.

Such persons included Iran's eminent scholar and philosopher, Professor Seyyed Hossein Nasr, the distinguished German scholar, the late Dr. Annemarie Schimmel; the Swiss academician, Dr. Hermann Landolt; the great French scholar of Iranian and Islamic philosophy, Henry Corbin; the Japanese Zen Buddhist and scholar of philosophy, Dr. Toshihiko Izutsu; American Islamic and Sufi scholars such as Profs. Carl Ernst, William Chittick, and James Morris; American poet Robert Bly; as well as Russian scholars in the field like Prof. I.M. Steblin-Kamensky. He became friend and mentor to western diplomats in Tehran, in particular, Sir Peter Ramsbotham of the United Kingdom and James George of Canada. He enjoyed warm relations with a number of other spiritual guides, such as Mme. de Salzman, head of the Gurdjieff movement at the time; Dr. Ganjavian, master of the Dhahabi Sufi Order of Iran; and the spiritual heads of the Ahl-e Haqq and Qadiri Sufi Orders in Iranian Kurdistan.

After obtaining his Psychiatric degree from the Sorbonne, Dr. Nurbakhsh was appointed professor of psychiatry at the Tehran University School of medicine, a position which he held until he retired, along with that of director of the Iranian Medical Council, president of the Iranian Association of Psychiatrists, and head of the Ruzbeh Psychiatric Hospital. He was also an honorary member of the American Psychiatrists' Association. He produced 37 scientific works in the field of psychiatry, as author, editor and translator, along with many articles in scientific journals and a compendium of instructional brochures for the use of researchers, professors and students.

Throughout his life Dr. Nurbakhsh wrote extensively on Iranian gnosis and Islamic Sufism. Besides publication of his prolific writings, including biographies of the masters of the path and the principles of the Nimatullahi Sufi Order, he also sponsored numerous international conferences and seminars, the papers of which have been compiled in three compendia in English. He was known for his "prodigious activity" (Henry Corbin's words) in the publication of classical Sufi texts. By 1979, when he went into voluntary exile in the West, he had published some eighty books. Besides his own prose and poetical works, Dr. Nurbakhsh edited and published the Divan and collected treatises (late 1970s, in 4 hefty volumes) of Shah Nimatullah, as well as many of the important works by nineteenth-century Nimatullahi masters, including collected works of Nur 'Ali Shah, and works by Mast 'Ali Shah, Muzaffar 'Ali Shah, Majdhub 'Ali Shah, Rawnaq 'Ali Shah, Mushtaq 'Ali Shah, and badr al-Mamalik Ardabili. He also edited and published critical editions of treatises and poetical works by classical Persian Sufi writers, such as Abdullah Ansari, Ahmad Ghazali, Ruzbihan Baqli, 'Iraqi and Mahmud Shabistari.

When the Nimatullahi Order began to set up branches in the West in the early 1970s, the Order's own 'Khanaqah-i Ni'matullahi Publications' in the United States translated and published scores of Dr. Nurbakhsh's own works.

Foremost among these should be listed: *Sufi Women* (New York 1983, reprinted 4 times and since translated into Spanish, French, Italian and German); *Jesus in the Eyes of the Sufis* (London 1983, reprinted once and since translated into Spanish, Italian and German); *Spiritual Poverty in Sufism* (London 1984, since translated into French, Italian and Spanish); *The Great Satan, 'Eblis'* (London 1986, since translated into Italian and German); and *The Psychology of Sufism* (London 1992, since translated into Italian, German, Spanish and Russian). Dr. Nurbakhsh's two volumes of Prophetic traditions used by the Sufis, published in trilingual texts (Arabic, Persian and English), his five-volume work entitled *The Gnosis of the Sufis* (*Ma'arif-i Sufiyya*), and his sixteen-volume work on Sufi technical terminology entitled *Sufi Symbolism* (*Farhang-i Nurbakhsh*) remain his most significant contributions to Islamic Sufi studies in the West to date.

His works have been translated from the original Persian into English, Spanish, Russian, French, German, Dutch, Swedish and Polish. In addition, he has published a quarterly journal with articles, features, fiction and poetry on Sufism and related spiritual paths, now in its twentieth year, with editions in Persian, English, French, Spanish and Russian. In the years up to 1979 he established 70 Sufi centres in most of the major cities and towns of Iran, all set up as charitable organisations according to civil and Islamic law. A great number of these have since been expropriated under the current regime. Since moving to the West in 1979 Dr Nurbakhsh has established 35 active centres across the rest of the world, including England, France, the Netherlands, Germany, Spain, Sweden, and Austria in Europe; Russia; the United States, Canada and Mexico in North America; Australia; and in the Ivory Coast, Benin, Mali, Burkina Faso, and Senegal in West Africa, each incorporated as an independent charity under the civil law of the respective countries.

Dr. Nurbakhsh made important advances in psychiatry in his native Iran, instituting improvements in the Ruzbeh Hospital which brought the institution into the forefront of psychiatric practice, including the construction of the first modern psychiatric clinic in Tehran. Under his leadership, the Order has provided financial and technical assistance to various charitable institutions in Iran and to two orphanages in Mexico as well as the founding and operation of two clinics in West Africa: in Abidjan, Ivory Coast, and in Porto Novo, Benin. Nimatullahi Sufi centres around the world reflect the vastness of his spirit and serve not only to promote the ideals of the Sufi path but also the Persian language, its literature, poetry and mystical opus through which the culture, music and art of Iran are celebrated. A formidable personality, he was known for his startling wit, constant rapturous laughter, mastery of the art of conversation and use of humour as a pedagogic device.

A ghazal in his lovely Divan of ecstatic Persian Sufi poetry concludes:

The world has been like a dream to you, Nurbakhsh

All the people therein bewitched and broken-hearted.

Dr. Nurbakhsh passed away in his retreat in the English countryside near the town of Banbury, Oxfordshire, where he spent his final years, and is buried there. He has been succeeded by his son, Dr. Alireza Nurbakhsh, a doctor in philosophy from the University of Wisconsin and a practising lawyer in London. His Sufi sobriquet is Reza 'Ali Shah. He is survived by his widow, Mrs. Parvaneh Daneshvar Nurbakhsh, three sons, and two daughters.

Selected Statements by Dr. Javad Nurbakhsh on Sufism and practice:

"The basis of Sufism is consideration of the hearts and feelings of others. If you haven't the will to gladden someone's heart, then at least beware lest you hurt someone's heart, for on our path, no sin exists but this"

"Sufism is a path towards the Truth where there are no provisions except Love. Its method is to look solely in one direction, and its objective is God."

"True lovers prefer the Beloved's desires to their own, being content with whatever the Beloved desires - 'be it cure or pain, union or separation.'"

"...if you encounter a human being who claims to be a Sufi and behaves contrary to the human code of ethics, do not ask, "What kind of Sufi is this?" Rather, it would be better to ask, "What kind of person would this have been had he not been a Sufi?"

"The capital of the Path is, in truth, nothing other than sincerity. Sincerity has been defined as `showing yourself as you really are' and `being inwardly what you show yourself to be'."

The teachings of the Qur'an; the *Sunna,* which is the example of Muhammad; and the example of all of the other

Prophets, form the basis for traditional Sufi *adab* — beautiful action, the form of behavior which creates the conditions in which the attributes of God may be clearly reflected.

Ibn 'Arabi stated that Sufism is "to assume God's character traits as one's own," and it has been said that all of Sufism is, in fact, *adab*. The primary meaning of the Arabic root of *adab* is "to invite," or "to gather together for a banquet." Hospitality is regarded as sacred duty in Islam, and this linguistic connection illuminates the significance with which the relationship of guest and host, and the sharing of sustenance, are regarded. Accordingly, early treatises on *adab* address such matters in great detail, as do the customs of many contemporary Sufi orders.

The 10th century traveler Ibn al-Husayn al-Sulami set forth many details of the *adab* of table manners and hospitality in his *Futuwah*. He advised, "Give elaborate feasts, be gracious when entertaining, and be generous to your guests." A host is instructed to serve all the food he has to his brother, even if this means only a drop of water. Sulami suggests that if a guest's gift of food in turn is offered to the guest by the host, one "must be extremely careful of your manners," and cites Muhammad's advice, "Don't count your friend's mouthfuls."

They must not inquire whence he has come or whither he is going or what is his name, but must deem that he has come from God and is going to God and that his name is "servant of God." [...T]hey should not eat alone, but should unselfishly share their food with one another; and when seated at table they should not be silent, and should begin by saying "Bismillah"; and they should not put anything down or lift anything up in such a way as to offend their comrades, and they should dip the first mouthful in salt, and should deal fairly by their friend. Sahl ibn Abdallah al-Tustari was asked about the meaning of the verse, "Verily God enjoins justice and beneficence" (16:92). He replied, "Justice consists in dealing fairly with one's friend in regard to a morsel of food, and beneficence consists in deeming him to have a better claim to that morsel than you."

Furthermore, the Sufi should eat with his right hand and should look only at his own morsel, and while eating he should not drink unless he is extremely thirsty, and if he drinks he should drink only as much as will moisten his liver. He should not eat large mouthfuls, and should chew his food well and not make haste; otherwise he will be acting contrary to the custom of the Apostle (peace and blessings upon him), and will probably suffer from indigestion. When he has finished eating, he should give praise to God and wash his hands.

Hujwiri

The 12th century scholar Abu al-Najib al-Suhrawardi also wrote a treatise on *adab* which included instructions for conduct at meals and with guests, many of which echo those of Hujwiri. First in importance was that one should eat in company whenever possible, whether informally with companions, graciously with guests, or generously with the poor, and always with impeccable courtesy. One should eat only when hungry, and stop before becoming full. Suhrawardi also advised that travelers not carry food on their journeys. To do so constitutes an exercise of the quality of *tawakkul* — wholehearted faith in Allah as Provider, humility in the face of that fact, and acceptance of what is given — into a context in which one is most vulnerable. Hungry strangers who consciously leave the provisioning to God expose and confront their dependence on Divine grace, generosity and protection. Consequently, the conditions are created for others to serve as vehicles of those qualities.

According to Suhrawardi, the Sufi must greet and honor all guests, and share with them whatever pure food or drink is available without fuss or ceremony. The guest, in turn, should sit where placed by the host, and express appreciation. After Muhammad's example, every meal should begin with:

Bismillah ar-Rahman ar-Rahim

In the Name of God, the Infinitely Compassionate and Merciful

He instructed that only the Shaikh (the spiritual leader) should invite those at the table to begin the meal; and no one, especially the leader of the group, should leave the table as long as anyone else is eating. This recalls the custom of Muhammad, who was always the last person at the table to finish lest any companion be embarrassed to eat more than him. No fault should be found with the food, nor should it be praised; in fact, too much discussion of food is considered equal to gluttony. In eating, one should only satisfy one's hunger, and better with a small amount of pure food than a feast of impure food. Following the Sunna, only three fingers of the right hand should be used for eating; small bites should be taken and the food chewed well. When sharing a common dish one should eat from the nearest side, not only out of courtesy and cleanliness, but because according to the counsel of Muhammad, *baraka,* the blessing power of God, descends first into the center of the dish. A meal should end with prayer, and might be followed by conversation, after which the guest should not leave until receiving permission from the host. In emulation of Muhammad's practice, the host should accompany the guest to the door.

The Nimatullahi Order's rules of the *adab* of service at dervish meetings offer a model of behavior relevant to life in the world at large. Those having the responsibility of service are chosen according to their inner potential, sincerity, good manners and gentle behavior; they are advised to treat everyone equally, regardless of wealth, parentage or social position. Neither must there be any discrimination on the basis of age; children are to be shown the same respect as adults. In distributing food and drink, the "dervishes of service" must "consider the circle" — the ancient Sufi custom of passing in a circular fashion, from right to left.

Although Hujwiri counselled dervishes to carry on the pleasant conversations with guests in some Sufi communities' meals traditionally have been taken in silence. Food is consumed to have the power to obey God. Hence that person who is engaged in eating with such an intention in mind is performing the essential act of obedience. And if someone is performing an act of obedience, for instance, saying prayers, how can he respond to the greeting of peace?

> Abu'l Qasim Nawrabadi
>
> When a Dervish is eating his food, it is his worship,
> and during the worship neither should he be saluted
> nor should he salute.
>
> Qutubuddin Bakhtiyar Kaki
>
> How could a morsel be digested without sight of Him,
> without the view of His roses and His rose-garden?
>
> Rumi

In many tariqats, the table is the setting for spiritual discourse: the Shaikh is the first to eat or speak, and participants pay close attention to exchanges with the Shaikh. Extraneous conversation is kept restrained and at low volume. The principle here is that without attention there can be no attunement, and without attunement there is no way to receive spiritual teaching and nourishment. Given the right circumstances, both food and exchange with one's spiritual teacher and companions — in words and in silence — may be transformed into energy, to be expended in conscious service.

Sufi teachings point to the potential nourishment in a meal beyond the bulk and chemical composition of the food. The senses are nourished by impressions arising from attention to the appearance, texture, flavor and aroma of food. Even subtler is the nourishment activated when food is prepared and eaten in a state of presence and love. And our hearts are nourished in loving exchange with our teachers and companions. Such nourishment feeds all centers of a human being.

The Mevlevi Order was founded by Sultan Veled, the son of Mevlana Jelaluddin Rumi. According to its custom, if a dervish wanted a drink of water during a meal, he would motion to the water server, the *saki*. All present would stop eating so that none would eat more than another. The saki would pour the water, kiss the glass, and offer it to the thirsty one. In silence the dervish would kiss the glass and drink. When the glass was empty, the Shaikh would say "*Ashk olsun*," then everyone would continue to eat.

This phrase, "*Ashk olsun*" — "May it become love" — is a declaration of a dervish's best vision of the fate of any sustenance: that it be transformed within the human heart into conscious awareness of the Divine love that provided it in the first place.

> Without Love, how could there be existence?
>
> By what power could bread have entered you and become you?
>
> Without your love and appetite, how could the bread
>
> have encountered the spirit of life?
>
> Love transforms dead bread into spirit:
>
> it makes mortal spirit everlasting.
>
> *Rumi*

The *Sunna* and *adab* contain the highest levels of metaphor. For instance, on the custom of eating with three fingers, the Ikhwan al-Safa wrote:

> One of the practices of the prophetic norm and the beautiful acts of right conduct is to use three fingers to partake of food, which is the nourishment of the body. In this custom the one who established the norm for souls seems to have made an allusion, admonishing and inciting them to seek knowledge from three routes. For knowledge is the nourishment of the soul just, as the food is the nourishment of the body. And the states of the soul are similar to the states of the body, because the connection between the two is so strong.
>
> One of the routes by which the soul partakes of knowledge is the faculty of reflection, through which the

soul perceives the intelligible existents. By this route the prophets take revelation from the angels. The second route is hearing, by which the soul receives the meanings of words and the tidings of absent things denoted by the sounds. The last is the route of sight, by which souls witness existent things that are present.

Ikhwan al-Safa

On one level, the use of the right hand for eating is a hygienic measure born of cultural necessity; it also carries the symbolism of right and left. The auspicious right hand is associated with goodness, happiness, cleanliness, purity, blessedness, and consciousness of God; the left is associated with the opposite qualities. This imagery suggests the choices that can be made by creatures with will and intelligence. In like manner, the image of the descent of *baraka* into the middle of a serving dish contains a reminder that the dimensionless center of the human being is where the presence of God is felt. The *Sunna* of accepting invitations acknowledges the value placed on community, sharing all levels of sustenance; in this context, refusal of an invitation implies alienation from community. The act of sharing food promotes remembrance of unity, and the interrelatedness of all creation.

For the Sufi, observance of *adab* forges links with a spiritual heritage. The extension of hospitality and sharing of meals offer opportunities to embody remembrance of God within traditions shared by generations of fellow travellers on the path. Sheikh Jalaluddin of Tabriz was one of the greatest saints... He had a cow, on the milk of which he usually breakfasted; and his practice was to sit up all night... He confines himself to the milk of his cow.

Ibn Batuta

Most early Sufis were well-known for their asceticism, both individually and in community. The early Sufi mystic and martyr Mansur al-Hallaj was said to have survived for seven years on a diet of bread and salt. The Chishti shaikh

Baba Fariduddin Masud frequently observed fasts, his *iftar* (fast-breaking meal) no more than a cup of syrup, at least half of which he would distribute among his companions. One 10th century traveler wrote of groups of Sufis whose only food was acorns split, sweetened, ground and mixed with wild barley. Qadiris of 17th century Sudan were known to subsist on nothing more than dates and acacia pods during retreats lasting three months or more.

Fasting is an essential Sufi practice, particularly in the context of the *chille*, the traditional forty-day retreat undertaken by initiates in many orders. However, such fasting does not involve total deprivation. In order to awaken subtle faculties, to reduce distraction, and to redirect the priorities of those on retreat, it often has been thought better to take a small amount of simple food rather than none at all. Protect yourself from the misfortunes of corrupt imaginings that distract you from remembrance. Be careful of your diet. It is better if your food be nourishing but devoid of animal fat. Beware of satiation and excessive hunger. Keep your constitution in balance, for if dryness is excessive, it leads to corrupt imaginings and long, delirious ravings.

Ibn 'Arabi

The soul-dog is better when its mouth is shut

by throwing a morsel into it.

Dara Shikoh

Whether fasting or not, Sufis have long been advised to eat in moderation. Men cannot dispense with nourishment, but moral virtue requires that they should not eat or drink in excess... Nothing is more hurtful to a novice in Sufism than eating too much. The seeker after truth should eat bread that is earned honestly by lawful means. He should eat just enough to help him to sustain himself and discharge his duties both towards his fellowmen and towards God. But he should never gratify himself to the maximum. The food must be simple. Since the appetites and passions are the natural propensities of nature, they cannot be uprooted; but the seeker after truth should, in the beginning, attempt to do so, so that he may come to achieve moderation. The secret of abstinence lies in gaining mastery over nature; when this is attained, further restraint is superfluous.

Muhammad al-Ghazzali

Austerity is not always called for, however, especially when guests arrive. In the late 10th and early 11th centuries CE, Abu Sa'id ibn Abil'Khayr engaged in extreme self-mortifications, and eventually alienated many of his companions. At the age of forty he experienced a spiritual transformation, and thereafter was renowned and controversial for his humor, generosity, joy, gratitude and girth. At Abu Sa'id's khanqah (Sufi center), food was served twice a day; the doors were open to all, without question. He is said to have prayed every night that God would give his disciples something good to eat. When there was no money, Abi'l Khayr and his disciples went hungry; when there was money, he spent it all on sumptuous feasts. In this way he cultivated detachment from both desire for food, and from identification with renunciation.

There are two stations on the Way to God,

but God is far aloof from them both,

and a dervish is dead to all stations and free from all states.

Abu Said ibn Abi'l Khayr

Abi'l Khayr established rules for his fraternity — one of the earliest Sufi brotherhoods — that were the foundation of later codes of dervish adab. Among them were that dervishes were never to eat alone, were to welcome anyone who joined their company, serve them with pleasure and patience, and offer even the smallest morsel of food to any person hungrier than themselves. Many early Sufis trod a middle path, neither ascetic nor extravagant. Such was Junayd of Baghdad, who was known for his moderation and generosity. His house was a center where Sufis held meetings and often stayed as guests. When Shaikh of Khorasan came to Baghdad with eight dervishes, Junayd lodged them in his home for a full year, offering them every day fresh food, new clothes and perfumes.

When asked "What is worship?," Muinuddin Chishti, founder of the Chishti Order, responded, To listen to the plight of the oppressed, to help the needy, and to fill the stomachs of the hungry. The man who does these three things may consider himself a friend of Allah. First he should have generosity like a river; secondly, kindness likes the sun and, thirdly, humility like the earth. The man who is blessed is the man who is generous.

Muiniddin Chishti

Muinuddin became legendary for his embodiment of this philosophy. It is said that so many meals were cooked every day in his kitchen that every impoverished person in the whole city could eat until satisfied. His custom was continued by his successors — any surplus at Chishti khanqahs was distributed to visitors and the needy. In emulation of their Shaikh, the Chishtis take to heart the hadith, "If someone visits a living man and gets nothing from him to eat, it is as if he had visited the dead." Bahauddin Naqshband, pir of the Naqshbandi Order, was so assiduous about the obligation to accept invitations that one Ramadan he is said to have agreed to share the fast-breaking meal, known in Arabic as iftar, with forty different friends — and to have been present at each of their gatherings. Though his disciples could hardly hope to reenact this legendary feat, they continue to be inspired by his example, set over six hundred years ago.

The Shadhiliyya Shaikh 'Abd al-Wahhab ibn Ahmad ash-Sharani ran a thriving zawiya (North African Sufi center) in Cairo during the 16th century. He, too, took great pleasure in generosity, and regarded as one of the blessings of Allah the fact that so many people were able to enjoy so much good food at his establishment during Ramadan, 'Id (the Islamic New Year), and other festivals. The 18th century Shadhiliya shaikhs of the Sudan were renowned for their generosity and graciousness, and regarded these qualities as the epitome of spiritual aspiration. Their schools, called khalwas, were centers of hospitality to visitors, travelers and traders.

The khalwa of Shadhiliya Shaikhs Idris al-Arbab and his son Hamad served a total of one hundred eighty meals every day of the year, and distributed to the poor all of the gifts that were received. When a scholar visited the khalwa and asked Shaikh Idris the ultimate goal of the Sufi's quest, the Shaikh brought him into the kitchen As they watched the women, servants and dervishes preparing sorghum pancakes for the guests, the Shaikh answered, "By God and by His Messenger, I have no name other than this dough!" Another shaikh, Hasan wad Hasuna, was also known for the feasts he would offer; he himself, however, ate bitter acacia pods with water as his guests enjoyed the more substantial food.

If one understands the inner significance of one's actions, observance of the *Sunna* and adab may help to cultivate an environment full of remembrance of God and of the unity of the manifest and the hidden levels of existence. From it grows the prayer:

May my imitation become real?

What is the spice of speech? Meaning and metaphor — and yours is a cook's garden of poetic herbs.

Repetitive? Yes, but one need not fear repetition in poetry which can only improve the more we read.

God seasons the pot of earth with tastes, smells, colours —apples, oranges, walnuts, quince and pomegranate; the grapes of the vine never clog your palate even if they taste the same as last year's or the year before... Nasir-i Khusraw

Sufi teachings and literature abound with metaphorical references to food and eating. Ibn 'Arabi identifies lubb, or kernel, as knowledge protected from hearts tied to the world. Lubb al-lubb, "the kernel of the kernel," is the substance of divine light. Simsimah, a sesame seed, is a realization too subtle for expression; and dhawq, or taste, is a human being's direct experience of Divine grace and unity.

Of dhawq and its companion shurb (drinking), Hujwiri wrote:

The Sufis call the sweetness of piety and the delight of miraculous grace and the pleasure of intimacy shurb — drinking — and they can do nothing without the delight of shurb. As the body's drink is of water, so the heart's drink is of spiritual pleasure and sweetness. Dhawq resembles shurb, but shurb is used solely in reference to pleasures, whereas dhawq is applied to pleasure and pain alike. One says dhuqtu'l-halawat, "I tasted sweetness," and dhuqtu'l-bala, "I tasted affliction;" but of shurb they say, sharibtu bi-ka'si'l-wasl, "I drank the cup of union," and sharibtu bi-ka'si'l-wudd, "I drank the cup of love," and so forth.

Hujwiri

More than eight centuries later, a Turkish Bektashi teacher expounded on the same subject:

One can go to the dictionary to learn what sugar is and how it is used. That is the shariat Gateway to knowledge. One feels the inadequacy of that once one sees and handles sugar. That represents the tariqat Gateway to knowledge. To actually taste sugar and to have it enter into oneself is to go a step deeper into appreciation of its nature, and that is what is meant by marifat. Should one go still further and become one with sugar so that one could say, "I am sugar," that and that alone would be knowledge of sugar. That is the haqiqat Gateway.

Bektashi Tradition

In another application of food as metaphor, the Bektashi poet Yunus Emre wrote, somewhat cryptically:

I climbed into the plum tree and ate the grapes I found there. The owner of the garden called to me, "Why are you eating my walnuts?" Yunus Emre, the Helveti Shaikh Niyazi

Misri offered this interpretation: Every tree of deeds has a special fruit. In the external world every fruit has a tree of its own; every deed has a means by which it can be reached... Yunus hints with "prune," "grape," and "nut" at the Divine law, sharia; the mystical path, tariqa; and the Divine Reality, haqiqa. For one eats the outside of the prune, but not its interior. The prune corresponds to outward actions. The grape is eaten, and many delicious things are made of it; but since a few kernels of hypocrisy, fame, vanity and ostentation remain, the grape refers to "interior acts," but not "Reality." The nut is a complete symbol of Reality: its interior is completely edible, and for how many illnesses is it a remedy! The master of the garden is the perfect mystical leader. One can discern the different fruits only with his help and eventually reach reality.

Niyazi Misri

The transforming power of love and gratitude is illustrated in Mevlana Jelaluddin Rumi's tale of Luqman. Though born a slave, Luqman "was the master of himself, and free from sensual desire." His master recognized his qualities, and sought to emulate him as a dervish might seek to emulate the Shaikh. Whatever food was brought to the master, he would first send to Luqman to eat; the master would then eat Luqman's leavings, and be overcome with rapture. If the slave rejected a food, his master would also refuse it or not enjoy it — "This is the sign of affinity without end." Given a melon, Luqman ate with pleasure all but the last slice. When the master tasted that slice, he was overwhelmed by its sourness. To the question, "How could you have eaten this poison?" Luqman replied:

I have eaten so much from your generous hand that I am bent over in shame. How could I refuse even one bitter thing from you? If I were to complain of bitterness, I should be engulfed in the dust of a hundred roads! Your sugar-scattering hand gave that melon its grace —how could any bitterness be left in it? By love the bitter is made sweet. Rumi

Food also plays a part in legends of the saints. Tales of miraculous feedings enrich the biographies of many Sufis and mirror similar stories from the life of Muhammad. Images of material abundance manifested by those of spiritual attainment are emblems of the potential of each human being to manifest Divine grace in his or her life. With such an abundance of food-related metaphors in the writings of its Pir, Mevlana Jalaluddin Rumi, it is not surprising that the Mevlevi Order traditionally valued the role of the head cook (Asci Dede or Sertabbah), second only to the Shaikh in rank. When the Shaikh died, more often than not it was the sertabbah who succeeded him.

The Sertabbah had overall responsibility for training new initiates, who would labor 1,001 consecutive days in service to the community. The last portion of this period was spent in the kitchen, after a ceremony in which the sertabbah presented the initiate to the Shaikh. In time, a Mevlevi dervish might serve as keeper of the cauldron (Kazanci Dede), sherbet-master (Serbetci Dede), table-setter (Somatci), coffee-maker (Iceri Meydancisi), coffee grinder (Tahmisci), or water server (Saki). The Bektashi cook (Asci Postu) held a status similar to the Mevlevi sertabbah. Kitchen-related posts include the Baker (Etmekci Postu); keeper of the cellars (Kilerci Postu); coffee-maker (Kahveci Postu). Other services are performed by the Sofraci, who sets the table; the Ibrikici, who pours water; and the Sakii Meydan, or cupbearer.

This high regard for the station of the cook, along with Bahauddin Naqshband's concern for the cook's level of concentration and emotional state, and the Ikhwan al-Safa's reference to the connection between states of mind and states of body, all point to the essential nature of the processes which the cook shepherds and embodies. The cook must be aware of the nature of the transformation of the coarse material of food into a finer state. In cooking the elements are marshaled to act upon the mineral, vegetable and animal kingdoms, maximizing their potential for human nourishment, for He changes every substance into Soul.

Rumi

This only happens with divine permission.

Air, earth, water, fire are His servants,

Dead to you and me, but alive to their Master.

Before Allah, fire writhes day and night, always ready to do His bidding.

Rumi

The cook must "have a mouth to taste the food." He or she must exercise the faculties of insight and discrimination, and be aware of the needs of the entire community. The cook must consider the qualities of foods and arrange them in combinations that promote balance and harmony in those who eat them, so that the nourishment of the body supports the nourishment of the soul. The cook must pay heed to the season, weather and time of day when food is to be served. Flavors, aromas, colors, textures and appearance must be appropriate and aesthetically pleasing. Equally important are the subtle attributes of foods — their heating or cooling, expanding or contracting effects; their influence on emotions; their tendency to promote vigor or calm, groundedness or etherealness; and their symbolic associations.

The results of this work enter the bodies of other human beings, and are transformed into energy and vitality, thought and spirit. It is a process requiring attention, discretion, creativity, presence, love, and patience — patience that accepts the manner in which all expressions of God unfold.

Be a skillful cook — let the kettle boil slowly,

For stew boiled in a great rush is of no use...

Why a child is created over nine months?

Because the King acts gradually.

Why Adam was created over forty mornings?

Because little by little, God was perfecting that clay.

You foolish one, you are rushing ahead —

Only a child, you make yourself out to be a sage...

But where is the spiritual warfare and combat to sustain you?

Rumi

The alchemy that takes place in the kitchen mirrors that which takes place in all creation. You have transmuted one handful of earth into gold, another into the Father of humanity. Your work is the transmutation of essences and the showing of generosity. My work is mistake and forgetfulness and error. Transmute my mistakes and forgetfulness into knowledge. I am full of heat and passion; make me patient and forbearing. You have made bread from the blackest earth; You have made dead bread into life... The heart's eye contemplates spiritual realities and sees in this world of form an unending alchemy. This body, this patched garment without stitches, holds its form through the transmutation of essences and Your all-embracing elixir.

Rumi

Sufi rituals evolved in recognition of the sacredness of the work of the kitchen. The Kara Kazan, or giant cauldron, of every Bektashi tekke is treated with great reverence and is reserved for special occasions only. The workday at the Istanbul Qadiri dergah kitchen begins with ablutions and recitation of the Fatiha, led by the recitation of a prayer by the head cook. This prayer ends with the invocation "Hu" — the non-gender-specific pronoun used only to refer to Allah.

Allah, Allah, zadallah, kesirallah, berekat-illah

Vakt-i serifler hayrola, hayirlar feth ola

Berekatillah Elhamdillah, pir askina

Hu diyelim, HU!

Allah, Allah, the sustenance of Allah

The benevolence of Allah, the blessing of Allah...

By the grace of God, praise be to God and our beloved Pir.

Let us say HU, HUUUU

Mevlevi Tradition

While preparing meals, Jerrahi cooks traditionally recite the prayer At-tahiyyat, the conversation held between Muhammad and Allah during the Miraj, the Heavenly Ascent, so that this heavenly blessing might be brought down to the kitchen and perpetuated. In Mevlevi tekkes, when a meal was ready the keeper of the cauldron would uncover it and recite:

> May its cooking be sweet;
>
> May God render it bountiful.
>
> By the breath of Hazrat-i-Mevlana [Rumi],
>
> By the mystery of Atesbaz-i-Veli [Rumi's cook],
>
> Let us all say Hu.

Following the meal, the dervishes would rise one at a time, and before leaving, bow at the threshold of the kitchen. Such customs recall the Latin word for hearth — focus — and the English definitions of focus as a point at which rays of light converge, a state of concentration and clarity. This etymology illuminates the traditional role of the hearth as the literal and symbolic focus of a spiritual education.

The truly virtuous are they who give food — however great be their want of it — unto the needy, the orphan, and the captive, saying, in their hearts, "We feed you for the sake of God alone: we desire no recompense from you, nor thanks: behold, we stand in awe of our Sustainer..." 80:7-10

One of the traditional roles of the dervish lodge was as community kitchen and hostel, providing food and shelter for the poor and for travelers. Many early Sufis were "sons of the road," wandering during the warm season, and relying on the grace of God and the spontaneous generosity of fellow Sufis for shelter and sustenance. Followers of other faiths also could count on such generosity, with no questions asked about their religion. One who entertains dervishes will be compensated in paradise.

Uthman Haruni

A kitchen in which meals were cooking around the clock was the hallmark of many Sufi saints. The great Chishti Shaikh Nizamuddin Auliya was known to entertain large groups of traveling dervishes — even thirty or more — for up to three days at a time. The three-day limit is in keeping with Muhammad's counsel: "Hospitality extends for three days, and anything beyond that is charity." Ibn Batuta enjoyed and documented such hospitality during his travels in the 14th century, as did Evliya Efendi in the 17th century.

The desire to share food was one basis for the development of communities — the Turkish word tekke referred to a refectory or dining hall long before it became exclusively identified with a Sufi establishment. With the development of orders and communities came a greater capacity to serve greater numbers; but no matter what its size, each Sufi center had lodgings reserved for guests, and a place of honor for them at the table.

The Persian word langar was synonymous with a soup kitchen and resting place for travelers, or a Sufi residence. Ahmed Uzgani's largely mythical "History of the Uwaysis," set in East Turkestan around 1600 CE, includes stories of Sufi saints who established langars and spent years in this way of service. Legend has it that the kitchen of one of them, Ghiyath al-Din of Shikarmat, was miraculously granted a limitless supply of fire and water. The many references to holy men and women engaged in such work reflect the great value attached to it, and the widespread presence of langars throughout Central Asia.

Abdul Qadir Gilani, pir of the Qadiri Order, was known as Ghauth al-'Azam, "The Great Helper," and was renowned for his charity. According to the Qadiris, he was 'born of love, lived in a perfect way, and died having achieved the perfection of love." One of his characteristics was generosity, and the tradition which he started of feeding the poor is perpetuated every year by his followers on his urs, the anniversary of his death. On the 11th day of Rabi'al-Thani, at his shrine in Baghdad and throughout the Muslim world, thousands of people gather at meetings and festivals to recite Qur'an, to honor the memory of Abdul Qadir Gilani, and to partake of the large quantities of food cooked and distributed in his honor.

Following the example of their founder, Muinuddin Chishti, Chishti khanqahs have always kept open kitchens and have provided vital services in public emergencies. In 1976, when monsoon floods destroyed many houses in Ajmer, India, the Chishti khanqah there fed and housed many of the homeless. For centuries the Ajmer Langar Khana has cooked and distributed twice daily barley porridge, itself known as langar. In 1904 the Rajputana District Gazetteer reported:

Two maunds and six seers of grain (178 lbs.) with six seers of salt (13 lbs.) are cooked and distributed to all comers before daybreak in the morning, and the same quantity before five o'clock in the evening... Besides the 1,570 maunds of grain (65 tons) which are thus yearly consumed, 644 maunds (27 tons) are annually distributed to infirm women, widows, and other deserving persons at their own houses.

Rajputana District Gazetteer

From the 15th to the 19th centuries CE, the Ansari caretakers of the shrine of Ali in Balkh (now Mazar-i-Sharif, Afghanistan) offered to all comers a meal of bread and soup every Friday and Monday evening; and when they could afford it, sweets and fruit were set out after Friday and Monday evening prayers. The 16th Century Helveti Shaikh Ibrahim ibn Muhammad Gulshani established a dergah in Cairo which became widely known for its public offerings of food; its staff included a baker, a cook, and a "tablesetter for the poor."

In Ottoman lands, the imaret was a public institution serving travelers, the needy, dervishes, and the keepers of the mosques. The public kitchens of the imarets and many of the Sufi tekkes and zawiyas (all of which had open kitchens) were supported by waqf, charitable foundations established by government, and by wealthy and prominent men and women. Support also came from private donations and from the dervish orders' agricultural activities and industries. (For instance, for centuries the Bektashi Order controlled the most productive salt mines in the Ottoman Empire; the salt from those mines was called Hajji Bektash salt.) In the 16th century, the Istanbul imaret of Sultan Mehmed II Fatih prepared meals for over 1,100 people every day; its guest house accommodated up to 160 visitors at a time. Stores of cheese, cream and honey were earmarked for guests, and those fortunate enough to attend a banquet there were served special rice dishes such as dane and zerde.

Sufis have carried this tradition of service into modern times. Although Kemal Ataturk outlawed the Turkish dervish orders in 1925, in the 1930's Mevlevi Shaikh Suleyman Loras was permitted to open the kitchen of a Mevlevi tekke in order to feed the poor. Three evenings a week the Karagumruk Helveti-Jerrahi dergah, located in a poor section of Istanbul, accommodates 500 or more diners. Many local community residents come for dinner and leave after the meal, to be replaced by others who come to participate in dhikr. The Jerrahi dergah in Spring Valley, New York, serves 125 or more diners every Saturday night, and even more — and more frequently — during the month of Ramadan. Once a month, community members directly distribute cooked meals, person to person, to local families in need.

In Rufai dergahs throughout Turkey, tables are routinely set for 200-250 people. During Muharram, the Tirana, Albania, Bektashi tekke prepares ashura, a pudding of legumes and dried fruits, for 600 people. Throughout the year at the Bawa Muhaiyaddeen Fellowship in Philadelphia, 50 to 200 people take their evening meal together every night.

In modern Egypt, offerings of food and hospitality are central to Sufi life. The Sufi center or saha offers meals and lodging to guests; some have enormous concrete tables accommodating one hundred of more diners at a sitting. At annual moulid observances honoring the anniversary of the death of Sufi saints, khidamat — hospitality stations — are set up in tents, at nearby buildings, or on simple cloths laid out upon the ground. Guests are offered food and drink, called nafha — a word with the dual meaning of "gift" and "fragrance." Nafha must be accepted, for not only is it a gift of the heart, but it carries with it the *baraka* of the saint being honored. Poor people partake of nafha for its nourishment; poor and rich alike partake of nafha for its *baraka.*

Dervish hospitality in the grand manner was described by an American guest of the Shaikh of the Tripoli Mevlevi tekke in the 1920's:

> [The Shaikh] shouted welcome in French and Arabic as he came, embraced Dr. Dray like a grizzly bear, shook hands with me, deplored the hot weather, and led us to a terrace where he hoped there would be a little breeze...
>
> We found ourselves [...] sipping a delicious pale-green liquid, mixed from freshly crushed white grapes and lime juice... The luncheon was an Arabian Nights feast of more than twenty courses and lasted for two hours. Whole roasted chickens, and chicken pilaf with rice, almonds, and raisins; lamb on skewers; lamb wrapped in grape leaves and cooked in olive oil, lamb stewed with eggplant; lamb cooked with peppercorns; delicious salads; cucumbers peeled at the table and eaten as we eat fruit; no less than six desserts, beginning with a great pan of custard, running the gamut of pastries with ground-up nuts and honey, to end at last with watermelons cooled in the fountain.
>
> [...] through all the exuberance of his welcome, through the elaborate material luxury of our entertainment and his obvious whole-hearted enjoyment of the delicious food, I sensed continually that there was another side to this man

and felt that his abundant physical vitality was not incompatible, perhaps, with powers which might be equally unusual in other directions. I had been told that he was a great mystic, and I was not prepared to doubt it on the superficial evidence.

William Seabrook

Six hundred years earlier, that Shaikh's Pir had written:

Sufis waits for the fulfillment of their desires — that's why they eat so much!

But the Sufi who takes nourishment from the light of God is free from the shame of begging.

Such Sufis are one in a thousand, the rest live under their protection.

Rumi

Both guest and host stand at the threshold between the known and the unknown worlds, between the mundane and the sacred. Whether the material setting be opulent or simple, the ultimate value of the relationship lies in the degree to which both are willing to reflect the divine qualities. The offering and acceptance of an invitation reflect the willingness of guest and host to render service and honor, to identify with each other, and to acknowledge that, in fact, there is no other. Knocking at the door, opening it in welcome, sharing company at the hearth, breaking bread in fellowship — these actions mirror the inner capacity for unconditional acceptance of the hospitality and sustenance God offers to all creatures. The epitome of such openness was depicted by the Hungarian traveler Arminius Vambery, who in 1862 was a guest in the tent of Allah Nazr, on the plateau to the north of Gomushtepe, Anatolia:

This old Turkoman was beside himself from joy that heaven had sent him guests; the recollection of that scene will never pass from my mind. In spite of our protestations to the contrary, he killed a goat, the only one which he possessed, to contribute to our entertainment. At a second meal, which we partook with him the next day, he found means to procure bread also, an article that had not been seen for weeks in his dwelling. While we attacked the dish of meat, he seated himself opposite to us, and wept, in the exactest sense of the expression, tears of joy. Allah Nazr would not retain any part of the goat he had killed in honor of us. The horns and hoofs, which were burned to ashes, and were to be employed for the galled places on the camels, he gave to Ilias; but the skin, stripped off in one piece, he destined to serve as my water-vessel, and after having well rubbed it with salt, and dried it in the sun, he handed it over to me.

Arminius Vambery

Whether he wore the robes of a Bektashi or not, it is clear that Allah Nazr understood the words of Hajji Bektash:

This is the state of the world: those who come shall pass away. Serve thou also. Lay out the meal. If you need help, seek it in generosity. When the people wanted courage and a miracle from 'Ali, he commanded Kanbar, saying, "Lay on the meal." Let all who would enter the tariqat and wear its dress seek out a traveler and serve him.

6

The Naqshbandiyah Order

Naqshbandi (*an-Naqshbandiyyah*) is one of the major tasawwuf orders (tariqa) of Islam. The order is considered by some to be a "sober" order known for its silent dhikr (remembrance of God) rather than the vocalized forms of dhikr common in other orders. The Naqshbandi order is also notable as it is the only Sufi order that claims to trace its spiritual lineage (*silsilah*) to Muhammad through Abu Bakr, the first Caliph. In contrast, most other turuq trace their lineage to Ali, Muhammad's cousin and son-in-law and the Fourth Caliph. The word *Naqshbandi* is Persian, taken from the name of the founder of the order, Baha-ud-Din Naqshband Bukhari. Some have said that the translation means "related to the image-maker," some also consider it to mean "patternmaker" rather than "image maker," and interpret "Naqshbandi" to mean "Reformer of Patterns", and others consider it to mean "Way of the Chain" or "Golden Chain."

Naqshbandi chain of transmission:

1. Muhammad
2. Abu Bakr
3. Salman the Persian
4. Qasim ibn Muhammad ibn Abu Bakr
5. Ja'far al-Sadiq
6. Bayazid Bastami

7. Abul-Hassan Kharaqani
8. Abu Ali al-Farmadi
9. Yusuf Hamdani
10. Abul Abbas al-Khidr (Spiritual Bayah)
11. Khwaja Abdul Khaliq Gajadwani
12. Khwaja Arif al-Riwakri
13. Khwaja Mahmood al-Injir al-Faghnawi
14. Khwaja Ali Ar-Ramitani
15. Khwaja Muhammad Baba as-Samasi
16. Khwaja Sayyid Amir Kulal
17. Khwaja Baha-ud-Din Shah Naqshband Bukhari - Namesake of Naqshbandi order

From here, the order branches into several sub-orders. One of the most important and widespread is the Naqshbandi-Mujaddadi branch founded by Ahmad Sirhindi. The chain between Bahauddin Naqshbandi and Ahmad Sirhindi continues below:

1. Khwaja Alauddin al-Bukhari al-Attar
2. Khwaja Yaqub al-Charkhi
3. Khwaja Ubaydullah al-Ahrar
4. Muhammad Az-Zahid
5. Darwish Muhammad
6. Khawaja al-Amkanaqi
7. Muhammad al-Baqi Billah
8. Ahmad Sirhindi Mujaddid Alf-thani

Sub-orders

There is no single authority for the Naqshbandi order today. Rather, there are numerous sub-orders which operate in autonomy. Among them are the Sardaria, Owaisiah, Haqqani, Aslamiya, Hijazi, Mujarradiya, Tahiri and Tauheedia branches. All the Sub-orders have altered the ways to suit the needs of the different communities thus making them into Naqshbandia Mujadidiyyah.

Naqshbandi Tahiri Branch

In Pakistan, Naqshbandi Order is mostly prevalent under this branch. Previously known as Ghaffari branch, the Naqshbandi Tahiri order belongs to a famous Shaikh of Pakistan, Shaikh Muhammad Tahir Abbasi Naqshbandi Mujaddidi, who is more famous with the name Mahboob Sajjan Saeen and the headquarter of this branch is at the Dargah in Allahabad, near Kandiaro, in the province of Sindh. This order is prevalent in all provinces of Pakistan, and many other countries such as the United Kingdom, Germany, Sweden, Spain, Australia, New Zealand and the USA. Shaikh Muhammad Tahir Abbasi belongs to the previously known as Ghaffari branch of Naqshbandi order; his lineage goes back to Shaikh Fazal Ali Qureshi. The lineage tree of this branch is the following:

1. Muhammad Ma'sum Faruqi
2. Sayfuddeen
3. Muhsin Dehlawi
4. Noor Muhammad Badyooni
5. Mirza Mazhar Jaan-I-Jaanan
6. Abdullah Shah, Muhaddis-e-deccan
7. Abu Sa'eed Ahmad
8. Ahmad Sa'eed
9. Dawst Muhammad Qandhaari
10. Muhammad Uthmaan Daamaani
11. Siraaj-ud-deen
12. Khwaja Ghareeb Nawaz Hadhrat Fazal Ali Shah Qureshi
13. Hazrat Khwaja Abdul Ghaffar, Pir Mitha
14. Hazrat Khwaja Allah Bakhsh, Sohna Saeen
15. Hazrat Khwaja Muhammad Tahir, Sajjan Saeen

Naqshbandi Mujaddidi branch:

1. Hazrat Muhammad Ma'soom Farooqui, Rehmatullah Allaih

2. Hazrat Sayfuddeen, Rehmatullah Allaih
3. Hazrat Muhsin Dehlawi, Rehmatullah Allaih
4. Hazrat Noor Muhammad Badyooni, Rehmatullah Allaih
5. Hazrat Mirza Mazhar Jaan-I-Jaanan, Rehmatullah Allaih
6. Hazrat Abdullah Shah, Muhaddis-e-deccan, Rehmatullah Allaih
7. Hazrat Abu Sa'eed Ahmad, Rehmatullah Allaih
8. Hazrat Ahmad Sa'eed, Rehmatullah Allaih
9. Hazrat Dawst Muhammad Qandhaari, Rehmatullah Allaih
10. Hazrat Muhammad Uthmaan Daamaani, Rehmatullah Allaih
11. Hazrat Siraaj-ud-deen, Rehmatullah Allaih
12. Khwajah Ghareeb Nawaz Hadhrat Fazal Ali Shah Qureshi Rehmatullah Allaih
13. Hazrat Saeed Qureshi, Rehmatullah Allaih
14. Hazrat Syed Zawwar Hussain Shah, Rehmatullah Allaih
15. Hazrat Prof. Dr. Ghulam Mustafa Khan, Rehmatullah Allaih, Hyderabad, Pakistan
16. Hazrat Dr Hafiz Munir Ahmed Khan, Damat e Barakatahu, Hyderabad, Pakistan

Naqshbandia Owaisiah Branch

Naqshbandi Order has another famous branch called Naqshbandia Owaisiah Order. The method of spiritual instruction is quite close to Mujaddidiyyah branch. However, there are two main differences. First Naqshbandia Owaisiah order uses the "Pas Infas" method of zikr. Secondly, the method of spiritual instruction is "Uwaysi", which means that the Shaikh can impart spiritual instruction regardless of physical distance and even difference of time period.

Seekers of Naqshbandia Owaisiah can obtain spiritual blessing from their Shaikh regardless of their location in the world. Owaisiah connection is also useful in obtaining spiritual blessings from Sufis of the Past. The Naqshbandia Owaisiah Order is based in Pakistan and its modern founder was Shaikh Allah Yar Khan. Current shaikh is Maulana Muhammad Akram Awan. Headquarters for this sect is Dar-ul-irfan, Minara, and Chakwal, Pakistan.

Naqshbandi Haqqani Golden Chain

The Naqshbandi Golden Chain is a lineage of Khalidiyya-Naqshbandiyya. It passes from Iraq under Khalid al-Baghdadi to Daghestan, where it remained through seven generations of Sufi masters, to finally return to the Middle East in Damascus with the emigration of Sharafuddin ad-Daghestani and his spiritual inheritor Abdullah al-Fa'iz ad-Daghestani, and then to Cyprus under Nazim al-Qubrusi, who is now the leader of the Naqshbandi-Haqqani order worldwide. Notable scholars who are Naqshbandi Haqqani, thus under the spiritual guidance of Shaykh Nazim, include Shaykh Hisham Kabbani, Shaykh Adnan Kabbani and Shaykh Gibril Haddad to name but a few.

Tauheedia Naqshbandia Branch

In 1955 Hazarat Kawajah Abdul Hakeem Ansari along with his only caliph Hazarat Abdul Sattar Khan (accompanied by Kawajah Sattar's wife and daughter) founded a new branch of the Naqshbandia Mujadidiah Order (chain mentioned below). He named it *Tauheediah*, with a focus on unity (Tauheed), truthfulness and love and making it more practical for modern Westernized society aiming towards unification of ummah... and development of humanity. It has a base in Lahore, and disciples throughout the world.

Naqshbandia Aslammiya Branch

In 1963 Shaikh Hazrat Khawjah Sufi Muhammad Aslam Rehmatullah Allaih came to spread the message of Islam and Prophet Mohammed (peace and blessings be with him) in the UK. He along with a disciple invited towards good until after 7 years, many people joined their gatherings. The order had Aslammiya put after its name because of its simplicity of Dhikr. In other Tariqas many Chakras had to be lit before annihilation but in this particular Group there was only one chakra which is the heart that made you Pure. It is now being led by their son Sufi Riaz Ahmed in Blackburn.

Naqshbandiyyah in Hyderabad, India

In the Hyderabad, India, there are many saints of Naqshbandiyyah such as Miskeen Shah Sahab, Saadullah Shah Sahab, Bukhari Shah, Syed Abdullah Shah Naqshbandi (He is very famous saint of the Naqshbandiya order. He is the first person in the whole Muslim Hanafi community, who authored a book on Hanafi Fiqh by name Zujajat al-Masabih in 5 volumes, and also he had many mureeds in Hyderabad and overall India), Khaleelullah Shah Sahab, Rahmatullah Shah sahib, Prof. Mohammed Abdus Sattar Khan sahib, Ex-Head department of Arabic, Osmania University, Anwarullah Shah Sahab, Shah Hussain Shaheedullah Basheer, Taskeen Shah Sahab.

Naqshbandia in the Western World

Abdullah Isa Neil Dougan learnt from the Afghani Shaikh Abdul al Khyum and taught in NZ from the early sixties until his death in 1987.

Political Aspects

In Syria the Alawi-dominated Ba'ath government is said to depend on the Naqshandi order for legitimacy. A prominent leader of the Naqshbandi order, Sheikh Ahmad Kaftarou, was grand mufti of Syria until his death in 2004.

The Naqshbandi Way of Dhikr

What are the difference between the Naqshbandi and the other Sufi ways? It is axiomatic that all Sufi paths lead to the Divine Presence. The Prophet (s) said, "The ways to God are as numerous as the breaths of human beings." The differences lie mostly in the realm of style and taste, and reflect the need to accomodate the variety of types among the aspirants. Differences also stem from the unique individualities of the great luminaries who imprinted each of the Tariqats — May Allah be pleased with all of them!

There are also some differences of approach. Most Sufi paths offer aspirants a gradual unveiling of the heart's eye, accomplished through the practice of Dhikr, the remembrance of Allah. This spiritual exercise may contain repetition of several of Allah's Holy Names. Some dhikrs involve practices designed to break the spell of mundane consciousness and propel the practicioner into a state of altered awareness. Such practices may include repetition of many thousands of holy phrases, sometimes connected with breathing exercises and often with physical movements. Without a doubt, through the steadfast and dedicated practice of these methods, the aspirant may experience spiritual states and attain stations unimaginable in a normal state of consciousness. The aspirant may feel himself to be flying towards the heavenly goals, beholding the wonders of the mysterious and hidden aspects of creation.

If your eyes have been thus opened, and if you are greatly enamored of the wide vistas you have beheld, then be warned. Should you embark upon the Naqshbandi path, your colorful plumage will be clipped and replaced with the humble cloak of obscurity. For the main difference between the Naqshbandi Way and others is that while they are giving, we are taking away. Everything must go, even your separate existence. First you will be without anything, and then you will be nothing. Only those who are prepared to take such a step can be real Naqshbandi murids. As long as a drop is falling from the heavens, it may be called a drop. When it falls into the ocean, it is no longer a drop, it is the ocean.

If anyone is interested in spiritual stations and powers, he may attain them through following any of the forty Sufi paths, as these ways are quite efficacious. Through the recitation of the most beautiful names of Allah everyone receives bountifully in accordance with his intention. In the end, however, the sincere seeker will be struck with remorse if he becomes fixated at the stage of stations and states. One day he will perceive how he has fallen victim to distraction and say: "Oh my Lord, I have been wasting myself and my efforts on something other than you." Should a seeker's life end while he is in those states, he will regret that they distracted him from seeking the Divine Countenance of His Lord. Therefore, GrandShaykhs have been ordered to strip their followers of their spiritual adornments, so that they may be presented to their Lord in perfect lowliness: "This is your servant, oh our Lord; accept him. He is lost to himself and exists only for You." This is their top priority, and helping their followers attain such a reality is their duty.

It is understood by all orders that the strange and enchanting experiences are the scenery of the journey, not the goal. The goal is to reach his Divine Presence by the attraction of the Beloved Himself. The Holy Prophet Muhammad (s) is the Guide and Example. On His miraculous Night Journey, in which He was conducted by the Angel Gabriel (s) first from Makkah to Jerusalem and then up to the Seven Heavens and into the Divine Presence, he passed trough the whole universe. Allah Almighty informs us in the Holy Qur'an that the Prophet's vision "neither swerved nor wavered" [53:2]. In other words, he looked and beheld but never let those sights distract him from ascending towards his most Exalted Destination.

The Holy Prophet was able to behold those sights without being distracted because His Heart was only for His Lord. He was the Beloved of Allah. As for ourselves, we are vulnerable and weak-willed. Those experiences and attainments may accord with our ego's desires, whereas annihilation is never an attractive proposition for the ego. Therefore, in order to provide maximum protection, the Naqshbandi Masters take a different approach to the unveiling of the heart's eye. There are 70,000 veils between us and the Station of the Prophet (s). A Naqshbandi Master rends these veils in descending order, starting with those closest to the Divine Presence and then successively downwards towards the level of the murid. This process continues throughout the training of the murid, until there is but one veil, the Veil of Humanity *(ijab al-bashariyya)*, restraining the murid's vision from contemplation of the Divine Reality. In order to protect the murid from attraction to something other than his Lord, however, the GrandShaykh does not rend that last veil until the murid reaches the highest state of perfection, or until his final seven breaths on his deathbed.

If the veils are removed from the bottom up by means of mystical practices, the murid beholds a succession of new panoramas. That very vision may keep him from progressing. Those who attain such stations during this life may discover that they have become powerful and famous among people. This is a danger. Power and recognition are conditions conducive to worldliness. The ego will never neglect such an opportunity to demand its share of the excitement and admiration, and by so doing taint the whole process of spiritual endeavor. The Sufi aspirant must seek his Lord, not fame. Look at history's most reknowned Holy Woman, the Virgin Mary, who once prayed (Surat Maryam, 23): "Would that I had been a thing forgotten and out of sight!" She has taught all mankind to seek only obscurity in the sight of the world, and not to look for recognition. The striving for power and fame is a heavy burden. The Sufi seeks rather to be forgotten in the Ocean of Unity of Allah Almighty.

The Naqshbandi Sufi Shaykhs say that whoever works according to the following series of recommendations, and acts on it, will attain the exalted stations, especially the Station of Closeness (Qurb) to Allah, Who is Powerful and Sublime, on the Day of Resurrection. The faithful and diligent application of these practices is certain to temper the influence of the lower elements which exist in every human being: the *nafs* (ego); *dunya* (worldliness); *hawa* (vain desires) and *shaytan* (the devil). A person who manages to keep these principles of the Naqshbandi Order will achieve the light of his Shaykh, who will lift him to the Presence of the Supreme Teacher, the Prophet (s), who in his turn, will lift him up to the Station of Annihilation in Allah.

Allah Powerful and Sublime taught the Prophet Muhammad (s) good manners, for which reason the Holy Prophet (s) said, "My Lord taught me good manners and perfected His Teaching." The best of manners is to keep the orders of Allah, and the seeker must follow the example of the Prophet in keeping the obligations of His Lord and in following the spiritual path. He must be persistent in keeping to the adab of the Order, until he attains the knowledge of the shari'ah and tariqat. The beginner must always begin at the beginning. He should recognize the difference between Shari^{c}ah and Tariqat. Shariah is a reality that is obligatory for every believing man and woman. Concretely speaking, the Shariah consists of practicing that which Allah has ordered and avoiding that which He has forbidden.

The believer relies on guides to indicate clearly to him what to discard and what to follow. The Qur'an and Sunnah are the foundation of all guidance. The Madhahib judgments of the four Imams, the writing of the scholars and their living inheritors relay and explain the guidance. Whoever keeps to this guidance will be on the *ira al-mustaqam,* the straight path. Tariqat is the firm intention *(^{c}azamah)* of the shara^{c}ah. It does not exist outside of shara^{c}ah. It is the resolution to follow the Sunnah of the Prophet (s) as completely as possible in every aspect, external and internal, exposed and hidden, exoteric and esoteric, physical and spiritual. To follow Tariqat the murid puts his trust in the judgment of the Shaykh for the correct understanding and application of the guidance of the Qur'an and the Sunnah. The murid places his hand in the hand of an authorized, living Shaykh and must procede as indicated by him.

He must be ready at all times to receive the orders of his

Shaykh, just as the Prophet (s) awaited the coming of Jibril with revelation from Allah, Almighty and Exalted. In the same way he must follow the Shaykh's orders, carrying them out to the letter. He must have the "adab of anticipation," which means that he must constantly await the orders of his guide. He must adopt the attitude of a hunter to its prey, being oblivious to all other directions. His sight, hearing, existence and thoughts should be ready to receive orders, and he should always be ready to carry out some new order. Such a man will be a master of the adab of the Exalted Naqshbandi Order, and this *tajalli* (manifestation) will become apparent in him.

The murid should keep to his daily dhikr and should obey the order of his Shaykh, without veering to the right or to the left. GrandShaykh Shaykh ᶜAbdullah ad-Daghestani said, "My tongue is the tongue of the secret of the shari'ah and of the secret of the Qur'an." Then he asked a question saying, "Who are the bearers and protectors of the Qur'an?" and answered himself: "The bearers and protectors of Qur'an are the ones who set foot in all the exalted stations and knew them with true understanding. And is it not right, my children that I should indicate to you that you should follow this path so that you may reach and discover these stations?"

Shaykh ᶜAbdullah ad-Daghestani continued saying, "Whoever receives the keys to the five stations *(maqamat)*: Heart *(qalb)*, Secret *(sirr)*, Secret of the Secret *(sirr as-sirr)*, Hidden *(khafa)*, Most Hidden *(akhfa)* is the one who takes care to perform the Adab and the Awrad in their correct manner. This enables him to reach the Station of Bayazid al-Bistami (q), in which he said, "I am also the Real *(al- aqq)*." Anyone who wishes to enter the Station of the Two Attributes of the Real, Almighty and Exalted: the Attribute of Beauty *(Jamal)* and that of Sublimeness and Glory *(Jalal)* must follow this Way.

Eleven Principles of the Naqshbandi Sufi Order

I have copied this page from the Haqqani Foundation website because of the importance of these principles to the

Naqshbandi order and because the background of the page on their site made it difficult for me to read. It appears largely to be taken verbatim from Trimingham, *The Sufi Orders of Islam* (pp. 203-204). The source for Triminghams's translation was Taj al-Din ibn Mahdi Zaman al-Rumi, *Risala fi sunan al-Ta'ifa al-Naqshbandiya,* which is a manuscript held in the Cambridge library and listed in the Add. (Additional or Added?) manuscripts #1073, pp. 4-5. There are a number of problems in Trimingham's translation. When I have the time, I will attempt to correct the translations, basing myself on sources that seem to have the much of the same material as Taj al-Din's *Risalah.* I will follow my corrections by "—ed," indicating that I, the editor, am responsible for the corrections.

The following eleven principles show the exercise-aims of the Tariqat Naqshbandiya. The first eight were formulated by Khwaja Abd al-Khaliq al-Ghujdawani, and the last three were added by Khwaja Bahauddin Naqshband.

Yad Kard

Remembrance- It means making mention, both oral and mental and always repeating the Dhikr imparted to you so that you may attain the beatific vision. Khwaja Bahauddin Naqshband said, "The aim in Dhikr is that the heart be always aware of al-Haqq [The Truth, a Beautiful Name of Allah], for its practice banished inattention."

Baz Gasht

Restraint- The person saying the Dhikr, when engaging in the heart-repetition of the blessed phrase [shahada] should intersperse it with such phrases as "my God you are my Goal and your satisfaction is my aim", to help to keep one's thoughts form straying. Other masters say that it means 'return' or 'repent', i.e, return to al-Haqq by way of contrition [inkisar].

Nigah Dasht

Watchfulness- Over wandering and passing thoughts when repeating the blessed phrase.

Yad Dasht

Recollection- Concentration upon the Divine Presence in a condition of Dhawq [zoq], foretaste, intuitive anticipation or perceptiveness, not using external aids.

Hosh Dar Dam

Awareness while breathing- The technique of breath control said, Khwaja Bahauddin Naqshband, "The external basis of this tariqa is the breath." One must not exhale in forgetfulness or inhale in forgetfulness.

Safar Dar Watan

Journeying in one's homeland- This is an interior journey, the movement from blameworthy to praiseworthy qualities. Others refer to it as the vision or revelation of the hidden side of the Shahada.

Nazar Bar Qadam

Watching one's steps- Let the salik [pilgrim] ever be watchful during his journey, whatever the type of country through which he is passing that he does not let his gaze be distracted from the goal of his journey.

Khalwat Dar Anjuman

Solitude in a crowd- The journey of the salik, though outwardly it is in the world, inwardly it is with God. Leaders of the Tariqa have said,"In this tariqa association is in the crowd [assembly] and disassociation in the khalwa." A common weekly practice was to perform the dhikr in the assembly.

Wuquf-e Zamani

Temporal pause [Awareness related to time—ed.]- Keeping account of how one is spending one's time, whether rightly and if so give thanks, or wrongly- and if so asking for forgiveness, according to the ranking of the deeds, for "verily the good deeds of the righteous are the iniquities of those who are near [to God]."

Wuquf-e Adadi

Numerical pause [Awareness related to number—ed.]. Checking that the heart dhikr [said in the heart, silently] has been repeated the requisite number of times, taking into account one's wandering thoughts. The *Rashahat* mentions that Khwaja Bahauddin Naqshband considered numerical awareness the first stage of esoteric knowlege.

Wuquf-e Qalbi

Heart pause [Awareness related to the heart—ed.]. Forming a mental picture of one's heart with the name of Allah engraved thereon, to emphasize that the heart has no consciousness or goal other than God. This is the meaning of the word "Naqshband".

Sufism and the Naqshbandi Order

Sufism has penetrated into the Western world at two far removed periods of history if we exclude the Muslim population of Europe in such lands as Albania and Bosnia. The first was what in the West is called the medieval period and in such lands as Spain and Sicily where Sufi orders flourished and even influenced certain esoteric currents of both Judaism and Christianity elsewhere in Europe. The second is the present century when Sufism has expanded much more widely into the Occident, including both Europe and America. During this second period, it was first of all the Shadhiliyyah Order which sank its roots seriously into the soil of the West and created a 'space' for Sufism in that world.

Other orthodox and traditional orders ...soon followed the Shadhiliyyah Order in creating branches in the West, including the Chrishtis, Rifa'is, Qadiris, Ni'matullahis and Khalwati-Herrahis. Finally, one of the most widespread of Sufi orders, the Naqshbandiyyah has come to Europe and American and begun to spread its teachings extensively especially during the past two decades. The Naqshbandiyyah Order was founded by Shaykh Baha al-Din Naqshband born in the 14th century near Bukhara in what is now called Central Asia, but which, at that time, was culturally a part of the Persian-speaking world.

The Order spread rapidly from its original home into the Eastern areas of Persia and present-day Afghanistan, and from there, into India which became the home of some of its greatest later figures. Also it spread eastward to China where it remains strong to this day and westward to the Ottoman Empire expanding rapidly into the Balkans as well where it survives to this day in Macedonia, Kosovo, Albania and Bosnia. The name of the Order, derived from its founder, means on one level, what is related to an embroiderer or literally one who casts patterns upon cloth (naqshband). But on a deeper level, it means bonding the heart with God through the imprint of His Name upon the human heart.

The Naqshbandis have always been very orthodox, staunch defenders of the Shari'ah and emulators of the Sunnah. Throughout Islamic history they have played a most important role in the preservation and spread of Islam especially under conditions of duress while of course having as their central aims the spiritual, inner perfection of their followers. But they have always sought to preserve a balance between the esoteric and exoteric, avoiding excesses which one might observe elsewhere. This fact is also reflected in the active role they have played politically on the one hand, and in their cultivation of the most esoteric doctrines of Sufism, on the other.

The Naqshbandi Sufi Way

The Naqshbandi Order is the way of the Companions of the Prophet and those who follow them. This Way consists of continuous worship in every action, both external and internal, with complete discipline according to the Sunnah of the Prophet. It consists in maintaining the highest level of conduct and leaving absolutely all innovations and all free interpretations in public customs and private behavior. It consists in keeping awareness of the Presence of God,

Almighty and Exalted, on the way to self-effacement and complete experience of the Divine Presence.

It is the Way of complete reflection of the highest degree of perfection. It is the Way of sanctifying the self by means of the most difficult struggle, the struggle against the self. It begins where the other orders end, in the attraction of complete Divine Love, which was granted to the first friend of the Prophet, Abu Bakr as-Siddiq. Historically speaking, the Naqshbandi Way can be traced back directly to the first of the rightly-guided caliphs, Abu Bakr as-Siddiq, who succeeded the Prophet Muhammad in his knowledge and in his role of guiding the Muslim community and indirectly to the fourth rightly-guided caliph, Ali Abi Talib.

Golden Chain—Transmission of the Teachings

The transmission of the teachings in this Order has been passed down in an unbroken line (referred to as The Golden Chain) from the time of the Prophet (pbuh) to the present living Master, Shaykh Muhammad Nazim Adil al Haqqani, who revived the Naqshbandi Order at the end of the 20th Century. He infused into the Community and the planet, love of God and love of the lovers of God. A prominent scholar of mainstream, traditional Islam, Shaykh Muhammad Hisham Kabbani has spent his life spreading the teachings of peace, tolerance, respect and love that are the message of Islam throughout the world. Here in the United States for the last eleven years, Shaykh Kabbani has continued to disseminate the light and peace of Islam's spiritual dimension to people of every background, ethnicity, race, and belief.

The history of the Naqshbandi order has to a great extent been recorded and studied by Western scholars as well as by the leaders of the order and their followers. Studies in this context are not, understandably, in proportion to the various periods of the history of the order or its geographical expansion. As far as Kurdistan and the Kurdish Naqshbandis are concerned, almost all of the studies have tended to focus disproportionately on Mawlana Khalid Sharazuri, the eponym and founder of the Khalidiyya suborder, and the early years in the development of Khalidiyya.

This chapter will be confined to studying the post-Mawlana periods of the Khalidiyya suborder, and in particular on the Naqshbandi shaikhs of Hawraman, the Siraj ad-Dini family, the most influential and prominent representatives of the Khalidiyya branch in Kurdistan and in the entire Middle-East. Emphasis will be placed on the family's role in spreading the Naqshbandi order from the time of Siraj ad-Din I onwards. The main features of the order that have been shaped in the span of more than one and a half centuries will be examined in light of, and in comparison with, the situation of the order during the time of Mawlana Khalid at the beginning of the nineteenth century.

Mawlana Khalid and Khalidiyya

The Naqshbandi order as introduced into Kurdistan in the beginning of the nineteenth century by Mawlāna Khalid had special features that, no doubt, contributed to its development and the spread of its teachings. Those features were, to a great extent, identical to mainstream Sufi views established and/or reestablished by Shaikh Ahmad Sirhindi (d. 1624) and his successors. It was therefore quite natural that Mawlana Khalid would represent the ideas and teachings of his masters in the subcontinent, by whom he was initiated to the path. But it is also true that Mawlana Khalid was not simply one of the hundreds or perhaps thousands of deputies who were initiated, trained and instructed by Shaikh Abdullah Dihlavi, also known as Shah Ghulam Ali, (d. 1240/1824). He was for several reasons, exceptional, in position, qualities and abilities.

Shah Ghulam Ali conferred upon Mawlana Khalid "full and absolute successorship" (khilafa tamma mutlaqa), a rank he seems to have denied to other deputies. There are statements by Shah Ghulam Ali in which he expressed his awareness of the unique position of Mawlana Khalid. After staying one year in the Khanaqah in Delhi, Shah Ghulam Ali, instructed Mawlana to return to Kurdistan. Prior to leaving, they engaged in an interesting conversation. Lastly Shah Ghulam asked him: "What else do you want?" Mawlana replied: "I want the religion (din) and I want the world (dunya) to strengthen the religion." The Shaikh told him: "Go, I gave (bestowed on) you the whole of it." Mawlana Khalid returned to Kurdistan in 1811 and left for Damascus in 1822. Even during those eleven years he spent more than five years of his life in Baghdad.

This period, although relatively very short, was quite important and decisive, for it was in these years that the order was firmly established and most of the great and prominent deputies were initiated. On his way to and from India through Iran, Mawlana Khalid was confronted several times by Iranian Shi'a scholars and had heated discussions with them concerning different religious questions. In Hamadan an attempt on his life was made, but he escaped death. The Naqshbandiyya-Mujaddidiyya was recognized as an anti-Shi'a order. This was in some measure due to the fact that there was a great Shi'a population in the original regions of the order in the Indian subcontinent, and daily confrontations strengthened that tendency. There were certainly historical reasons for the tension in relations between the Naqshbandis and the Shi'a. But when Mawlana Khalid returned to Kurdistan, this aspect was totally minimized. There was no need to emphasize anti-Shi'ism because there was no longer direct confrontation with the Shi'a.

On the other hand the Indian Mujaddidis were on good terms with the leaders and followers of the Qadiriyya order, and Mawlana got his Khilafa even for the Qadiriyya order. But once Mawlana returned to Sulaymani he was confronted with great rivalry by the leader of the Qadiri order; Shaikh Ma'ruf Node (Nudahi). The Qadiri order was well established in Kurdistan at that time and had great influence upon the people and the rulers of the Kurdish Baban principality as well. The return of Mawlana Khalid and the rapid spread of the Naqshbandiyya-Mujaddidiyya as a new and energetic order disturbed the Qadiri leaders, who resisted Mawlana Khalid strongly. The rivalry escalated to a degree that even Mawlana's trustworthiness as a Muslim was questioned by Shaikh Ma'ruf, who accused him of being a liar and a heretic.

It should be mentioned that the political factor in this conflict was not only present but also effective. The Baban Mahmud Pasha harboured ill will against Mawlana Khalid and feared his influence upon his brothers and cousins. It is not unlikely that the Pasha played a role in deepening the dispute between the two orders to benefit his political ends. Although Mawlana Khalid was deeply touched by the circumstances, he nevertheless displayed great restraint and never let himself be driven into polemics. He expressed his willingness to have discussions and dialogue with his opponents. In letters to one of the Baban princes, 'Uthman Pasha, he suggests that Shaikh Ma'ruf and "great scholars" should come to meet him and he would debate and converse with them (in faqir ba Uha mubahatha va guftgu mikunam). He suggests further that the Pasha himself would be present in the meeting.

Mawlana Khalid's attempts to achieve a peaceful solution seemingly did not meet with success. He chose to leave Sulaimani and to reside in Baghdad where he stayed for about three years. When Mahmud Pasha succeeded his father, Abd ar-Rahman Pasha (d. 1228/1813), as the ruler of the Baban principality, he visited Baghdad and invited Mawlana to return to Kurdistan. He did so in 1231/1816 or 1232/1817. Apparently the situation was not proper for Mawlana to stay for a long time; therefore he left Sulaimani forever on the 25th of October 1820. Apart from the summer months of 1821 and 1822, which Mawlana spent in Hawraman, he remained in Baghdad. After spending the summer of 1822 in Kurdistan he left via Urfa and Dayr az-Zur for Damascus where he arrived most probably in late November 1822.

It is often indicated that Mawlana left Kurdistan, and Baghdad, for Damascus to escape the Qadiris' hostility. Considering the situation from an historical perspective, it is borne in one's mind that it was necessary for the order to expand widely and not to be limited to Sulaimani or Baghdad. A settlement of sorts was, however, reached with the Qadiri leaders while Mawlana was still alive, and Shaikh Ma'ruf Node declared his repentance in his letters to Mawlana and by sending his envoys to him asking to meet and reconcile, and to forgive his, Shaikh Ma'ruf's, shortcomings.

The time between Mawlana's return to Kurdistan as a Sufi guide and his death was relatively short, but he succeeded in establishing the Naqshbandiyya-Mujaddidiyya as the most powerful and influential Sufi order in the Middle East. He is compared in this respect to Shah Ghulam Ali. In 1820, when he was still living in Kurdistan, the number of his disciples was estimated at 12,000. This of course is difficult to either confirm or disprove. One thing is certain: no other Naqshbandi-Mujaddidi Shaikh before him succeeded as he did in initiating as many great and distinguished scholars to the order.

The Siraj ad-Dini Shaikhs

The Siraj ad-Dini sheiks have been the most prominent representatives of the Khalidi sub-order in Kurdistan since Mawlana Khalid left Kurdistan for Damascus at the end of 1237 A. H./autumn, 1822. Indeed Shaikh Uthman Siraj ad-Din I (1195/1781-1283/1867) was the most important figure among Mawlana Khalid's disciples even at a time when Mawlana was still living in Kurdistan and/or in Baghdad. The two men knew each other as students of Islamic sciences (faqe in Kurdish), and they met once again in Baghdad in 1226/1811 when Mawlana stayed in the mosque of Shaikh

Abd al-Qadir al-Gaylani for five months, shortly after his return from India to Sulaimani. It was then that Faqe Uthman, later known as Siraj ad-Din I, was initiated to the path by Mawlana. After two years of spiritual training, he was the first person to become a khalifa (deputy) of Mawlana. He was then thirty-three years old.

Shaikh Uthman Siraj ad-Din was born in Tawela, in Hawraman region, near Halabja. According to many sources his parents were descendants of the Prophet Muhammad. The family is thus a Sayyid family. But the Siraj ad-Dini Shaikhs never claimed to be Sayyids. Shaikh Uthman signed his letters with his own name followed by al-Khalidi al-Mujaddidi an-Naqshbandi. Shaikh Uthman accompanied his preceptor during the years in which Mawlana was twice obliged to leave Sulaimani for Baghdad. In Sulaimani Shaikh 'Uthman usually substituted for Mawlana in the khatm assemblies. The disciples were instructed by Mawlana to attend Uthman's khatm circles. Among these were outstanding names such as Sayyid Isma'il Daghistani, Mulla Abd al-Hakim Kashghari and Shaikh Muhammad of Halabja.

Apparently Mawlana Khalid, who had a good deal of organizational ability, was preparing his disciple to succeed him and to take the difficult and crucial responsibility of spreading the order in Kurdistan. When Mawlana left Sulaimani for Baghdad for the last time in 1820, Shaikh Uthman did not follow him. He moved instead to his home region, Hawraman, and began there to establish a strong base for the order. Hawraman became one of the most important centres for the Khalidi suborder in the entire Middle East and continued to be so until the 1950s. This center not only contributed greatly in spreading the Sufi teachings of the Naqshbandi order, but also produced a number of poets whose poems are examples of the most significant and marvellous Sufi poetry.

This indispensable position of Siraj ad-Din for Mawlana and for the order becomes clearer when we know that during the summer months of 1236/1821 and 1237/1822 Mawlana left the heat of Baghdad for the summer resorts of Hawraman. There he met Siraj ad-Din and supervised the Naqshbandi networks in Kurdistan. Shaikh Uthman also visited Mawlana in Baghdad at least once during this period. It was from Kurdistan, not from Baghdad, as is commonly, but wrongly, accepted in the sources on the Khalidi suborder, that Mawlana Khalid went to Damascus. After leaving Sulaimani in 1236/1822, Mawlana was represented in his Sulaimani khanaqa by Shaikh Abdullah Hirati (d. 1245/1839-40), who was assisted by Shaikh Muhammad Sahib (d. 1283/1866), the brother of Mawlana. When Mawlana died in 1242/1827, Hirati, and shortly thereafter, Sahib, left for Damascus.

A few years later, in 1254/1838 the Baban Ahmad Pasha invited Shaikh Uthman to take charge of the Khalidi khanaqa in Sulaimani. The Shaikh accepted the task and supervised the khanaqa, but he did not abandon Hawraman, where he often returned. With the exception of those two years, Shaikh Uthman lived in Tawela and Biyara, in Hawraman, from 1236/1820, the year Mawlana left Sulaimani for Baghdad, until his death, i.e. Shaikh Uthman's death, in 1283/1867. In nearly half a century he was the most prominent khalifa of Mawlana Khalid in Hawraman and Baban regions. The Shaikh had a great number of khalifas and mansubs /deputies and affiliates from different regions in Kurdistan and the Middle East. In his hagiography about Mawlana Khalid and the Naqshbandi Shaikhs of Hawraman, Mala 'Abd al-Karim-i Mudarris enumerates 96 khalifas and 33 mansubs of Shaikh Uthman.

Among them we find many great 'ulama and poets but also two powerful rulers; Ahmad Pasha of Baban and Rizaquli Khan of Sina (Sanadaj) in Ardalan. This is contrary to what many researchers have inferred: that the Naqshbandiyya was only an assembly for opposition sects in Kurdish society. In addition to his letters there are a few lines of poetry and ten advisory articles by Shaikh Uthman, in which he instructs his disciples in the issues of the order. In one of these articles, dated 1272/1856, he appoints his sons, Muhammad Baha' ad-Din and Abd ar-Rahman, as his deputies and successors and advises his followers to obey them.

Shaikh Uthman Siraj ad-Din I was succeeded in turn by five Shaikhs in his family. But it should be indicated also that other members of the family have been in charge of the path in different periods, each with own disciples and khanaqas. He was succeeded directly by his son Shaikh Muhammad Baha' ad-Din. Although in his testament Siraj ad-Din had appointed two of his sons; Baha' ad-Din and Abd ar-Rahman Abu al-Wafa to be his successors, apart from a very short time, Shaikh Abd ar-Rahman declined the position and resided in Baghdad. He was a creative poet. The small number of poems to which we have access today, some 70 poems in Persian, mostly ghazals, indicates his talent as a Sufi poet. Baha' ad-Din was also a poet, although only a few of his poems are extant.

The third Shaikh in the Siraj ad-Din silsila (initiating chain) was Shaikh Umar Zhia' ad-Din. He was distinguished from his predecessors in some respects. It was in his time as a Shaikh that dhikr-i jahr (vocal remembrance) was practiced besides dhikr-i khafi (silent remembrance). He was known for his enthusiasm for science and education, and for culture as a whole. He built several new khanaqas in Khanaqin, Kifri, Qizrabat, Biyara, Tawela and Sardasht. He was a brilliant poet in Kurdish, Persian and Arabic. In his poems he used "Fawzi" as his takhallus (pen name). We have access also to some fifty letters written by him to his deputies or to the great men of his time, among whom we find the Qajari Shah Muzaffar ad-Din (reigned 1896-1907) and the Ottoman Sultan Abd al-Hamid II. There are, moreover, three treatises on Sufi teachings. A remarkable feature in the life of Shaikh Umar Ziya' ad-Din was his good relation to the Qadiri Shaikhs and their disciples and followers, which will be dealt with later.

The immediate successor in the chain was his son Shaikh Najm ad-Din who was known for his zuhd (renunciation). The Ottomans wanted to give him a monthly salary to use it for the khanaqa and its visitors, but the Shaikh rejected the offer. He had great interest in intellectual conversations with the scholars who so often visited the khanaqah in Biyara. He was a poet, but the number of the poems available to us is very small. Shaikh Najm ad-Din was succeeded by his brother Shaikh Muhammad Ala' ad-Din. He wrote a treatise in Arabic entitled Tibb al-Qulub (Healing the hearts), which contains advices and recommendations. He was a well-known physician who helped thousands of people in the region and he prescribed them herbal medicine.

When Shaikh Ala' ad-Din died in 1954 he was succeeded by his son Shaikh Muhammad Uthman Siraj ad-Din II, who was already a well-known and established Sufi leader. Shaikh Uthman II was deeply learned in Islamic theology as well as in Kurdish and Persian poetry. He was moreover a skillful physician with wide knowledge of herbal medicine. When the monarchy in Iraq was overthrown by General Abd al-Karim Qasim, Shaikh Uthman left Iraqi Kurdistan in 1959 and resided in Iranian Kurdistan about two decades. After the Iranian revolution he came back to Hawraman, Iraqi Kurdistan, but he soon left it for Baghdad. He spent the last seven/eight years of his life in Istanbul, where he died on 30 January 1997. He was buried inside his residence, close to the khanaqa in Istanbul. Shaikh Uthman was also a poet; two volumes of his poems, in Kurdish and Persian, are published, as well as a volume of his treatises and letters entitled Siraj al-Qulub "Lantern of Hearts" of which an English translation is also published.

Shaikh Uthman died almost simultaneously; as his brother Shaikh Mawlana Khalid, also a Sufi leader, in Sanadaj, Iranian Kurdistan. No one of them knew, at least outwardly, about the death of his brother, and thus a great wish of their lives was fulfilled. Both had wished that he might never experience (the usual Kurdish expression here is not to see) the death of his brother. In tens of poems and hundreds of letters that were coming and going between them in the span of the last 70-80 years, they expressed that wish time and again. This was one of the last wondrous deeds (karamat) so often attributed to them throughout their lives. Shaikh Uthman was 101 years old when he died and Shaikh Khalid was 99. Shaikh Uthman was named after his great-grandfather Uthman Siraj ad-Din I and Shaikh Khalid was named after Mawlana Khalid.

The role of the Naqshbandi Shaikhs of Hawraman in spreading and establishing the Naqshbandiyya-Mujaddidiyya-Khalidiyya in Kurdistan and in parts of the Middle East is of central importance. It was under the guidance of them and their deputies that the order reached most of the regions in Iraqi and Iranian Kurdistan, Turkman Sahra in Iran, Northern Syria, Lebanon and Bosnia. Nevertheless, they still identify themselves as Khlaidis and Mujaddidis, and never invented, or claimed to have invented, a new sub-order.

Post-Mawlana Naqshbandi-Mujaddidi in Kurdistan

The characteristics of the Naqshbandiyya-Mujaddidiyya that Mawlana Khalid introduced in Kurdistan were not everlasting; they were, to some extent, the products of the Central Asian and Indian circumstances. The new Kurdish environment obviously had its impact on the development of the Khalidiyya suborder and shaped it to adjust to the Kurdish reality. It should be emphasized here that the adjustment did not involve the principal conceptions or teachings of Sufism, but mostly concerned the practical aspects; silent or vocal remembrance, the attitude towards other sects and communities; the Shi'a and the Qadiris, or the stance that should be adapted on politics and political authorities. The only exception, probably, is the opinion about Ibn Arabi and his theory of wahdat alwujud, which is not properly relevant in this case.

The first great problem to face Mawlana Khalid and his newly established suborder was the hostile attitude taken by the leader of the Qadiri order in Kurdistan, Shaikh

Ma'ruf Node with all the complicated consequences the conflict implied, as was mentioned previously. Shaikh Uthmin Siraj ad-Din I had to deal with this conflict and with the new situation as a whole when Mawlana Khalid left for Damascus and died thereafter in 1242/1827. The reconciliation reached at between Mawlana Khalid and Shaikh Ma'ruf, obviously, put an end to any open dispute between the two men and their followers further. The position of Siraj ad-Din as the main representative of the order in Kurdistan necessitated starting new and friendly relations with the Qadiri order. This new attitude marks the two orders' relations in the coming decades and among the succeeding generations.

Among the letters sent by Siraj ad-Din to different people we find a letter to Haji Shaikh Kak Ahmad, son of Shaikh Ma'ruf Node, which contains many friendly and sincere expressions. Shaikh Abd ar-Rahman Talabani of Karkuk (Kirkuk) was one of the prominent leaders of the Qadiri order, with whom Siraj ad-Din was on good terms. This relation was developed further when Siraj ad-Din sent his son Umar to study at the Talabani Takya (takka) in Karkuk, where he lived within Shaikh Abd ar-Rahman's family and studied in the company of his son, 'Ali, who afterwards succeeded his father and became the leader of the Qadiri order. Shaikh Umar Ziya' ad-Din later married a niece of Shaikh Hasan Qarachewar of Qadir Karam, Karkuk, who also was a leader of the Qadiri order.

In a letter to the Naqshbandi deputies and novices in the Juwanro region, Shaikh Uthman Siraj ad-Din reminds them that their order is a combination of five orders, including the Qadiri and that Shaikh Sirhindi regarded Hadrat-i Ghawth, i. e. Shaikh Abd al-Qadir Gilani, the all-embracing means without whom nobody would be favoured on the path. Apparently some people have behaved rudely with the dervishes of Shaikh Abd ar-Rahman (probably Shaikh Abd ar-Rahman Talabani). The Shaikh orders his followers "to treat them as a beggar treats a king." He further tells them that he regards himself as the ground under the feet of the lowest of the Shaikh's dervishes (Khak-i qadam-i 'adna darvishi ... danesta va midanam).

Shaikh Umar Ziya' ad-Din, in a letter to one of his deputies, emphasizes that there is no difference between the Qadiri and the Naqshbandi orders, and whoever makes such a difference, he bears the signs of misfortune. In another letter, addressed to Shaikh Hasan Qarachewar, a leader of the Qadiri order, he begs him for tawajjuh (attention) and describes himself as a servant (chakar). This genuine and friendly relationship between the Qadiris and the Naqshbandis was not limited to the leaders of the two orders. The Kurdish Sufi poet Mawlawi (1221/1806-1300/1882) was a deputy of Shaikh Uthman Siraj ad-Din I and his son Shaikh Muhammad Baha' ad-Din, but, at the same time, he was a good friend of Shaikh Abd ar-Rahman Talabani and Shaikh Kak Ahmad, both great leaders of the Qadiri order, visited them and sent letters to them.

He wrote poems praising Shaikh Abd ar-Rahman and wrote two elegies when the Shaikh died. His friendship with the family continued even after the death of the Shaikh. Mawlawi visited Shaikh Ali Talabani and on one occasion he stayed several months in the Qadiri takya in Karkuk. The third and fourth generations of Qadiri and Naqshbandi Shaikhs kept all the ways and bridges between them open, further developed their relations, and cooperated even on the political level when the circumstances of the Kurdish liberation movement demanded such cooperation. Shaikh Uthman Siraj ad-Din II, praises Shaikh Mahmud Hafid (1881-1956), king of Southern Kurdistan (October 1922-August 1923) in one of his poems and wishes to sacrifice his head, fortune, heart and soul for him.

These were not merely words of courtesy or politeness since we know that the Naqshbandi Shaikhs of Hawraman supported Shaikh Mahmud politically and militarily. In May 1919 Mahmud Khan Dizli, a chief from Hawraman, encouraged directly by the Naqshbandi Shaikhs, came with 300 of his men to Sulaymani. After clashes with the British troops he occupied the city and took the British officers as prisoners. This operation enabled Shaikh Mahmud to strengthen his authority as the governor of Southern Kurdistan. It was during the same period that another Naqshbandi Shaikh, Shaikh Ahmad of Barzan, the elder brother of the legendary Kurdish leader Mustafa Barzani, started a campaign among the tribes in his region to support Shaikh Mahmud and his uprising against the British colonialists.

Relations between the Qadiri and Naqshbandi orders took a political and organizational form in the middle of the 1940s when there was a need to build a new party to lead the Kurdish struggle in Iraqi Kurdistan. Mala Mustafa Barzani, a general in the army of the Kurdish Republic in Mahabad in 1945-46, sent his representatives to Iraqi Kurdistan to build such a party. In his absence—since he was outlawed by the Iraqi and British authorities—he appointed Shaikh Latif Hafid (1917-1972), son of Shaikh Mahmud, as the first vice chairman of the Kurdistan Democratic Party (KDP) founded on 16 August 1946. This decision was signifi-cant both historically and politically. Barzani evidently wanted to mark the new party as a continuation of the Kurdish aspirations of which Shaikh Mahmud was a great symbol.

Moreover it was of great importance to include Shaikh Latif in the leadership of the party not only to ensure support from different regions of Iraqi Kurdistan, but because he was an outstanding figure among the Qadiri Shaikhs, including the Hafid Shaikhs in Sulaymani, whose influence, socially and politically, needed to be taken into consideration. This symbolic significance was reassured a half century later when the remains of Mustafa Barzani were brought to the Great Mosque in Sulaymani and placed beside the graves of Shaikh Kak Ahmad and Shaikh Mahmud for one night, before he was moved to Barzan to be buried in his native village, in 1992. Even in our days we find that one of the three political advisors of Mas'ud Barzani, chairman of the KDP, is a professor of law from Karkuk who belongs to the Qadiri Shaikhs.

As mentioned above, Shaikh Umar Ziya' ad-Din was sent by his father to study at the Qadiri takya in Karkuk, where he was treated as a member of the family and established a friendship with Shaikh Ali Talabani that lasted throughout their lives. This intimate acquaintance with the Qadiri order had an impact on the practical aspects of the Naqshbandi order. When Shaikh Umar succeeded his father as the leader of the Naqshbandiyya-Khalidiyya he introduced the vocal remembrance (dhikr-i jahr) into the order besides the silent remembrance (dhikr-i khafi) that has been, and still is, characteristic for the Naqshbandiyya. The Siraj ad-Dini Shaikhs, who were always identified as Naqshbandis, began to initiate their disciples to the Qadiri order and to consider themselves as leaders for both orders. Shaikh Muhammad Ala' ad-Din was the first to use the title, Khadim at-Tariqa an-Naqshbandiyya wal-Qadiriyya (servant of the Naqshbandi and Qadiri orders).

Attitude towards Ibn Arabi and His Doctrine of Wahdat al-Wujud

The earlier leaders of the Naqshbandiyya were apparently acquainted with and interested in the teachings of Ibn Arabi, especially his doctrine of wahdat al-wujud (the unity of being), in as early as the eighth/fourteenth century. This familiarity with Ibn Arabi and his teachings can be traced in the numerous treatises written by the prominent Naqshbandi Shaikhs in Transoxiana, or by their disciples and deputies. Mulla Abdullah Ilahi (d. 896/1490), a deputy of Khwaja Ubaydullah Ahrar (d. 895/1490), was the first to introduce the Naqshbandi order in the Ottoman lands. Ilahi, who was trained by Ahrar and had contact with Abd ar-Rahman Jami (d. 898/1492), was greatly influenced by the teaching of the Shaikh al-Akbar, which impacted on his writings. The Naqshbandis in Kurdistan were not far from that influence. Evidently the works of Ibn Arabi were read and studied in the Sufi and intellectual circles in Kurdistan and there was a serious interest in them among the educated Kurds.

A literary and poetic expression of Ibn Arabi's ideas, especially the doctrine of wahdat al-wujud, is found in the poems of the Kurdish Sufi poet Mala-ye Jaziri (1570-1640). These teachings are also artistically interwoven with the events of the Kurdish national epic Mam u Zin by Ahmad-i Khani (1651-1707). The first Naqshbandi leader who took a critical attitude towards Ibn Arabi's doctrine of wahdat al-wujud was Shaikh Ahmad Sirhindi, the Mujaddid. This attitude marked to some extent the order in the Indian subcontinent after Sirhindi, the post-Sirhindi period that was called thenceforth Naqshbandiyya-Mujaddidiyya. As far as the Khalidiyya branch of the order is concerned, it is obvious that Mawlana Khalid Shahrazuri was an initiatic descendant of Shaikh Ahmad Sirhindi by five generations, and an enthusiastic Mujaddidi. It is therefore presumed that he was influenced by the teachings of Sirhindi.

We do not find in the letters of Mawlana Khalid, of which nearly three hundreds are extant, or in his treatises, any indication to Ash-Shaikh al-Akbar and his teachings. But on the other hand, he wrote several times to his deputies and disciples advising them to read works written by leaders of the tariqa and scholars who were known for their enthusiasm for Ibn 'Arabi and his teachings, such as Ubaydullah Ahrar, 'Abd ar-Rahman Jami, 'Abd al-Ghafur Lari and Abd al-Ghani an-Nabulusi. It is only in later hagiographies that a critical attitude concerning Ibn 'Arabi's wahdat al-wujud is ascribed to Mawlana Khalid. Mala 'Abd al-Karim Mudarris in his Yad-i Mardan quotes Shaikh Shahab ad-Din Alusi as stating that he had heard that Mawlana Khalid forbade his disciples to read Ibn 'Arabi's Futuhat al-Makkiyya and Fusus al-Hikam.

Alusi was himself a mansub of Mawlana Khalid and studied Islamic law under him. Nevertheless, when relating Mawlana's attitude towards Ibn 'Arabi's works, he states that he had heard about it. The Iraqi historian Abbas al-Azzawi indicates in an article that he had seen a list of the books belonging to Mawlana Khalid, in which he did not find anything of the books by the extremist Sufis (al-ghulat min al-mutasawwifa). Then, praising Mawlana Khalid, he adds, "far be it from him that he inclines to such books." The sentence here is not clear since Azzawi does not specify what "such books" means. But in the preceding pages in the same article, he quotes the above-mentioned Shaikh Alusi, stating that Mawlana Khalid had a pure faith, and "he did not believe in unity, unification and incarnation", which explains Azzawi's doubts. This is undeniably contradictory to the assertions of other sources that several of Ibn Arabi's works were in Mawlana Khalid's library.

Although most of the leading Siraj ad-Dini Shaikhs have been good poets and active letter writers, there is not a single comprehensive work about the philosophical and theoretical aspects of the Naqshbandi order among their writings. Most of the letters and treatises were written to reply to deputies, followers and friends. In many cases they are devoted to explain questions related to the shari'a, or simply to give instructions on everyday issues. A number of these letters were written to the rulers of the time (including the Ottoman Sultan and the Qajar Shah) to ask a favour or simply to send them a few words of courtesy. The letters and treatises of Shaikh 'Umar Diya' ad-Din are probably the most comprehensive among the writings of the Siraj ad-Dini Shaikhs. In a few of them he discusses briefly the questions of fana' and lata'if and other related topics, but the question of wahdat al-wujud is not dealt with anywhere.

Cultural Heritage

In addition to hundreds of letters and a great number of treatises, Mawlana Khalid also wrote tens of poems in Kurdish, Arabic and Persian. These were collected and printed in Istanbul in 1260/1844, only eighteen years after his death. Even in his letters, Mawlana Khalid usually quotes lines of poetry. Often these are lines by known poets such as Hafiz, Mawlana Jalal ad-Din Rumi, Shah-i Naqshband, Shabustari, Jami, Bidel-i Bukhari and others. But he enriches many of his letters with lines of his own poetry. The addition of these lines of poetry clearly indicates Mawlana's sophistication and appreciation of poetry and the impact of words as a whole. This tradition was further developed by the Naqshbandi Shaikhs of Hawraman, the Siraj ad-Dini Shayk family. Already in the 1830s Shaikh Uthman Siraj ad-Din I had turned his home region into an important center of Sufism and culture attracting a great number of poets and scholars. Shaikhs in the family who succeeded him during the last one and a half centuries continued to promote Kurdish culture.

Among their disciples there have always been great scholars and poets who participated in the spreading of the order, creating great works that constitute the grounds of Kurdish Sufi literature, which is an important feature of Kurdish culture as a whole. Many of these poets and scholars dwelled permanently in the Naqshbandi khanaqahs or visited frequently and stayed for long periods. Mala Hamid-i Katib was initiated to the path by Shaikh Uthman Siraj ad-Din I in 1250/1834 and remained with the family until his death. He served the Shaikh and his sons Muhammad Baha' ad-Din and Umar Ziya' ad-Din as their katib. Mala Hamid was a writer and poet, but his poems are mainly devoted to recording social events, including the births and the deaths of prominent members of the Siraj ad-Din family or of the order in general.

His works include six books; perhaps the most important being the interpretations of the Mathnawi-ye Ma'nawi of Jalal ad-Din Rumi, in three volumes, his commentary on Gulshan-e Raz by Mahmud Shabustari and Riad[section] al-mushtaqin, a hagiography about the lives of Mawlana Khalid and Shaikh Uthman Siraj ad-Din I. Not one of these works is printed, but manuscripts are extant. Two great Kurdish Sufi poets are certainly Sayyid Abd ar-Rahim Mawlawi, also known as Ma'dumi, and Shaikh Muhammad Mahwi (1830-1906). Undoubtedly both merit thorough study as examples of excellent and significant Sufi literature.

Other important poets and scholars affiliated with the Naqshbandi Shaikhs of Hawraman are Hajj Sayyid Hasan Chorri (d.1323/1905), Mala Abdullah Jali Koyi (1250-1326), Shaikh Salim Takhtayi, also known as Salim-i Sina (1845-1909), Shaikh Muhammad Am1 'n Hawleri (Al-Kurdi al-Arbilli), Shaikh Umar Ibn al-Qaradaghi (1303-1353), Shaikh Baba Rasul Bedani (1303-1363), Shaikh Abd al-Karim Ahmadbirinda (d. 1361), Mala Mahmud Bekhud (1878-1955), Shaikh Ahmad Shakali (1903-1982) and Mala Abd al-Karim Mudarris (born 1901). The return of Mawlana Khalid in 1811 from India marked the beginning of a new period in the history of the Naqshbandi order in the Middle East. Although a representative of the Mujaddidi branch of the order, the charismatic character of Mawlana Khalid made him the eponym of a branch that is called Khalidiyya that spread rapidly in the whole Middle East.

Many of the leaders of the Khalidiyya played an important role in the political history of Kurdistan in different stages. Shaikh Ubaydullah Nahri (in 1881), Shaikh Sa'id Piran (in 1925) and Mala Mustafa Barzani (1945 until 1975), leaders of the Kurdish liberation movement, belonged to the Mujaddidi-Khalidi branch of the Naqshbandiyya. The role of the order in the development of Kurdish culture was even greater, since many significant scholars and poets were among the deputies and disciples of the Khalidiyya. The first deputy of Mawlana Khalid was Shaikh Uthman Siraj ad-Din I, the founder of the Siraj ad-Din I Shaikh family, also known as the Naqshbandi Shaikhs of Hawraman.

The Naqshbandi center started in Hawraman in the 1830s has continued to be the most important Sufi and cultural center in Kurdistan during the last one and a half centuries. In 1997 one of the most influential Sufi Shaikhs of Hawraman, Shaikh Muhammad Uthman Siaraj ad-Din II, died in Istanbul, without appointing any of his sons or deputies to succeed him. This was an unprecedented event in the history of the family. There are now speculations that the leading role of the family has come to an end. It is not obvious; however, to what extent this will affect the development or the survival of the Khalidiyya-Mujaddidiyya in Kurdistan.

7

Sufism in the Indian Subcontinent

Mystic interpretation of Islamic life within the bonds of religious orthodoxy is known as Sufism, which was initially launched by God fearing people of Perso-Arab world. They renounced the world and devoted themselves to His service. As the seekers of Tawhid (Unity in God) they helped in spread of Islam through mystic movement with intellectualisation of Sunnah (The orthodox customs of Islamic world) as one of its basic principles. The Sufis either in their lifetime or their tombs after death became a symbol of supernatural power with metaphysical features ascribed to them under the guidelines of Quran and Sunnah. The disciples of Sufis adopted the path of peace or even armed jehad for Shariatisation of the whole world as a mission of holy duty. "Seekers of Tawhid should strive to dedicate themselves to the Prophet Mohammad, so much so that their entire selves, including their hearts and their spirits, were free of thoughts other than of God".

"Mysticism is a practical spiritual discipline based on the insight of illuminated seekers after truth". It is in fact a mission of higher religious order of any faith, which disdains strife and conflict in any form. Joy of self-realisation being the essence of religion is experienced after a long spiritual practice. The mystics discard outward form of religion once they attain such joy. The concept of Sufism was therefore, to focus the mystic power on the spiritual dimension of Islam with a view to shield the believers from the outwardly and unrealistic dogma of the faith.

Sufism-Spiritual or Politics

Contrary to the spiritual mission of Sufism, the cult was primarily introduced in India for spread of Islam with a view to help the Muslim rulers for political domination. By and large the spiritual successors of mystic Islamic saints enjoyed the royal favour of Muslim rulers and gave moral support to the atrocious Muslim invaders and looked other way to ignore the growing social conflict. They also guided the State in political affairs with their experience of regular interaction with common people.

The way Sufis' tombs emerged as a place of pilgrimage suggests that the missionary objective of the Islamic mystics was formulated mainly for conversion and to establish the Perso-Arabian cultural domination in South Asia. Even though the Sufi saints got convinced with non-Islamic worldview on metaphysics in course of their interaction with non-Muslim saints, they did not allow their followers to accommodate it in the straight jacket of Islamic theology. Sufi saints commonly viewed as symbol of secularism however, never opposed Jejiya (Tax imposed on non-believers) levied on Hindus in Islamic India. Sufis had accompanied the Muslim marauders in their conquest and brought Islam in contact with Hindu priests and saints.

They were receptive to some of the local Hindu traditions may be for a tactical reason to entice the locals towards Islam but ensured that local norms are not accommodated against the watertight Islamic belief, dogma and practice of Quran, Hadith and Sharia which were the fountainheads of Sufism. Their deeply rooted belief and practice of Islamic norms within Perso-Arabic traditions remained the bedrock of the mystic movement. Therefore, in stead of advising the Muslim marauders against their inhuman deeds, the Sufis overlooked the plight of Hindu priests and saints, who were forced to flee and hide themselves. Passion to the essential spirituality of life was hardly found in any Muslim ruler or Prince except Dara Shikoh (1615-1659). He was perhaps the only sincere Muslim prince, whose "effort was to find a common ground between Hindu and Muslim religious thought".

For this he was accused of heresy. Under the patronage of the State under Muslim rulers, the Sufi mystics while offering spiritual guidance and support to the Hindu subjects allured them for adoption of Muslim identity, superiority of Arbo-Persian-Turkish tradition and accordingly transplanted them in the cultural tradition of India. "The establishment of Sufi orders in India coincided with the rising political power of Muslims. Despite the fact that except Prophet Mohammad, the sainthood in Islam has been a debatable issue, Sufism of various orders in the name of their founder saints has become a universal aspect of Islam. Sufis are known as Islamic spiritualists and the Muslims commonly view them as intermediaries between God and individuals.

Sufism is the Sultanate Period

During the period of Sultanate in India these mystics were supposed to guarantee the prosperity to Islamic kingdom. They were patronized by the state for spreading Islam among the non-believers with their acclaimed spiritual influences in the mass. The gift and land provided to the Islamic mystics were used for hospice and their tombs became a place of pilgrimage after their death. "On paper, the Sultanate seemed to be a perfectly Islamized state (but) religious leaders often of Arab origin and the religion (Islam) were subordinated to the political exigencies of the Turko-Afghans, who were in power". "No document attests to the peaceful preaching of the Sufis that most defenders of Islam put forward today" (Ibid. Page 33). "The attraction exercised by the politico-economic benefits that Islam offered seemed to have been the primary motivation for conversion, which particularly affected the middle strata of society" (Ibid.page 33).

Even though the majority of Sufi orders have a Sunni orientation, early Shia Imams were also revered commonly in Sufi circles. However Nakshbandi order of Sufism, which reached the Prophet via Abu Bakra, was notably known for anti-Shia views. Suhrawardiyya and Naqshbandiyya orders of Sufism had more support of Muslim political powers in India." The numerous Sufi religious establishments in India were the major means of spreading Islam and adapting it to indigenous cultural tradition" (Islamic Mysticism in India by Nagendra Kumar Singh, former Chairman, Islamic Research Foundation, Delhi).

Various Sufi Orders

Of the various Sufi orders, Muslims of India prominently follow Chistiyya, Naqshbandiyya, Qadiriyya and Suharabardiyya. Of them the impact of Chisti order is visible even in small villages of Indian subcontinent. Kwaja Moin-ud-Din Chisti, a disciple of Khwaja Abu Abdal Chisti, the propounder of this order introduced it in India. Born in Afghanistan in 1142 AD, he came to India with the army of Shihab-ud-Din Ghuri in 1192 AD and selected Ajmer as his permanent abode since 1195. His shrine became a place of pilgrimage largely with the support of Muslim rulers. Akbar used to have annual pilgrimage there.

Four Islamic mystics from Afghanistan namely Moinuddin (d. 1233 in Ajmer), Qutbuddin (d. 1236 in Delhi), Nizamuddin (d.1335 in Delhi) and Fariduddin (d.1265 in Pattan now in Pakistan) accompanied the Islamic invaders in India. All of them were from the Chistiyya order of Islamic mysticism. Radiating from Delhi under Nizamuddin and following the trail of Mohammad ibn Tughlaq towards the south, the Chistiyya spread its roots all across India. Internationally famous Sufi Shine at Ajmer Sharif in Rajasthan and Nizamuddin Auliya in Delhi belong to this order. A section of Sufis under Chistiyya order was not against adjustment with Hindu saints of Bhakti cult and used even Hindi language for Islamic devotional songs. However, the orthodox Ulama with royal support forced the Sufis to raise the slogan of "back to Shariat" Even though Ulama had certain differences with Sufis over theological and mystic issues; Shariat remained a cementing force between them. Later both the Islamist groups joined together to woo the rulers with a view to furthering their self-seeking interest.

Suharawardy order of Sufism was founded by Shihabud-Din Suharawardy of Baghdad and introduced in India by his disciple Baha-ud-Din Zakariya of Multan. Suharawardiyya order of Sufism became popular in Bengal. Qadiri order founded by Abdul Qadir whose tomb is at Baghdad and its influence is extensively among the Muslims of south India. Baha-ud-Din Naqshband (1318-1389) of Turkistan founded Naqshbandi order of Sufism. Insistence on rigid adherence to Shariat and nurturing love for prophet was the essence of this order that established its hold in India under the patronage of Mogul rulers, as its founder was their ancestral 'Pir' (Spiritual guide). "The conquest of India by Babur in 1526 gave considerable impetus to the Naqshbandiyya order".

Its disciples remained loyal to the throne because of the common Turk origin. With the royal patronage of most of the Mogul rulers Naqshbandi order served the cause for revival of Islam in its pristine form. Khwaja Mohhammad Baqi Billah Berang whose tomb is in Delhi introduced Naqshbandi order in India. Though, the Sufis of this order were lying low during the period of Akbar, Khalifa Shaikh Ahmad Sirhindi, (1564-1624), a favourite disciple of Baqi Billah achieved increasing importance and popularised this order when the Great Mogul became bed ridden. Baqi Billah nicknamed him as 'Mujaddid (Reformer or reviver of Islam for the second millenium).

Sufi Thinkers

The Sharia-guided mystic influence of Sufis produced the Muslim thinkers like Shaikh Ahmad Sirhindi, Shah

Wali Ullah, Sayied Ahmad Barelavi, Karamat Ali, Sir Sayed Ahmad Khan, Allama Iqbal and Maulana Maududi. They used the mystic philosophy befitting to the political exigencies of the time for revival of political supremacy of Islam. Of them the Sufis like Sirhindi and Wali Ullah, who politicised the mystic ideology for political domination of Islam. They were projected as Islamic reformists for purifying Islam from any extraneous influences. They conveyed the political aspect of Islam to Muslim masses so aggressively that it created a permanent imprint on their psyche. It is therefore said that the Sufi Islamists saved the Islam but failed to save the downfall of Mogul Empire.

The mission of Shaikh Sirhindi popularly knows as Mujaddid was to purify Islam from the influence of Akbar with a view to counter his policy of "the Hindu wielding the sword of Islam" and "Peace with all". Unhappy with the regime of Emperor Akbar for withdrawal of Jejia tax imposed on the Hindus, Sirhindi made hectic effort to purge Islam of all extraneous influences. He viewed Hindu mystics like Guru Nanak and Sant Kabir contemptible, as they did not follow Sharia. With contempt against old schools of mysticism for tolerance, Sirhindi condemned the reign of Akbar for his 'broadmindedness' and policy of 'peace with all'. Propagating against the contemporary socio-cultural situation Sirhindi, felt that the attitude of Akbar "sullied the purity of Islam and the political social and cultural life of Muslims".

During the closing years of Akbar reign; when his son Salim had revolted against him, Sirhindi spread the virus of communalism with some success "in the beginning of Jehangir's reign". He strongly criticised freedom of worship granted to the Hindus. Hate-Hindu syndrome was so deep in him that "death of Akbar (1605) filled Shaikh Ahmad with hopes that the pristine purity of Islam would be implanted in India". "Misguided and greedy Ulama, he (Sirhindi) believed, were responsible for the alleged downfall of Islam in Akbar's regime". With his strong contempt against Shia and the Hindus, Sirhind wrote several letters to the nobles in the court of Jehangir for guiding the emperor on the path of Shariat, and for removal of Qafirs (Shias and Hindus) from the administration. He was dead against any honourable status of Hindus in Islamic government. Sirhind wanted the religious freedom enjoyed by the Hindus during Akbar regime to be curbed.

Enraged with his too much interference in administration, Jehangir imprisoned him in Gwalier but released him after one year. Sirhind not only "injected communal virus into the body politic of the country but also generated hatred, mutual distrust and discord among the various sections of Muslims". Despite this anti-Hindu tirade of Sirhindi, Maulana Abul Kalam Azad in 1919 eulogiged the role of Mujaddid (Sirhind),"who did not see eye to eye with the policy of state". Shah Wali Ullah, a prominent Muslim thinker of eighteenth century who shaped the destiny of Indian Muslims was also a Sufi of Naqshbandi order. His contempt against the Hindus was identical to Shaikh Ahmad Sirhindi. The rise of two Hindu rebellious groups namely Marathas and Jats against the Muslim rulers in 1750s stirred the mystic spirit of Wali Ullah and he invited Ahmad Shah Abdali, the Afghan ruler to invade India to save the Muslims from the subjugation of Hindus. While formulating the contours of his mystical ideology, he transformed the Islamic mysticism to a theo-political concept for supremacy of Islam and for political power to the Sunnis.

Wali Ullah started a tradition of reformed Sufism in which Islamic mysticism was far superior to other form of mystic philosophy. His reform in Sufi cult made the spirituality of Islam subservient to Political Islam. His doctrine for internal unity of Muslims through complete adherence to pure Islam was only to fight against the infidels and for reestablishment of assertive Islamic political power. His ideology had no scope to accommodate any order of non-Islamic mysticism, which he regarded unhealthy. He tried to comb out all the foreign influences, such as neo-platonism and Vedantism from Islamic mysticism. Carving out a new path for Sufism he became an active Islamist with a sole objective for resurgent Sunni political power in Delhi.

Bridging the gulf between the Islamic clerics and Sufis, Wali Ullah infused new vigour in practice of Naqshbandi Sufi order. He synthesised the disciplines of the three major Sufi orders namely Qadari, Chisti and Naqshbandi with a view to unite the Muslim society against the Hindus. Like Shaikh Ahmad Sirhind he was also against the presence of Hindu employees in the administration of Muslim rulers as he viewed it detrimental to the purity of Islam. His attempt was to purify Islam from the mystic influence of Hinduism. Under the influence of Serhindi whose belief that Islam is a complete way of life stirred the Muslims to retrieve the medieval glory of the faith in this sub continent. The exclusivist Ideology of Wali Ullah, which sowed the seed of Muslim separatism in South Asia, had nothing to do with the secular intellectual approach towards spiritualism.

Against the total rejection of Sufism by his contemporary radical Islamist Wahhab of Saudi Arabia, Waliullah used his mystic ideology for political domination of the Muslims in the region. However, the spirit and aim of both were for adherence to pure Islam. He was the main guiding source for Muslims after the decline of Islamic rule in Indian subcontinent. Contrary to the commonly viewed Sufi tradition he was not receptive to the spiritual tradition of local Hindus in any form. His main spiritual concerns if any were for revival of Islamic India.

The Muslim ruler under the influence of the doctrine of Shah Wali Ullah patronised Islamic learning and "took away the administrative and economic power that had passed into the hands of Hindus". "For Shah Wali Ullah, the decline of Mogul political power and the spiritual decadence of Indian Islam were closely related ". Sayyid Ahmad Barelavi, a disciple of Abd al Aziz, (the son of Shah Wali Ullah) continued the tradition of Waliullah by synthesising the three major Sufi orders". He launched armed jehad against the non-Muslims but was killed in the battle of Balkot against Sikh leader Ranjit Singh. Karamat Ali, a disciple of Sayed Ahmad Barelavi further developed the ideology for purifying Islam from the influences of Hindu custom and tradition. "His work largely paved the way for the establishment of the organisation which has more recently been developed under the name of Ahl-I-Hadith". It was a neo-Sufi concept of Islam interpreted by Shah Wali-Ullah.

The leaders of Deoband movement were also under the influence of both Wali Ullah and Wahhab and accordingly they resisted against the British and were critical of Aligarh movement because of its leader Sir Sayed Ahmad being loyal to it. Protracted struggle with the concept of greater jehad was the basic creed of Deoband movement, which is a synthesis of Wahhab and Wali Ullah. Deobandis extreme austere approach towards Wahhab and harsh condemnation of the much popular practice of Sufism in India are being viewed as a totally anti-Sufi movement. Ahmad Riza Khan Barilavi, the founder of Barelavi movement was the defender of traditional Sufi movement but Mohammad Ilyas, a pietistic missionary group though, appropriated the ethical emphasis of Sufism rejected its ritual, metaphysics and sainthood.

Sufi during British Rule

Sufi movement became dormant with the decline of Muslim power in India. With the failure of armed resistance against the British and Sikh- Hindu combined, the followers of hard line Sufism were forced to adjust with the ground reality of non-Muslim occupation of Indian subcontinent but did not reconcile with it. The failure of Sepoy mutiny and consolidation of British power in Indian subcontinent was a further jolt on the radical Islamists but all the Islamic revivalist movements like Deoband, Aligarh and Pakistan drew their inspirations from the anti Hindu syndrome of Sufi saints like Sirhind and Shah Wal Ullah. Khilafat movement and subsequent Pakistan movement were the outcome of the jehadi interpretation of Walli Ullah brand of neo-Sufi jehad against the political domination of non-believers. The resistance of Muslims against the British and subsequently against the Indian National Congress was due to deep and hard line influence of Shah Wali Ullah over them.

Before the failure of 1857 Sepoy mutiny Sir Sayed Ahmad Khan was a follower of the neo-Sufi cult of Shah Waliullah. Elizabeth Syrriyeh (Sufis and Anti-Sufis, 1999) maintained that Syed Ahmad Khan gradually distanced himself fro Shah Wali ullah. But firmly rooted in the Indian Islamic mysticism he was deeply pained with the plight of Muslims after the collapse of Sepoy mutiny of 1857. He therefore, took up the challenge of modern education and transformed the revolutionary mystic ideology of Shah Wali Ullah for revitalisation of Islamic glory through western education. Had he distanced himself from Wali Ullah, he would not have initiated the two-nation theory on the line of this Sufi Islamist to promote the movement of Muslim separatism through his Aligarh movement.

Sir Sayed's philosophy was a synthesis of progressive and orthodox Islam. On one hand he favoured modern education on European pattern and on the other he supported Islamic orthodoxy for superior religious identity of Muslims. He reinterpreted the cultural heritage of Islam within the mystic ideological frame of Wali Ulla, His Aligarh movement was a tactical but a hidden alliance of the Muslims with British under latter's sovereignty to revive the supremacy of Muslims. He advocated for free discussion on Islam but due to his communal obsession he did not strive hard to prove his point for the socio-religious integration of Indian society. His excluvist belief of Muslims' superiority was based on the mystic ideology of Wali Ullah. It was against the unity of Indian society.

According to Allama Iqbal, "he (Wali Ullah) was the first Muslim to feel the urge for rethinking the whole system of

Islam without in any way breaking away from its past". In fact Wali Ullah and Abd al Wahhab recommended religiously approved jehad against unbelievers (non-Muslims) but rejected the commonly viewed difference between lesser jehad and greater jehad. "This physical armed struggle had commonly been termed 'lesser jihad' (al-jihad-al -asghar), the greater jihad (al-jihad-al akbar) being the struggle for the interior spiritualisation of individual battle waged against the base self rather than exterior armies". Iqbal was a known follower of Islamic mysticism of Qadiriyya order. He, synthesied the mystic ideology of Wali Ullah and the modern view on Islam of Sir Sayed Ahmad Khan and made his Islamic mystic approach completely subservient to political domination of the Muslims.

Applying modern philosophy in his intellectual exploration of Sufism he gradually turned to an anti-Sufi philosopher. He said, "The present day Muslims prefer to roam about aimlessly in the dusty valleys of Hellenic - Persiam mysticism, which teaches us to shut our eyes to the hard reality around, and to fix our gaze on what it describes as 'Illuminations' a blue, red and yellow reality springing up from the cells of an overworked brain". "Sufi shaikhs constituting a spiritual aristocracy, Iqbal appealed to Muslim youth to cast off the Sufi noose from their neck". For Iqbal Sufism was a formulation of Islamic Persianism. It was contrary to the purity of Arabic faith in its original version. His rejection of Sufism was influenced by Wahhabi movement of Saudi Arabia, which was more concerned with Islamic power following the decline of Muslim power in eighteenth century.

The concept of Tawhid (Unity in God), which is the real formulation of Sufism suggests that Islamic mysticism has no difference with the formulations of other non-Islamic faiths about the oneness of God. On this basis Sufism became popular in India during the period of Muslim rule. But when the Sufis supported the Muslims in their political conflict with the Hindus and played important role in conversion of indigenous people to Islam, it gave birth to politicisation of religion, which generated communal tension between the two major religious communities. The movement for purifying Islam from extraneous influences, which was launched by the Sufis like Saikh Ahmad Sirhindi and Shah Wali Ullah, was against the spiritual doctrine of 'Tawhid' (Unity in God). Creating a far-reaching impact on the psyche of Indian Muslims it continues to keep the Muslim mass away from the modern global changes.

Sufism in India has commonly been viewed as a secular attempt for eternal quest of the soul for its direct experience of the ultimate Super power. For centuries the Hindus accepted Sufi shrines as symbol of communal harmony. A large number of them have been offering prayers in Sufi shrines without any reservation but this liberal gesture has not been reciprocated Muslims. Had Sufism as commonly been viewed as an attempt to adapt Islam in Hindu tradition, the philosophy of two-nation theory would not have emerged. The Hindu revivalist movement like Arya Samaj was a reaction to politicisation of the doctrine of Sufism, which widened the gap of mistrust between the two major religious communities of South Asia.

Contrary to the common perception that Sufism tried to unify the Hindu-Muslim spirituality for a communal harmony, the political Islamists of Sufi background used the doctrine of Tawhid to accelerate the process of Muslim separatism in Indian subcontinent. Their movements were the by-products of Sufi tradition of Islam. They were basically the mystics for the political domination of Islam activists. The basic creed of mystic movements is unity of God irrespective of religious connotation. Unity of God denotes social unity and universal brotherhood. But these political mystics not only divided the society on the basis of religion but their doctrine created a permanent Hindu-Muslim conflict in the region.

The spirit of mysticism is to resolve any dilemma confronting the society. But Sufi movement failed to resolve confronting Hindu-Muslim dilemma in Indian society. In practice they launched a movement for systematic dehumanisation of Islam and negated the concept of Islamic spiritualism of Tawhid (Unity of God). Islamic spiritual traditions in the Indian subcontinent developed features uniquely their own, but as was the case in other parts of the Islamic world, they remained deeply rooted in the Quran, Hadîth, and the teachings of the righteous caliphs and those of Ali ibn Abu Talib's descendants.

The spiritual guide of the great Persian Sufi Bayazîd Bastami was Abu 'Ali Sindî. In ca. 292/904, on his second pilgrimage to Mecca, Mansur al-Hallaj with his four hundred disciples traveled through Gujarat, the Lower Indus Valley and the northern Indian borders to Khurasan and Turkestan. From time to time other Sufis also moved to different parts of Sind and the Punjab, but the contributions of only those Sufis who settled in India after the conquest of the Punjab and Sind by Sultan Mahmud of Ghaznah (388/998-421/1030) are documented.

The Kâzirûniyyah Tòarîqah

By the fourth/ tenth century, the Sufis had formed several orders and fraternities. One of them was founded by Shaykh Abû Ishòaq Ibrâhîm ibn Shahriyâr (d. 426/ 1035), who died at Kazirun, situated between Shiraz and the Persian Gulf coast. He ordered his nephew Shaykh Safî al-Dîn to mount a camel and travel in whatever direction the animal took him; he was then to remain where finally the camel halted. The camel stopped at Uchh (Upper Sind in Pakistan), where Sòafî al-Dîn founded his khanqah. The shaykh died in Uchh, but the influence of his uncle penetrated very deeply into the life of seamen and mariners who undertook hazardous voyages from the Persian Gulf to China through the Indian Ocean and the Indonesian archipelago. Ibn Batatu, who traveled along the Indian coasts on his way to China between 743/1342 and 747/1346, stayed in the Kazirûnî khanqahs in Calicut and Quilon on the Malabar coast and at Zaitun in China. A modern scholar compares the chain of Kazirûnî khanqahs with an insurance corporation, but none can doubt the devotion of seamen who returned to their homes safely because of what they believed to be the efficacy of Shaykh Abû Ishòâq's prayers.

The Junaydiyyah Fraternity

Before long, Lahore also became an important Sufi center. Abu'l-Fadòl Muhammad ibn al Hasan Khuttalî, a disciple of Hucrî (d. 371/ 981-82) of the school of Junayd of Baghdad, is the first known Sufi to have ordered a disciple, Shaykh Zanjânî, to move to Lahore. Later Khuttalî asked his young disciple, Abul-Hòasan 'Alî Hujwîrî to follow Hòusayn Zanjanî. It would seem that he arrived at Lahore in 426/1035, the same day Zanjânî died. Born at Ghaznah in about 399/ 1009, Hujwîrî had studied under many teachers, but Khuttalî of Syria was his main spiritual guide. From Lahore, he made long tours of the Islamic world at least twice during his lifetime. According to A. Nicholson, he died sometime between 465/ 1072-73 and 469/ 1076-77 at Lahore. Later Muslims posthumously conferred on him the title, Dâtâ Ganj Bakhsh (distributor of unlimited treasures). Among the early mystics who undertook hard ascetic exercises at his tomb was Khwâjah Mu'în al-Dîn Chishtî, the founder of the Chishtî Order in the Indian subcontinent.

Hujwîrî wrote books on Sufism in both prose and poetry. His Kashf al-mahòjûb (Rending of the Veiled) is the first known manual of Sufism written in Persian. Composed toward the end of his life, the work draws on the vast source material available in Arabic and is a most authoritative exposition of the sober Sufism of Junayd's school. It indicates that Lahore had become an important center of Sufism, some Sufis being profoundly aware of Hindu spiritual traditions. One of them who were an expert in Quranic exegesis held that baqâ (abiding in Allah) meant God's subsistence in man. Some Lahore Sufis identified gnosis with divine revelation.

Some Sufis believed in the superiority of saints over prophets. It was an uphill task for Hujwîrî to convince them of the true meanings of Sufism. He considered himself a "captive among uncongenial folk" in Lahore. It would appear that from its very inception, Sufism in India developed conflicting trends, mainly because of the challenges from movements among local mystics. The analysis of Sufism, its history, and its principles discussed perceptively in the Kashf al-mahòjûb went a long way toward stabilizing Sufi thoughts, not only in India but even in Persia and Central Asia.

The Suhrawardiyyah

The only other work able to match the Kashf al-mahòjûb in popularity and utility in India was the 'Awârif al-m'ârif by Shaykh Shihâb al-Din Abû Hòafs 'Umar (539/1145-632/1234), the founder of the Suhrawardî Order. He obtained training under his uncle Shaykh Dòiyâ' al-Dîn Abu'l-Najîb Suhrawardî (490/1097-563/1168), who built a hospice on a ruined site on the Tigris in Baghdad. The caliph al-Nâshir li-Dîni'Llâh (575/1180-622/ 1225) appointed Shaykh Shihâb al-Dîn as his ambassador to different courts of important rulers and built an extensive khânqâh for him in Baghdad, which included luxurious bathhouses and gardens. He traveled extensively and made several pilgrimages to Mecca, accompanied by his eminent disciples.

Sufis from all over the world flocked to his khânqâh to obtain initiation from him. One of them was Shaykh Bahâ'al-Dîn Zakariyyâ', who was born at Kot Karor near Multan (now in Pakistan) in about 578/1182-83. After studying at different centers of Islamic learning, he arrived in Baghdad. His training period under Shaykh Shihâb al-Dîn lasted for only seventeen days, to the utter disgust of the senior disciples, but the Shaykh silenced them by saying that when they had first come to him they had been like green wood which would not catch fire, whereas Bahâ' al-Dîn had been like dry wood, which had begun to burn with a single breath.

In Multan, the eminent Sufis and *'ulamâ'* stubbornly opposed Shaykh Bahâ' al-Dîn, but his scholarly attainments and a distinctive position among the disciples of Shaykh Shihâb al-Dîn Suhrawardî soon made him a principal figure in Multan. It appears that merchants from Iraq and Khurasan were attracted to him in large numbers. The Shaykh built an extensive *khânqâh* on the pattern of his spiritual guide's *khânqâh* in Baghdad. He fearlessly opposed Qubâchah, the ruler of Multan, and espoused the cause of Sultan Shams al-Dîn Iltutmish (607/1211-633/1236) of Delhi, who seized Multan in 625/1228. The repeated Mongol invasions of Multan made the life of the townsfolk miserable, but the fame of Shaykh Bahâ' al-Dîn's piety in Khurasan and Transoxiana facilitated successful negotiations with the Mongol invaders.

Shaykh Bahâ' al-Dîn strongly discouraged Sufis from seeking guidance from a number of different *pîrs* (spiritual guides), urging them to lay their heads on one rather than a number of thresholds. He placed great stress on performing obligatory prayers and assigned a secondary place to supererogatory prayers and dhikr. He ate normally and did not indulge in incessant fasting. In Sòafar 661/ December 1262 he died at Multan, and his tomb became a center of pilgrimage in the region. He was succeeded by his own son, Shaykh Sòadr al-Dîn 'Ârif (d. 684/ 1286). Shaykh Bahâ' al-Dîn Zakariyyâ's disciple and son-in-law, the poet and mystic Shaykh Fakhr al Dîn Ibrahîm, popularly known as 'Irâqî (d. 688/ 1289) spread his fame from Syria to Turkey. Irâqîs Lama'ât (Divine Flashes), based on lectures by Shaykh Sòadr al-Dîn Qûnawi (d. 673/ 1274) on his master Ibn 'Arâbî's Fulû al-hòikam, made a deep impact on the spiritual discipline of the Indian Suhrawardiyyah.

Shaykh Sòadr al-Dîn 'Ârif was fortunate to have the poet Amîr Husayn Hòusaynî (b. 671/1272-73) as his disciple. Husaynî works, such as âd almus Ãfirin (Provision of

Travelers), Nuzhat al-arwâhò (Pleasure of Spirits), and Kanz al-rumûz (Treasury of Mysteries) are devoid of 'Irâqî's spiritual sensitivity, but their deep ethical teachings are of far-reaching importance.

Shaykh Sòadr al-Dîn's son and successor, Shaykh Rukn al-Dîn Abu'l-Fathò, revived the political and spiritual glory of his grandfather. From the reign of Sultan Alâ' al-Dîn Khaljî (695/1296-715/1316) to his own death in 735/1334-35 in the reign of Sultan Muhammad ibn Tughluq (725/1325752/ 1351), Shaykh Rukn al-Dîn was deeply revered by all the reigning monarchs of the Delhi sultanate. Whenever he visited Delhi, he never forgot to call on the great Chishtî Shaykh Nizòân al-Dîn Awliyâ', but he did not care for the latter's strained relations with the sultans. Petitioners filled Shaykh Rukn al-Dîn's palanquin with petitions on his way to the sultan's court. The latter read them carefully and granted the petitioners' requests, thanks to Shaykh Rukn al-Dîn's influence. The shaykh's fame reached as far as Alexandria and Ibn BaTò+016BCatah was recommended to see him.

The works of the shaykh do not survive, but some of his authentic conversations with Sufis tend to indicate that he regarded possession of wealth, scholarship, and mystical enlightenment as indispensable for the Sufis. The Chishtîs, however, never agreed with the Suhrawardis on the question of the accumulation of wealth. Some of the Suhrawardî saints were, however, great ascetics. One of them was Shaykh 'Uthmân Sayyâh (d. 738/ 1337-38) (the traveler) of Sunnam in eastern Punjab. He was a disciple of Shaykh Rukn al-Dîn. With his pîrs, he departed on a pilgrimage to Mecca without carrying even so much as a waterpot. After his return from Mecca, his pîr allowed him to live in Delhi, where he spiritedly defended the Chishtî practice of Sama' (spiritual music).

Reverting back to Shaykh Shihâb al-Dîn's disciples, who strengthened the Suhrawardî spiritual movement in India, we may mention Qâdòî Hòamîd al Dîn of Nagawr in Rajasthan, not to be confused with the Chishtiyyah Shaykh

Hòamîd al-Dîn Sòûfî. His family had migrated from Bukhara to Delhi before its conquest by the Turks. He completed his education in Delhi and was appointed the qâdî of Nagawr. After three years of service, he was disgusted with it and left for Baghdad, where he became Shaykh Shihâb al-Dîn's disciple. He visited Mecca and Medina, traveled to many parts of western Asia and then arrived in Delhi around 618/ 1221. He was a firm friend of the Chishtî Khwâjah Qutòb al-Dîn Bakhtiyâr Kâkî and enthusiastically participated in Sama' sessions in Delhi.

His wit, in conjunction with his deep knowledge of Islamic Law, frustrated the 'ulamâ''s efforts to defeat him on legal issues. His thirst for unqualified and nondelimited love in his three surviving works, the 'Ishqiyyah (Pertaining to Love), the nawâli' al-shumûs (Risings of the Suns) and the Risâlah min kalâm (Treatise of Kalâm), is very profound. In the 'Ishqiyyah he says that although Lover and Beloved appear to be different, they are in fact identical. Whoever sees them as two is confused and whoever does not see them at all is insane. One who is lost in being is a part of God's Attributes. This stage makes Sufis present everywhere. The extinction of "I" leads to the predominance of "He." Both Lover and Beloved mirror each other. Love is the source of everything that exists. Fire is the burning quality of love, air is its aspect of restlessness, water is its movement, and earth is its immutable aspect. In the Tawâli' al-shumûs, the Qâdòî spells out the mystery of the Names of Allah. He says that the greatest Name of God is Huwa (He) and it indicates His eternal nature, hallowed and free from decline and fall. The Qâdòî died in 643/1245-46.

The disciple of Shaykh Shihâb al-Dîn Suhrawardî who made Islam popular in Bengal was Shaykh Jalâl al-Dîn Tabrîzî. He excelled all the shaykh's disciples in serving his pîr. Migrating to Bengal, he built a khânqâh at Deva Mahòal near Pandua in northern Bengal and converted a large number of Hindus and Buddhists to Islam. In the Rihòlah

(Travels) of Ibn Batòtòûtòah, Shaykh Jalâl of Sylhet whom he visited has been confused with Shaykh Jalâl Tabrîzî and the mistake has been repeated by several scholars. The early Suhrawardîs and the Chishtîs had divided different regions of the Indian subcontinent into spheres of their respective spiritual influence and refrained from interfering with those of others. Despite their humility and self-abasement, the Chishtîs encouraged their disciples to exhibit the utmost veneration to their pîrs and even permitted the performance of sajdah (prostration) before them, but Shaykh Bahâ' al-Dîn Zakariyyâ' expected his disciples to greet him with the customary al-salâmu 'alaykum (peace be upon you).

He also urged his disciples to finish their obligatory religious duties first and to greet him afterward. The Suhrawardî view of the function of the state, envisaged by Shaykh Shihâb al-Dîn's disciple, Shaykh Nûr al-Dîn Mubârak Ghaznawî, who settled in Delhi and died there in 632/1234-35, encompassed the prosperity of the Sunni upper classes alone; Shî'îs and Hindus were permitted to survive, provided they did so in a deprived economic state. The Suhrawardîs, as depicted in the legends surrounding Shaykh Jalâl al-Dîn Tabrîzî's activities in Bengal, and those of Makhdûm Jahâniyân, as we shall see, were unhesitating in their proselytizing zeal. By contrast, the Chishtîs believed that only the company of pious and ascetic Muslims prompted others to accept Islam. To them, their main mission was to work for the integration of those Hindus who embraced Islam in an attempt to make them genuinely pious Muslims and save them from emulating the example of the haughty governing classes.

Makhdûm Jahâniyân Sayyid Jalâl al-Dîn Bukhârî was a grandson of Shaykh Bahâ' al-Dîn Zakariyyâ's disciple, Sayyid Jalâl al-Dîn Surkh. Sultan Muhòammad ibn Tughluq, who initiated the policy of controlling the appointment of the heads of Sufi khânqâhs, had made him the head of the khânqâh of Sehwan. Before long, however, Makhdûm Jahâniyân embarked on a pilgrimage and later traveled to many parts of the Islamic world, earning the title Jahângasht (world traveler) for himself. During the reign of Sultan Fîrûz Tughluq (752/1351-790/1388), he settled down in Uchh and occasionally visited Delhi. A notorious puritan, Makhdûm Jahâniyân strongly deplored the Indian Muslim religious customs and ceremonies which had been borrowed from Hindus and were an Indian accretion.

He urged that dervishes, Sufis, and 'ulamâ' visit rulers and government officials in order to elicit assistance for the downtrodden sections of Muslims. He introduced among his disciples the spirit of the akhî and futuwwah (spiritual chivalry) organizations of Anatolia, Khurasan, and Transoxiana. After his death in 785/1384, he was succeeded by his brother, Sadr al-Dîn, who achieved fame under his nicknames Râjû and Qattâl (slayer) for his militant evangelism. A grandson of Makhdûm Jahâniyân moved to Gujarat and before long came to be known as Qutòb-i 'Âlam (The Pole of the Universe). He settled in Ahmadabad, the newly founded capital of an independent provincial ruling dynasty of Gujarat. He died in 857/1453 and was succeeded by his son, who came to be known by the illustrious title Shâh-i 'Âlam (The Emperor of the World), and was also called Shah Manjhan. Qutòb-i 'Âlam, Shâh-i 'Âlam (d. 880/ 1475) and their disciples made Gujarat a leading Suhrawardî Sufi center of India.

The influence of Shaykh Samâ' al-Dîn and the fame of his disciple Shaykh Jamâlî transformed Delhi into an important Suhrawardî center. Jamâlî (d. 942/ 1536) was passionately fond of traveling and, starting with a pilgrimage to Mecca, he traveled through western Asia and the Maghreb. At Herat he called on the great Persian poet Jâmî and held lively discussions, particularly on 'Irâqî's Lama'ât. Jamâlî was the author of several Persian mathnawîs in which he lyrically delineated the theme of spiritual transmutation through love. The biographical notes on the Chishtîs and Suhrawardîs which he wrote in his Siyar al-'ârifîn (Biography of the

Gnostics) comprise a wealth of information which he collected during his travels to Persia and Iraq. In the eighth/ fourteenth century a Suhrawardî center was established in Kashmir, strengthening orthodox Sunnism there.

The Firdawsî Branch of the Kubrawiyyah

Shaykh Najm al-Dîn Kubrâ (540/1145-618/1221), the founder of the Kubrawî Order, was the disciple of Shaykh Ismâ'îl Qadrî (d. 589/ 1193) of Khuzistan and Shaykh 'Ammâr ibn Yâsir al-Bidlîsî (d. 597/ 1200), who in their turn were disciples of Shaykh Abu'l-Najîb Suhrawardî. A galaxy of eminent Sufis flocked to Kubrâ as disciples and a number of branches of his order spread to Baghdad, Khurasan, and India. One of Kubrâ's eminent disciples, Shaykh Sayf al-Dîn Bâkharzî (d. 658/ 1260) ordered his disciple, Khwâjah Badr al-Dîn Samarqandî Firdawsî to settle in Delhi. After his death in Delhi, he was succeeded by Khwâjah Najîb al-Dîn Firdawsî and Khwâjah Rukn al-Dîn.

The Firdawsîs would have remained unknown, had Khwâjah Najîb al-Dîn not been so fortunate as to find a disciple of the fame of Shaykh Sharaf al-Dîn Ahòmad ibn Yahòyâ Munyarî (also known as Maneri) Ahmad was born in Munyar, near Patna in Bihar, where he obtained his early education. He then moved to Sunargaon, near modern Dacca in Bengal, with Shaykh Abû Tawwâmah of Bukhara, and studied under the latter until his own father's death in 690/ 1291. From there he visited Delhi and Panipat and finally became Khwâjah Najîb al-Dîn's *khalîfah* and returned to Bihar. Instead of going to his village, the shaykh chose to do ascetic exercises in the lonely Rajgir hills of Bihar, where Buddhist monks and Hindu sages loved to establish their hermitages. He would go to Bihar Sharif near Patna each Friday for congregational prayers, returning to the Rajgir forest afterward. Later, in 782/1381, he was forced to settle down in Bihar Sharif, where he lived throughout the greater part of the reign of Muhòammad ibn Tughluq.

His teachings are embodied in several collections of his letters to his disciples, both 'ulamâ' and Sufis. He also wrote to the state dignitaries and even to Fîrûz Tughluq. One of the collections comprising one hundred letters was compiled in 747/1346-47, and the other, containing 151 letters, was compiled in 769/1367-68. His Malfûzòât (Discourses) were also compiled and give an authentic picture of his spiritual contributions to his contemporaries and to posterity. Through Quranic verses, ahòâdîth, anecdotes and parables from classical Sufi works, he discussed the religious and spiritual duties of Islam and the social and ethical responsibilities of Muslims in a vocabulary enriched by his own contemplative vision of the realities of things. Frequently quoting the Quranic verse "Despair not of the mercy of Allah" (XXXIX, 53), he used to affirm that the divine fire consumed the root of despondency and the young shoots of desperation. Mystical knowledge was the seed of love.

All those who penetrated deeply into the realm of mystical knowledge were engulfed by the fire of love and obtained increasingly great delight and distinction from the face of the Beloved and from the sight of the Desired One. Although the shaykh strongly advocated adherence to the Sharî'ah, he failed to concede the superiority of the 'ulamâ' over Sufis. He avoided, however, expressing his ecstatic feelings and spiritual experiences and advised his disciples to keep their own knowledge of such experiences secret. He was appalled at the execution by Sultan Fîrûz of his friends and the enraptured Sufis (majdhûbs) Shaykh ' Izz Kâkû'î and Shaykh Ahmad Bihârî. But for the timely intervention of Makhdûm Jahâniyân, he would also have met the same fate. The number of the shaykh's disciples was quite large; among them Shaykh Muzòaffar Balkhî was most prominent. A network of small khânqâhs stretching from Bihar to Bengal and reaching many areas of the Indian subcontinent disseminated the shaykh's spiritual teachings as embodied in his letters.

The Kubrawiyyah of Kashmir

The Kubrawiyyah Order was introduced into Kashmir by Mîr Sayyid 'Alî Hamadânî, who was initiated into it by Shaykh Sharaf al-Dîn Mahòmûd Nizòâm al-Dîn Mazdaqânâ, a disciple of the great Shaykh 'Alâ' al-Dawlah Simnânî. At his pîr's bidding, Mîr Sayyid 'Alî studied under a number of important disciples of Shaykh 'Alâ' al-Dawlah, but he was not converted to the view of wahòdat al-shuhûd (unity of consciousness), although before the death of the aged shaykh, he went to Simnan and completed his final training with him. He was imbued, however, with the shaykh's missionary fervor and sense of social responsibilities. The Mîr left Simnan with Muhòammad Ashraf Jahângîr Simnânî (d. ca. 840/ 1436-37), a Kubrawî who, after settling down in Kichawcha in the Sharqi sultanate of Jaunpur in India, founded the Ashrafî branch of the Kubrawî Order. One traveled slightly ahead of the other, shortly before Shaykh 'Alâ al-Dawlah's death.

Travelling through Uchh, Mîr Sayyid 'Alî arrived at Srinagar in 783/1381. He was accompanied by a considerable number of sayyids. Their missionary zeal took the form of temple demolition and the enforced conversion of many Hindus. After a stay in Kashmir of about three years, Sayyid 'Alî left Srinagar and died en route in 786/1385 after having passed through Pakhli near Kunar. His body was taken to Khuttalan, now part of the Soviet Union, where it was buried. Mîr Sayyid 'Alî has been credited with the authorship of 170 treatises, generally short in length, of which about fifty have survived. He translated the Fucûc al-hòikam (Bezels of Wisdom) into Persian and wrote a religiopolitical treatise entitled the Dhakhîrat al-mulûk (Provision of Kings). The clarity of expression and the force of his arguments in the short treatises dealing with Muslim ethics and spirituality are remarkable.

His interpretation of the "oneness of being" is accompanied by a mystical portrayal of the "reality of the perfect man." He identifies the latter with the "Muhòammadan Reality," which acts as a receptable for all of being's perfec-tions. His treatises entitled the Akhî (Brother) and the Futuwwah (Spiritual Chivalry) are designed to arouse devotion in 'Alî ibn Abî âlib's futuwwah, which in turn was based on forgiveness in place of revenge, patience in the time of anger, wishing an enemy well, and preference for the needs of others over one's own. The Mîr believed that spiritual beings whose earthly existence had been completely effaced, who swam in the ocean of ahòadiyyah (oneness, unicity) and flew into the realm of huwiyyah (Divine Ipseity) belonged to a supernatural category, but those who remained steadfastly dedicated to ordinary people and looked after the comfort of mankind were true members of futuwwah.

When Sayyid 'Alî left Kashmir, only a handful of Persian sayyids were allowed by him to accompany him back to Persia. After 796/1393, the migration of Mîr Sayyid 'Alî's son, Mîr Sayyid Muhòammad, provided them with much-needed leadership. Sultan Sikandar (788/1386-813/1410), nicknamed But Shikan (destroyer of idols), became his disciple, and the sultan's Brahmin vizier, Suhâ Bhatta, embraced Islam after instruction by Mîr Muhammad. Many ancient temples were destroyed and puritanical and discriminatory state laws were introduced for the first time in Kashmir.

Mîr Sayyid Hiq ârî, a disciple of Mîr Sayyid 'Alî who had earlier moved to Kashmir and had lost his influence with the court was deeply upset with the aggressive evangelism of his pîr's son. Before long he was able to reassert himself at the court and Mîr Sayyid Muhammad left Kashmir after a stay of some twelve years. By that time, the Kubrawî Order was firmly established there. Their role in converting the Kashmîrî Brahmins to Islam is overestimated, but the devotion to 'Alî ibn Abî âlib and his descendants inculcated in the Muslims of Kashmir by the Hamadânâ Kubrawâs made Kashmîrî spiritual traditions unique in the subcontinent.

Among Mîr Sayyid 'Alî's disciples was Khwâjah Ishòâaq al-Khuttalânî, who was executed by the Tîmûrid Sultan

Shâhrukh (807/ 1405-850/ 1447) in 826/1423 for leading an unsuccessful revolt against the sultan. His impact on the spiritual life of Khuttalan and the Balkh region was most profound. His disciple Sayyid Muhòammad Ahòsâ'î, on whom he bestowed the title *Nûrbakhsh* (Bestower of Light) and whom he considered to be the Mahdî of the Sunni tradition, was hounded from place to place by Shahrukh.

This harassment and persecution helped to make the sayyid famous throughout Persia, Central Asia, and Kashmir. In 869/ 1464-65 he died at Rayy near Tehran, but his son, Shâh Qâsim Faydòbakhsh, who lived in the reigns of Sultòân Hòusayn Bâyqarâ (873/1469-911/ 1506) of Herat and Shah Ismâ'il Sòafawî (907/ 1501-930/ 1524) of Persia, transformed the Kubrawî teachings on the devotion to 'Alî ibn Abî âlib into Ithnâ 'Asharî Shî'ism. His disciple, Mîr Shams al-Dîn 'Irâqî, introduced Shî'ism into Kashmir. Although Shî'ism was strongly opposed by the Suhrawardî leader Shaykh Hamzah Makhdûm (d. 984/ 1576) and later by the Naqshbandiyyah, the spiritual framework of the Kubrawiyyah in Kashmîr remained deeply rooted in the *awrâd* (litanies) of Mîr Sayyid 'Alî Hamadânî. These were deeply impregnated with the spirit of the invocations to Allah ascribed to 'Alî ibn Abî âlib's disciple Kumayl ibn Ziyâd. The latter's impact on the Kubrawiyyah was indelible.

The Shatòtòâriyyah

The Shatòtòâriyyah drew inspiration from works of mystic exegesis on divination ascribed to Imâm Ja'far al-Sòâdiq (d. 148/ 765), the sixth Imam of the Shî'ites. Another influence on the order came from mystical stories about the life of Abû Yazîd Bastòâmî. In Ottoman Turkey the order was known as the Bastòâmiyyah and in Persia and Turkey it was known as 'Ishqiyyah. The Indian branch of the order founded by Shah 'Abd Allâh preferred to call itself the Shatòtòâriyyah. Shah 'Abd Allâh moved from Bukhara—where he perfected his mystical training—to India in the early ninth/ fifteenth century.

The incredible speed with which Sufis trained in this order were able to solve the paradox of Unity in multiplicity prompted Shah 'Abd Allâh to call the order that of the Shatòtòârs (those who moved fast). During his travels the shah marched in royal fashion with his disciples dressed in black uniform, holding banners and beating kettledrums. He proclaimed that he was engaged in a quest to discover more of the secrets of wahòdat al-wujûd from anyone who was more perfect than he. At the same time, others in their turn could learn from his perception. He traveled in northern India as far as Bengal, where the leading Sufi, Shaykh Muhòammad 'Alâ', known as Shaykh Qâdin, ignored his challenge. Sorely disappointed, the shah retreated to Malwa in central India and settled down in its capital, Mandu, in 846/1442-43; he died there in 890/1485.

The local sultans were deeply devoted to the shah, and seekers after spirituality from all over India sat at his feet. Shaykh Qâdin also arrived from Bengal and apologized for his earlier rude behavior and enrolled himself among his disciples. The Latòâ'if-i ghaybiyyah (Subtleties of the Invisible World), of which the shah was the author, outlines the basic framework of Shatòtòâriyyah teachings and practices. In it, Shah 'Abd Allâh divides Muslim spiritual devotees into three categories: akhyâr (the chosen ones), abrâr (the dutiful ones) and shatòtòâr (the swift-paced ones). Of these, the Shatòtòâriyyah were superior to all, for they obtained direct training from the spirits of great saints of the past and thus were able to traverse the path of Sufi ascension rapidly.

Shaykh Qâdin's influence made the Shatòtòârî Order considerably successful in Bengal. His disciple, Shaykh Zòuhûr Hòâjjî Hòamîd Hudòûr of Gwalior, lived for a long time in Medina and in his old age returned to Gwalior, where he trained two young boys, Shaykh Muhòammad Phûl and Shaykh Muhòammad Ghawth. He then took both of them to Bihar. At his instigation, Shaykh Muhòammad Ghawth plunged himself into hard ascetic exercises in a cave in Chunar near Banaras. A number of Brahmin sages and Nâtha siddhas had also made the region their hermitage. Shaykh Muhòammad Ghawth lived there for more than thirteen years.

The Mughal Emperor Humâyûn became Shaykh Phûl's disciple. In 946/ 1539, Humâyûn's brother, Mîrzâ Hindâl, killed Shaykh Phûl in Agra for political reasons. Before Humâyûn's exile from Agra in 947/ 1540, Shaykh Ghawth moved to Gujarat. There the greatest 'âlim of the region, Shaykh Wajîh al-Dîn Gujarâtî (d. 997/ 1589), became his disciple. Shaykh 'Alî MutòtòAaqî (d. 975/ 1567), the great Indian scholar of Hòadîth, and some other eminent members of the 'ulamâ' and Sufis resolutely opposed Shaykh Ghawth for the claims he made in his Risâla-yi mi'râjiyyah (The Treatise of Nocturnal Ascent) that his own mystic ascent enabled him to arrive near Divine Proximity and to hold a conversation with God. Shaykh Wajîh al-Dîn's influence in Gujarat, however, saved his spiritual guide. After Akbar's accession to the throne, the shaykh returned to his khânqâh at Gwalior and died there in 970/ 1563.

The works and disciples of Shaykh Wajîh al-Dîn Gujarâtî ensured the popularity of the Shatòtòârî Order throughout India, and its disciples in Mecca and Medina initiated Sufis from the Malay and Indonesian islands into the order. They, in turn, disseminated the Shatòtòârî teachings in their homeland. Of all the works written by Shaykh Ghawth, it was his Jawâhir-i khamsah (The Five Substances) that left the most indelible mark on Sufism on the Indian subcontinent, as well as in Malaya and Indonesia.

It was first authored in 929/ 1522-23, and in 956/ 1549-50, at the request of his disciples, it was edited and some new material added, superseding the earlier version. Before long it was translated into Arabic and obtained considerable popularity in Arabic-speaking countries. Its third jawhar (substance or section), dealing with invocation of the Names of Allah and the mystical importance of Arabic letters, numbers, and rubrics, gained great popularity with those Sufis who were keen to gain supernatural power.

Its fourth section discusses the advanced stages of the mystical achievements of the Shatòtòâr, which, according to the contemporary Shatòtòâriyyah scholar Ghawthî Shatòtòârî, was the legacy of Imam Ja'far al-Sòâdiq and Bâyazîd Bastòâmî. Its fifth section deals with the ontological perfection manifested by the Divine Names, leading to the stage wherein the attributes of the mystics become the theophany of the Divine Attributes.

Shaykh Muhòammad Ghawth retranslated the Bahr al-hòayât (The Ocean of Life), on yogic practices, by Qâdòî Rukn al-Dîn Samarqandî (d. 615/ 1218). The work, which was originally translated into Arabic from the Sanskrit Amritkunda, was designed to integrate more firmly yogic practices and principles with Shatòtòârî spiritual discipline.

The Qalandariyyah

The founding of Sufi orders synchronized with the movement of itinerant dervishes who did not observe the customary rules of Sufi life and normal social behavior. They considered khânqâh life sacrilegious and profane. The Chishtî records portray them as being extremely rude to the Suhrawardî leaders, but somewhat more considerate toward the Chishtiyyah because of their humility. Fakhr al-Dîn 'Irâqî visited Shaykh al-Dîn in the company of qalandars. Another exception made by Shaykh Bahâ' al-Dîn was in the case of his most famous disciple, Mîr Sayyid 'Uthmân of Marwand in Sistan, who came to be known as Lal Shahbâz (The Red Falcon). He established his khânqâh at Sehwan in Sind at the site of an old Shaivite sanctuary.

Incredible miracles are said to have been performed by him, and even his tomb in Sehwan is known for innumerable miracles. Verses said to have been composed by the members of the Sehwan khânqâh tend to indicate that they were very deeply devoted to ' Alî ibn Abî âlib and reinvigorated

Hòallâjian traditions in their poetry. His disciples developed bî-shar' (indifferent to Sharî'ah) practices and came to be known as malangs. Their annual fair in the month of Shawwâl attracts enormous crowds in Sehwan from all parts of Pakistan. The Haydarî and Jawâliqî branches of qalandars also made a deep impact on Indian spiritual life.

Wandering from place to place throughout India, the qalandars who sang love songs and walked on burning fire and ate redhot charcoals presented a staggering spectacle to the urban and rural population of the country. They did not fail, however, to arouse spiritual sensitivity among the Muslim converts, who had not forgotten the siddhas and yogis of their Hindu milieu. Like the Suhrawardîs, the Chishtîs also initiated the qalandars into their orders. One of the most prominent qalandars of the Chishtiyyah Order was Shaykh Abû 'Alî Qalandar. His letters explain Sufism and its many controversial aspects. Although a Dîwân ascribed to him is apocryphal, some verses and quatrains which appear genuine remind the reader of Ahòmad Ghazzâlî and 'Irâqî. He died at Panipat in 724/1324.

The Majdhûbs (Enraptured Sufis)

In Sufi traditions, the malâmatîs are holy men who deliberately led an outrageous life in order to conceal their spiritual achievements. The malâmatiyyah, however, hardly found any respite from their admirers. The same was the case with the majdhûbs or enraptured mystics. Many Sufis lived in a state of ecstasy for shorter or longer periods, but some never regained mental stability. Just as there was no external criterion by which to judge a true Sufi or by which to distinguish him from a charlatan, so it was difficult to distinguish a majdhûb from a lunatic. In the popular mind, however, majdhûbs were supernatural beings who could perform incredible miracles, and both Hindus and Muslims vied with one another in exhibiting devotion to them.

In all decades and in all centuries, there was no dearth of majdhûbs. Preposterous stories are told about their spiritual achievements. Biographical notes on some of them are available in even sober hagiological literature, but none could surpass Muhòammad Sa'îd Sarmad in his contribution to the colorful mystical life and exuberance of emotions in poetry. He was an Armenian Jew who came from Kashan but embraced Islam under the influence of his teachers, Mullâ Sòadrâ and his contemporary Mîr Findarskî. The hòikmat al-ishrâq and wahòdat al-wujûd became the breath of his nostrils. He earned his living as a merchant and amassed a considerable fortune from his overseas trade. In 1042/ 1632-33 he visited Thatta, where he fell violently in love with a Hindu boy, Abhai Chand by name. In 1044/ 1634-35, Sarmad went to Lahore and from thence to Hyderabad, Deccan.

Around 1064/ 1654, Sarmad reached Delhi, where Prince Dârâ Shukûh became his devotee. The depths of Sarmad's ineffable experience in the mysteries of Divine Love have been articulated in his quatrains of indescribable beauty, although they tend to offend orthodox sentiments. In 1071/ 1660-61 Emperor Awrangzeb, in his bid to weed out Dârâ Shukûh's influence completely, passed orders to execute Sarmad. When Sarmad was taken to the gallows, the executioner proceeded to cover his eyes, but Sarmad, preventing him from doing so, cast a glance at him and said, smiling, "Come in whatever garb you choose, I recognise you well," and recited the following verse:

There was an uproar and we opened our eyes from the eternal sleep,

Saw that the night of wickedness endured, so slept again.

You have seen kings, dervishes and qalandars,

Come, see the intoxicated Sarmad in his wretched condition.

Mythical stories were also associated with Sarmad and his quatrains. Both in the history of Sufism and in the popular mind, Sarmad came to occupy the same status that was held by Hòallâj. Rightly did one of his verses earlier prophesy?

A long time since the fame of Mansûr became an ancient relic,

I will exhibit with my head the gallow and cord.

Sufi Poetry in Indian Languages

Eminent Sufi saints expressed their ideas generally in Persian poetry and prose, but what made Sufism a household word and a mass movement in the Indian subcontinent was the poetry in its regional languages.

The Chishtîs, both the eminent leaders in cities and village Sufis, were pioneers in the movement, writing mainly in Hindâwî or Hindi; later, Sufis in other parts of the country began to give vent to their emotions in touching Hindi poetry.

The Shatòtòâriyyah wrote both Hindi and Râjasthânî poetry. The Hindi mathnawî, Madhu-mâltî, which Shah Manjhan Shatòtòârî (d. 1001/ 1592-93) composed in 952/ 1545, reiterates in a most artistic and lyrical style the Sufi and Hindu bhaktî (devotional) theory of the self-manifestation of the Absolute. The Shatòtòârî Sufis, like the Chishtiyyah, freely borrowed symbols and mythological stories from their local Hindu environment, but gave them an Islamic color to delineate their involvement with the splendor of their radiant love for the Divine.

The Nâtha theory of the unity of being did not differ from the Sufi perception of the wahòdat al-wujûd, and the Shatòtòâriyyah therefore had no difficulty in delving deep into Nâtha terminology in order to make their own realization of Reality known to the common people. Nevertheless, they never subscribed to the Hindu belief in the transmigration of the soul. Their main concern was with selfrealization through Yoga or love, or both and this goal was realized within the bounds of Islam, although the poetic frameworks were Hindu or Buddhist.

The Kashmîrî poetry of Shaykh Nûr al-Dîn Rishî (779/ 1378-842/ 1439) saw the cross-fertilization of Sufi beliefs with those expressed by Lâl Ded or Lalla, a Kashmîrî Shaivite woman whose Supreme Reality, identified as Shiva, was Eternal, All-Pervading and All-Transcending. Some of

Shaykh Nûr al-Dîn's verses are almost identical to those written by Lalla, but those which are attributed only to the shaykh exhibit him as an ardent devotee of the Absolute, trying to reach the Unknowable in the heart by lighting the lamp of love. To him, the repetition of the Islamic profession of faith was incomplete without a valid realization of the reality of the self. He admitted that although eating meat was permitted by the Sharî'ah, to him it was cruelty to animals. His disciples invented a distinctive dress for their followers and transformed the teachings of their master into an organized Rishî (ascetical Sufi) movement.

The poets and authors of the movement believed they were duty bound to turn Kashmir into a heaven—although they themselves led harshly austere lives—planting fruit trees for the benefit of the common people. In Bengal, the Hòusayn Shâhî sultans (897/ 1494-945/ 1538) gave considerable encouragement to Bengali literature, but a real flouri-shing of Bengali Sufi poetry took place mainly from the tenth/ sixteenth century on in the Chittagong region and at the Arakanese court. Some works translate the Nâtha Panthî literature from Sanskrit into Bengali and try to reconcile them with Sufi maqâmât (stages) and teachings. A distinctive contribution of the Bengali Sufi poets involved the creation of a corpus of mystical and legendary mathnawîs on the model of those written in Persian by Nizòâmî, 'Atòtòâr, and Jâmî.

Sayyid Sultòân (957/ 1550-1058/ 1648) of Chittagong, a leading Sufi in that region, had obtained a profound mastery over arousing human emotions through the use of the most poignant diction. He composed a number of Bengali mathnawîs on themes relating to the life of the Prophet Muhòammad and his family members, borrowing similes and metaphors from the Hindu epics and legends. His mystical poems such as GnânChautîsa Chautîsa and Gnân Pradîp were believed to have been written in his old age in an attempt to harmonize Hatha-Yoga with Sufism.

The Bengali poets exhibit considerable literary skill and

aesthetic taste in depicting their perception of al-nûr al-muhòammadî (literally, Muhòammadan Light) or the precreation light from which everything was created. In the Nûr-nâmah (Treatise on Light) or the Nûr-kandîl (Lamp of Light), Sayyid Murtadòâ (998/ 1590-1072/ 1662) passionately makes the Prophet both the cause and the goal of creation. The hòadîth, anâ Ahòmad bilâ mîm (I am Ahòmad [Mu%ammad] without the letter m, i.e., Ahòad=One) is represented by many Bengali Sufi poets in Hindu symbols, and some even go to the extent of anthropomorphizing the concept.

The earliest known Sòufi poets of the Punjab were Bâbâ Farîd of Pakpattan and his descendants. Mâdho Lâl Hòusayn (946/ 1539-1001/ 1593) was the most colorful of the Punjabi Sufi poets. His verses called kâfîs give emotional expression to the doctrine of wahòdat alwujûd. The folktales of Hîr and Rânjhâ and Sohnî Mehanwâl are also sung in his poetry. Nawshâh Ganjbakhsh (d. 1064/ 1654) was deeply influenced by the pioneers of Hindu devotional movements, Kabîr (828/ 1425-911/ 1505) and Gurû Nânak (873/ 1469-946/ 1539). He wrote many Panjabi dôhas (couplets) in which he answered questions earlier posed by Kabîr. Nevertheless, he strongly criticized the Hindu belief in the transmigration of the soul. Sultan Bâhû (d. 1102/ 1691) was the author of the Punjabi Sîharfîs (Golden Alphabets) ending with the exclamation Hû (He). Not only were his verses welcome at the Sama' gatherings but they were—and still are—upon the lips of all sections of the Punjabi community.

They deal with the self-manifestation of the Absolute and the preeminence of the life led in spiritual dedication and asceticism. The greatest Sufi poet of the Punjabi language was, however, Mîr Bullhe Shah Qâdirî-Shatòtòârî (1091/ 1680-1165/ 1752). His imageries on wahòdat al-wujûd are both novel and frank. Around 1180/ 1766, Wârith Shah, a famous Chishtî Sufi, re-versified the celebrated Punjabi folk story, Hîr-Rânjhâ. In it, the yogi Bîlnath exercises his spiritual power in collaboration with five pîrs (Khwâjah Khidòr, Bâbâ

Farîd Shakarganj, Lâl Shahbâz Qalandar, Shaykh Bahâ' al-Dîn Zakariyyâ', and Makhdûm Jahâniyân) to bless Rânjhâ. The poet repeatedly portrays the unio mystica throughout the mathnawî.

As was the case in other regions of India, the Sama' gatherings of Sind reverberated with Sufi music in the Sindhi language. The foremost Sufi poet of Sind was Shah 'Abd al-Latòîf (1102/ 1690-91-1165/ 1752). The melodies of his poetic works called Risâlo (The Book) embodying the folk ballads of Sind are very emotive and stirring. Among the different romantic stories chosen by the Shah to invite Sufis to concentrate on Divine Love is the Sasui-Punhûn Punhûn. He does not give the details of the story but masterly portrays only some thrilling episodes in order to use them as the background for his mystical perception of quest, separation, and death.

The twelfth/eighteenth century also saw the crystallization of the poetic form of Urdu, spoken both by Hindus and Muslims. The greatest Sufi poets of the period were the Naqshbandî Sufis Khwâjah Mr Dard and Mîrzâ Jân-i Jânân Mazòhar. The thirteenth/nineteenth-century poet Mîrzâ Asad Allâh Khân Ghâlib (1212/ 1797-1286/ 1869) did not lead a khU+000101nqâh life and was known for his gaiety, but his Urdu poetry is marked by a deep spiritual sensitivity. He also wrote profound ghazals in Persian. Sir Muhammad Iqbal (1294/ 1877-1357/ 1938) also wrote poetry in both Persian and Urdu. He strongly criticized the degenerate Sufism of his own day and considered it a threat to Islamic dynamism and the self (khwudî).

Role of Sufis in Bijapur Adil Shah Era

Islam's normative vision of society and piety was mediated to the masses in large part by Sufi shaikhs, heirs to Islam's rich mystical tradition. Although anthropologists have examined the social roles played by Sufis in some contemporary societies and few historians have done the same for earlier periods, in any part of the Islamic world is an attempt to fill this gap by scrutinizing the social careers of Sufis of a single city-state, the Deccani kingdom of Bijapur, from the early fourteenth to the late seventeenth centuries. The aim is two-fold: first, to identify the dominant social roles played by Sufis of Bijapur; and second, to explain why certain kinds of Sufis appeared when they did. The section thus blends cultural history with social biography during a critical period of Deccani history.

W. Chittick explains the position of Sufism and Sufis this way: In short, Muslim scholars who focused their energies on understanding the normative guidelines for the body came to be known as jurists, and those who held that the most important task was to train the mind in achieving correct understanding came to be divided into three main schools of thought: theology, philosophy, and Sufism. This leaves us with the third domain of human existence, the spirit. Most Muslims who devoted their major efforts to developing the spiritual dimensions of the human person came to be known as Sufis.

This school of thought is widely known as SUFISUM in Islam. Before and during the time of Adil Shahs many such Sufi saints came and settled in Bijpaur and around and brought peace and submission to God through proper teachings of Islam. They came from different parts of the Islamic world from Iraq, Iran, Arab penunsilla, Turkey, Yeman, and North Africa. They learned the local languages Deccani Urdu, Marathi and Kannda. They lived within the common folks rather than living the offered comfort palaces by the Adil Shahi Kings. They made their own shcools knwon as Khankas or darsgahs (meaning place of learning lessons). The common men and the royal men attracted towrds these noble people and learned the lessons of life to become successful here and here after. Still today the platu Deccan Bijapur witnessed the last resting places of these sufis. Some of the families of these great suffis leneage is exists and trying their ways to continue to give the similar services for humanity.

Sufi centers had existed in the Deccan since the early fourteenth century conquests of the Delhi Sultanate. The first Sufi order to be transplanted to the peninsula was that of the Chishtis, the most popular group in the north. Members of other Sufi orders migrated to the Deccan from the Middle East or from other areas of the subcontinent slightly later, in the fifteenth and sixteenth centuries. By the seventeenth century, Sufis in Bijapur were varied in affiliation and diverse in their interests, as Richard M. Eaton's work has demonstrated. Some Bijapur Sufis worked closely with the court and received land grants in return; this intimate link with Sufis and their ideas is revealed in the painting, poetry, and prose produced by the court elite. Other Bijapur Sufis shunned contact with the courts and instead focused on spreading their ideas through literature. They wrote not only in Persian but also in a form of proto-Urdu known as Dakani. Dakani resembled north Indian languages in grammar and syntax, but incorporated many words from the Arabic and Persian languages and was written in the Perso-Arabic script. Because it combined elements drawn from both the Indic and Islamic traditions, Dakani was a perfect vehicle for the composite culture that flourished in the early modern Deccan Sultanates.

Sufism in Islam

Hazrath Ali is respected not only as a warrior and leader, but as a writer and religious authority. Many Sunnis believe that Muhammad told about him "I'm the city of knowledge and Ali is its gate..." Ali told people about him "Ask me before you miss me." Muslims consider him as a foremost authority on the Tafsir (Quranic exegesis), Fiqh (Islamic jurisprudence) and religious thought. Ali was also a great scholar of Arabic literature and pioneered in the field of grammar and rhetoric. His speeches, sermons and letters served for generations afterward as models of literary expression. He also has a high rank position in almost all Sufi orders which trace their lineage to Muhammad through him. Therefore various groups of Muslims have attempted to collect his quotations, narrate his life and recite his sermons. Historians have paid attention to his government, religious scholars tried to learn his knowledge and the men of literate collected his speeches. Sunnis have narrated many hadith trough him from Muhammad in their authentic books. Shias have narrated his quotations in specific books such as "Ghorar Alhakam". In the 7th century Sulaym ibn Qays and `Abd Allah ibn `Abbas narrated his speeches and manners as well as the events which had happened in his life in their works. In the 8th century his descendants such as Muham-mad al Baqir and Jafar as Sadiq narrated his quotations which had learnt from their fathers. Some historians such as Abu Mikhnaf narrated the story of major events of Ali's life in his books like Kitab al Jamal, Kitab al-gharat and so on.

Numerous short sayings of Ali have become part of general Islamic culture and are quoted as aphorisms and proverbs in daily life. They also have become the basis of literary works or have been integrated into poetic verse in many languages. Already in the 8th century, literary authorities such as 'Abd al-Hamid ibn Yahya al-'Amiri pointed to the unparalleled eloquence of Ali's sermons and sayings, as did al-Jahiz in the following century. Even who works in the Divan of Umayyad recited Ali's sermons to improve their eloquence? Of course Peak of Eloquence (Nahj al-Balagha) is an extract of Ali's quotations from literal viewpoint as its compiler mentioned in its preface. While there are many other quotations, prays (Du'as), sermons and letters in other literal, historic and religious books. In later Islamic philosophy, especially in the teachings of Mulla Sadra and his followers like Allameh Tabatabaei Ali's sayings and sermons were increasingly regarded as central sources of metaphysical knowledge, or divine philosophy. Members of Sadra's school regard Ali as the supreme metaphysician of Islam.]

Sufism is a mystic tradition within Islam that encompasses a diverse range of beliefs and practices dedicated to Divine love and the cultivation of the elements of the Divine within the individual human being. Practitioners of this tradition are known as "Sufis" generally, though some senior members of the tradition reserve this term for those who have attained the goals of the tradition. Although some people refer to this tradition as Sufism, others refer to it as the Sufi Way. They draw this distinction because they feel that the term "Sufism" refers to a philosophy or a school of thought like capitalism or socialism, and they feel that the Sufi Way describes a practical path to follow.

Sufism has been defined as a type of knowledge by the great Sufi masters. Shaykh Ahmad Zarruq, a 15th century Sufi who wrote The Principles of Sufism, defined Sufism as "a science whose objective is the reparation of the heart and turning it away from all else but God." Ibn 'Ajiba, one of the best known Sufi masters, defined Sufism as "a science through which one can know how to travel into the presence of the Divine, purify one's inward from filth, and beautify it with a variety of praiseworthy traits." The Tariqas, or Sufi orders, may be associated with Sunni Islam or Shia Islam. It has been suggested that Sufi thought emerged from the Middle East in the eighth century, but adherents are now found around the world. A number of Sufism adherents, mostly in the West, believe or assert that Sufism is a projection of "the perennial philosophy" of man's true nature to the Divine and as such forms a subterranean current in many religions and mystical traditions and practices. This viewpoint is denied, often with great energy by a substantial number of other Sufis Etymology.

The conventional view is that the word originates from Suf, the Arabic word for wool, referring to the simple cloaks the early Muslim ascetics wore. However, not all sufis wear cloaks or clothes of wool. Another etymological theory states that the root word of Sufi is the Arabic word safa, meaning purity. This places the emphasis of Sufism on purity of heart and soul. Others suggest the origin is from "Ashab al-Suffa" ("Companions of the Veranda") or "Ahl al-Suffa" ("People of the Veranda"), who were a group of Muslims during the time of the Prophet Mohammad (S.A.W) who spent much of their time on the veranda of the Prophet's mosque devoted to prayer. Yet another etymology, advanced by the 10th century author Al-Biruni is that the word, as 'Sufiya', is linked with Sophia, the Greek term for "wisdom" - although for various reasons this derivation is not accepted by many at the present. In the introduction to The Sufis, Idries Shah writes that the word Sufi has no etymology. A few etymologies for the word Sufi (Arabic, ta awwuf - Kurdish: 'sofîtî, f' -, Sufi gari - Turkish: 'Tasavvuf') or Irfan have been suggested.

Basic Beliefs

The essence of Being/Truth/God is devoid of every form and quality, and hence un-manifested, yet it is inseparable from every form and phenomenon either material or spiritual. It is often understood to imply that every pheno-menon is an aspect of Truth and at the same time attribution of existence to it is false. This apparent paradox of the relationship of creator and created is the basis of Sufi metaphysics. The chief aim of all Sufis then is to let go of all notions of duality, including a conception of an individual self, and to realize the Divine unity. Sufis generally teach in personal groups, as the counsel of the master is considered necessary for the growth of the pupil. They make extensive use of parable, allegory, and metaphor, and it is held by Sufis that meaning can only be reached through a process of seeking the truth, and knowledge of oneself. Although philosophies vary among different Sufi orders, Sufism as a whole is primarily concerned with direct personal experience.

A significant part of Oriental literature comes from the Sufis, who created books of poetry containing the teachings of the Sufis. Some of the more notable examples of this poetry are the Walled Garden of Truth, Rubaiyat of Omar Khayyam, the Conference of the Birds and the Masnavi.

Sufism is generally believed to have originated among Muslims near Basra in modern Iraq, though there is a history of Sufism in Transoxania dating from shortly after the time of Muhammad. Almost all traditional Sufi schools (or "orders") trace their "chains of transmission" back to Muhammad via his cousin and son-in-law Imam Ali ibn Abi Talib; the Naqshbandi order is a notable exception to this rule, as it traces its origin to Caliph Abu Bakr. From their point of view, the esoteric teaching was given to those who had the capacity to contain the direct experiential gnosis of God, which was passed on from teacher to student through the centuries. Worth noting is that the original Islamic scriptures (Qur'an, tafsir Ibn Ishaq, tafsir al-Tabari) have no mention whatsoever of Sufi traditions or practices. Some Orientals scholars believe that Sufism was essentially the result of Islam evolving in a more mystic direction for example according to Louis Massignon: "It is from the Quran, constantly recited, meditated, and experienced, that Sufism proceeded, in its origin and its development.

Great Masters of Sufism

The Sufis dispersed throughout the Middle East, particularly in areas previously under Byzantine influence and control. This period was characterized by the practice of an apprentice (murid) placing himself under the spiritual direction of a Master (shaykh, pir or murshid). Schools were developed, concerning themselves with topics of mystical experience, education of the heart to purify it of baser instincts, the love of God, and approaching God through progressive stages (maqaam) and states (haal). The schools were championed by reformers who felt their core values and manners were threatened, as the material prosperity of society seemed to them to be eroding the spiritual life.Uwais al-Qarni, Harrm Bin Hian, Hasan Ul-Basri and Sayid Ibn Ul Mussib are regarded as the first mystics among the "Taabi'een" in Islam. Rabia was a female Sufi and known for her love and passion for God. Junayd was among the first theorists of Sufism; he concerned himself with 'fanaa' and 'baqaa', the state of annihilating the self in the presence of the divine, accompanied by clarity concerning worldly phenomena derived from the altitude of that perspective. Some believe that Sufism was first formed as a belief in South Asia when Islam mixed with the Hindu, Sikh, and Buddhist Cultures.

The Chishti order was founded by Abu Ishaq Shami ("the Syrian") who brought Sufism to the town of Chisht, now Afghanistan. The Chishti Order was first introduced in India by Khwaja Moinuddin Chishti (1143-1223 AD) and is the oldest known order. Some of the Sufi orders started in India. Chishti Order (India)(1143-1223 AD), Suhrawardi Order (India)(1234-1335 AD), Qadriya Order (Iraq) (1430-1517 AD), Naqshbandi Order (Afghanistan)(d.1642 AD), Nimatullahi Sufi Order(Iran) (at the end of the 14th century AD), Shattari Order(India)(d.1485 AD)

Formalization of Philosophies of Sufism

Al Ghazali's treatises, the "Reconstruction of Religious Sciences" and the "Alchemy of Happiness," argued that Sufism originated from the Qur'an and was thus compatible with mainstream Islamic thought and theology. It was around 1000 CE that early Sufi literature, in the form of manuals, treatises, discourses and poetry, became the source of Sufi thinking and meditations.

Propagation of Sufism

Sufism, during 1200-1500 CE, experienced an era of increased activity in various parts of the Islamic world. This period is considered as the "Classical Period" or the "Golden Age" of Sufism. Lodges and hospices soon became not only places to house Sufi students, but also places for practicing Sufis and other mystics to stay and retreat. The propagation of Sufism started in Baghdad in Shiah majority areas, such as Iraq and Khorasan, and spread to Persia, the Indian subcontinent, North Africa, and Muslim Spain. There were tests of conciliation between Sufism and the other Islamic sciences (sharia, fiqh, etc.), as well as the beginning of the Sufi brotherhoods (turuq). One of the first orders to originate was the Yasawi order, named after Khwajah Ahmed Yesevi in modern Kazakhstan. The Kubrawiya order, originating in Central Asia, was named after Najmeddin Kubra, known as the "saint-producing shaykh", because a number of his disciples became shaykhs. The most prominent Sufi master of this era is Abdul Qadir Jilani, the founder of the Qadiriyyah order in Iraq. Others included Rumi, founder of the Mevlevi order in Turkey, Sahabuddin Suharwardi in Iran, Moinuddin Chishti and Makhdoom Ashraf in India.

Sufism's Role in the Expansion of Islam

Sufism has some roots in the Shamanic traditions of Middle Asia, and is flexible in terms of religious materiality. These two characteristics of Sufism attracted the nomadic people of middle-western Asia (mainly the current Iranic and Turkic republics of Iran, Afghanistan, Pakistan, India, Turkmenistan, Uzbekistan, Tajikistan, and Kyrgyzstan). Sufism also spread quickly among the Anatolian Turkmen and among Balkan peoples of modern Albania, Bosnia, Macedonia, and Bulgaria. The mystics of Khorasan like Ahmad Yasavi and Haci Bektas-i Veli were influential in the spread of Sufist Islam first in Asia Minor and then in Eastern Europe as the Selcuk Turks and Ottoman Turks extended their empires.

Sufi Philosophy

Realities of The Heart: Drawing from Qur'anic verses, virtually all Sufis distinguish Lataif-e-Sitta (The Six Subtleties), Nafs, Qalb, Ruh, Sirr, Khafi & Akhfa. These lataif (singular: latifa) designate various psycho spiritual "organs", or faculties of sensory perception. Sufic development involves the awakening of these spiritual centers of perception that lie dormant in an individual. Each center is associated with a particular color and general area of the body, oftentimes with a particular prophet, and varies from order to order. The help of a guide is considered necessary to help activate these centers. After undergoing this process, the dervish is said to reach a certain type of "completion."

The person gets acquainted with the lataif one by one by Muraqaba (Sufi meditation), Dhikr (Remembrance of God) and purification of one's psyche of negative thoughts, emotions, and actions. Loving God and one's fellow, irrespective of his or her race, religion or nationality, and without consideration for any possible reward, is the key to ascension according to Sufis. These six "organs" or faculties: Nafs, Qalb, Ruh, Sirr, Khafi & Akhfa, and the purificative activities applied to them, contain the basic orthodox Sufi philosophy. The purification of the elementary passionate nature (Tazkiya-I-Nafs), followed by cleansing of the spiritual heart so that it may acquire a mirror-like purity of reflection (Tazkiya-I-Qalb) and become the receptacle of God's love (Ishq) and illumination of the spirit (Tajjali-I-Ruh). This process is fortified by emptying of egoic drives (Taqliyya-I-Sirr) and remembrance of God's attributes (Dhikr), and completion of journey by purification of the last two faculties, Khafi and Akhfa.

Sufi Cosmology

Although there is no consensus with regard to Sufi cosmology, one can disentangle at least three different cosmographies: Ishraqi visionary universe as expounded by Suhrawardi Maqtul, Neoplatonic view of cosmos cherished by Islamic philosophers like Ibn Sina and Sufis like Ibn Arabi, and Hermetic-Ptolemaic spherical geocentric world. All these doctrines (each one of them claiming to be impeccably orthodox) were freely mixed and juxtaposed, frequently with confusing results – a situation one also encounters in other esoteric doctrines.

Dhikr

Dhikr is the remembrance of God commanded in the Qur'an for all Muslims. To engage in dhikr is to have awareness of God according to Islam. Dhikr as a devotional act includes the repetition of divine names, supplications and aphorisms from hadith literature, and sections of the Qur'an. More generally, any activity in which the Muslim maintains awareness of God is considered dhikr. The practice of Muraqaba and Dhikr has very close resemblance with the practices of the Jewish mystics. Muraqaba is very similar to the Merkavah practice, which is one of the meditations used by Kabbalists to attain higher states of consciousness. Some Sufi orders engage in ritualized dhikr ceremonies, the liturgy of which may include recitation, singing, instrumental music, dance, costumes, incense, meditation, ecstasy, and trance.

Hadhra

Hadhra is a form of dhikr practiced primarily in the Arab world. The word Hadhra means Presence in Arabic.

Qawwali

Qawwali is a form of devotional Sufi music common in Pakistan, India, Bangladesh, Afganistan, Iran and Turkey. It is known for its secular strains. Some of its modern-day masters have included Nusrat Fateh Ali Khan and the Sabri Brothers. Amir Khusro, a disciple of Nizamuddin Auliya, of the Chishti Order, is credited with inventing Qawwali in the 14th century.

Sama

Sama or Sema' (Arabic "listening") refers to Sufi practices which can involve music and dance. In Uyghur culture, this includes a dance form also originally associated with Sufi ritual.

Khalwa

Khalwa refers to a form of retreat, once widespread but now less common. A khalwa may be prescribed by the shaykh (spiritual advisor) of the murid or talib (student). Muslims believe that most of the prophets, and also Maryam (Mary) the mother of Issa (Jesus), lived in some form of seclusion at some point in their life. Prophet Muhammad, for example, used to retreat to the cave on Mount Hira where he received his first revelation – but had been going there for many years prior to his meeting with the angel Gabriel. Similar examples include Moses' going into seclusion for 40 days in a cave in Mt. Sinai. Mary was in seclusion in the Jewish temple for a year, where only Zakariya was permitted to see her.

Sufi Poetry

Sufism has produced a large body of poetry in Arabic, Kurdish, Persian, Punjabi, Sindhi, Turkish, Pashto language and Urdu languages which notably includes the works of Jalal al-Din Muhammad Rumi, al-Hallaj, Ibn al-Farid, Hafez, Jami, Ibn Arabi, Shah Syed Muhammad Noor Baksh,Farid Ud-Din Attar, Abdul Qader Bedil, Bulleh Shah, Amir Khusro, Yunus Emre, Shah Abdul Latif Bhittai, Sachal Sarmast, Sultan Bahu, Muhammad Iqbal, Hussain Baksh Malang as well as numerous traditions of devotional dance, such as Sufi whirling, and music, such as Qawwali.

Langar

Langar is a fundamental element of Indian Sufism, especially the Chishti Order. Langar is served in the precincts of a Sufi Dergah, and is served out of a massive pot called a "Deg," and is not necessarily vegetarian. Langar is not only available for all but is actively distributed to the poor.

Orders of Sufism

Traditional Orders

Dervishes used these bowl during begging, which was a process of overcoming personal vanity and arrogance for dervishes in Sufi culture of the time. The traditional Sufi orders emphasise the role of Sufism within Islam. Therefore, the Sharia (traditional Islamic law) and the Sunnah (customs of the Prophet) are seen as crucial for any Sufi aspirant. Among the oldest and most well known of the Sufi orders are the Qadiri, Chisti, Oveyssi, Shadhili, Jerrahi, Ashrafi,

Bektashi, Nimatullahi and Mevlevi. One proof traditional order assert is that almost all the famous Sufi masters of the past Caliphates were also experts in Sharia and were renowned as people with great Iman (faith) and excellent practice. Many were also Qadis (Sharia law judges) in courts. They held that Sufism was never distinct from Islam and to fully comprehend and practice Sufism one must be a practicing Muslim obeying the Sharia.

Traditional Islamic Schools of thought and Sufism

Islam traditionally consists of a number of groups. The two main divisions are the Sunnis and the Shia. Shia and Sunni Islam consist of a number of schools of legal jurisprudence (called Madhabs). Sufis do not define Sufism as a madhhab — what distinguishes a person as a Sufi is practicing Sufism, usually through association with a Sufi order. In this sense, traditional practitioners of Sufism don't see it as an exclusive group but just as a form of training necessary to cultivate spirituality and Ihsan in their lives.

8

Indo-Muslim Spirituality and Literature

When Islamic conquest did begin to occur, however, it was not of the original Arab variety. It came during the period of the 'Abbasid Caliphate (750 - 1258), and more than that, during a late phase of the 'Abbasid dynasty in which a number of independent succession states had emerged, one of which on the far eastern end of the Islamic world, namely, that of the Turko-Afghan Ghaznavid state, was to be the first agent of Islamization on the subcontinent. By the time of the 'Abbasid Caliphate, Islamic culture and civilization had become a cosmopolitan, imperial presence throughout the Middle East and the Mediterranean world, and had indeed become the heir of the heritage of Middle East civilizations, including Jewish, Christian, Hellenistic, Byzantine and Sasanian cultural components. When it entered India, in other words, it brought with it a much richer heritage than the original Arab faith of the founder, Muhammad.

This is not at all to suggest that all of this came with the invading forces of Mahmud of Ghazni and Sultan Muhammad of Ghur in the eleventh and twelfth centuries. It was, however, the beginning of a cultural invasion and cultural transformation the likes of which the subcontinent had not experienced in over two thousand years of previous history. Mahmud of Ghazni and Sultan Muhammad of Ghur, in other words, may have appeared to be only two more outside invaders on analogy with so many who had come before. This time, however, there was a profound difference.

This time it was not simply an invading force to be absorbed or accommodated, sooner or later, into the dense and rich subcontinental civilization. This time an entire civilization, at least as dense and rich as the subcontinental, was making an appearance, and the encounter and accommodation would be exceedingly fruitful, albeit also deeply frustrating and painful. From 997 onwards, Mahmud of Ghazni, a Turko-Afghan Muslim from Afghanistan, led his armies in some seventeen bloody attacks, not only in the Punjab region but well into North India as well. A number of important Hindu religious sites were attacked and plundered, including those at Thanesar, Kanauj, Mathura and the famed temple at Somnath. The Ghaznavids, however, made no attempt to hold extensive portions of the subcontinent beyond some areas in the Punjab and Sind.

It was over a century later, when Ghazni itself was conquered (1173) by another Central Asian Muslim, Sultan Muhammad of Ghur, that North India became the target for permanent conquest and settlement. In 1192 at the second battle of Tarain the Rajputs under Prithiviraja were completely defeated. Thereafter most of North India was open to permanent conquest by the Muslim armies. Sultan Muhammand of Ghur himself withdrew from North India and returned to Ghur, leaving the task of the further conquest of North India to his most favored Turkish commander, Qutb ud-din Aibak, and, as was mentioned above, when Muhammad of Ghur was assassinated in 1206, Qutb ud-din Aibak claimed the title of Sultan for himself in Delhi and began the series of Turko-Afghan Sultanates called simply the Delhi Sultanates (1206 - 1526). These Sultanates ruled most of North India from the Punjab in the North-West to the borders of Bengal in the North-East, but they were for the most part simply large regional polities.

There were a number of other regional powers during the period, Hindu as well as spin-off Muslim politities, including the Rajput Confederacy (Hindu) in the West (the Rajasthan region), the Bahmani (Muslim) dynasty in the Deccan, the Ilyas Shahi (Muslim) dynasty in Bengal, the Vijayanagar (Hindu) dynasty in the Karnataka region, and so forth. When yet another Turkish line, the Timurids or Mughals, founded in 1526 by Babar (purportedly a descendent of both Timur on his father's side and the great Chingis Khan on his mother's side), supplanted the last of the Delhi Sultanates (the Lodi dynasty, 1451 - 1526), the battle was not just with the Lodis. The Rajput Confederacy under the Rana Sanga of Mewar (the region of Rajasthan) was at least as formidable as the weakened Lodis. In any case, Babar was finally successful after a series of major encounters in the North with various regional polities.

The most important of the Mughal rulers included, in addition to Babar himself (ruled 1526-30), his son Humayun (1508-56, ruled from 1530), the great Emperor, Akbar (ruled 1556 - 1605), Jahangir (ruled 1605-1627), Shah Jahan (ruled 1628 - 1658, builder of the Taj Mahal), and Aurangzeb (ruled 1658 - 1707). Under Akbar the Mughal dynasty achieved its greatest success and coherence, controlling most of North India from the far North-West to the far North-East, although much of the South remained outside of Mughal control. With Aurangzeb the extent of Mughal power covered almost the entirety of the subcontinent (including most of the South), but the control was loose at best and decline was already setting in. By the end of Aurangzeb's rule, the empire was overextended, financially weak, and, therefore, in serious decline, and thereafter the dynasty continued largely in name only until its final representative, Bahadur Shah II, was deposed in 1858 by the British (at the conclusion of the North Indian rebellion, 1857-1858).

Sunni, Shi'a and Sufi

As mentioned above, apart from some early contacts on the western coast by Arab traders, the vehicle for the transmission of Islam into the subcontinent was not the original tradition of the Arabs but, rather, the much more cosmopolitan and sophisticated Islam of the 'Abbasid caliphate. The tradition of the original religious Arab Islam was simply (a) that there is only one God (Allah), (b) that God is revealed in the sacred text of the Qur'an, (c) that Muhammad is the final messenger (*rasul*) or prophet of this God and his revelation, that is to say, the final prophet or "seal of the prophets" in a long line of previous prophets or messengers who brought new revelations leading back through (the Christian) Jesus to the ancient (Hebrew) prophets or messengers, Abraham and Moses, (d) that all believers are equal before God and must together exercise total submission (*islam*) to God and have faith (*iman*) in Him, his angels, his revelation, and his lordship over corporate life (that is, all of history, including family, society and state), (e) that believers should obey the law (*shari'ah*) as determined by the Qur'an, the traditions of the prophet (*hadith*), the consensus of the community (*ijma*) and basic custom or "orthodoxy" (*sunnah*), and (f) that believers should observe the five "supports of the religion" (*arkan ad-din*), namely, the "witnessing" or credo that there is only one God (*shahadah*), daily "prayer" (*salah*), "fasting" (*sawm*) during the month of Ramadan, "almsgiving" (*zakah*), and "pilgrimage" (*hajj*) to the sacred city of Mecca.

It was a faith that enabled a broader vision of communal life than the constraints of older Arab tribalisms and that provided a powerful rationale for conquest and proselytization in order to establish a universal "abode of peace" or "house of Islam" (*dar al-islam*). One other interesting historical development should also be mentioned which coincides with the appearance of Islamic culture in India, and again, it has to do with the 'Abbasid Caliphate. Just as the 'Abbasids had provided a context for the diffusion of a common culture, the collapse of that same Caliphate in its later phases, after the tenth and eleventh century, provided the occasion for many scholars, artists, intellectuals, and religious leaders in the eastern regions of the learned Islamic world to seek refuge in India.

The subcontinent, fortunately, with the exception of some portions of the Punjab, escaped the Mongol invasions, and the Delhi Sultanates (1206 - 1526) of North India became a place where Islamic culture could develop in new and intriguing ways. Sunni, Shi'a and Sufi forms of Islam, all of which had developed into mature traditions by the twelfth century, long before the appearance of Islam as a conquering force in India, underwent a new and vigorous development on the subcontinent.

Sunni Islam was the main "orthodox" tradition. The term "sunni" is the adjective derived from the word "*sunnah*," meaning "custom." Sunni Muslims accept the first four Caliphs (*kalifah* or "deputy," namely, Abu Bakr, 'Umar, 'Uthman and 'Ali). They do not ascribe any special spiritual powers to 'Ali (as do Shi'ites and Sufis), and they follow one or the other of the four Sunni Schools of Law (the *shari'ah*): the Hanafi, Hanbali, Maliki or Shafi'i (representing mainly variant traditions in geographic regions). They accept, of course, the Qur'an and the *hadith* ("authentic traditions" about the Prophet) as authoritative revelation, but Sunni Islam also puts great importance on the notion of the "consensus" (*ijma'*) of the community, either the collective consensus of the legal specialists or learned men of the community (the *'ulama'*) or the corporate Muslim community as a whole (the *umma*). The great majority of all Muslims (well over 80%) through the centuries have been Sunnis. The majority tradition in India has always been Sunni, and Sunni Muslims in India have followed the Hanafite School of Law. Shi'ite Islam represents a minority of about 10% of the Muslim world, and it has three major divisions, the largest of which is Twelve Imam Shi'ism.

This latter has had its base primarily in Iran (Persia) and Iraq. There are two other smaller groups, namely, the Five Imam Shi'ites in theYemen and the Seven Imam Shi'ites or Isma'ilis, largely in India. Shi'ism became an important force in the spin-off (from the Delhi Sultanates) Muslim regional polities in the Deccan in the sixteenth century. Also,

Bairam Khan, the guardian and minister of the Mughal emperor, Akbar, was a Shi'ite. The Shi'ites (from the term "shi'ah," meaning "partisan," and more specifically, "shi'at 'Ali," the "party of 'Ali") believe that 'Ali was the first legitimate Caliph, since he was in the blood-line of descent (a cousin) of the Prophet. 'Ali was assassinated, and his oldest son, Hasan (through his wife, Fatimah, the daughter of the Prophet), was coerced into abdicating the Caliphate to Mu'awiyah, the founder of the Umayyad dynasty in 661. When Hasan finally died, Husayn, 'Ali's second son by Fatimah, proclaimed himself Caliph, but Husayn and his small band of followers were ruthlessly massacred on the battlefield of Karbala (in Iraq) in 680 by Yazid, the son of Mu'awiyah.

This massacre (commemorated on the 10th day of Muharram in the ritual calendar) is the most important symbolic event for Shi'ism, since it marks the martyrdom and sacrifice of the 'Ali line. Shi'ites believes in a line of spiritually empowered "Imams" in the 'Ali blood-line of descent from the Prophet who preserve and transmit the esoteric or "inner" truth of Islam. It is a messianic form of Islam. The Twelve Imam tradition in Iran and Iraq believes that the last Imam is currently in "occultation" and will return at the end of the age as "*al-Mahdi*" ("the guided one") to restore righteousness and the legitimate Caliphate. Sufism (probably from the term "*suf*," meaning "rough wool" worn by early Muslim ascetics) represents the mystical tradition within Islam, influenced probably by Neo-Platonism from the Hellenistic tradition and possibly by older traditions of Indic mystical thought from Central Asia (via Buddhism and Iranian Manichaeism). Like Shi'ism it focusses on the "inner" truth of Islam with special emphasis on a living, personal relationship with Allah.

Mystical traditions appeared very early in the history of Islam and developed considerably after Islam expanded into Iran or Persia in the late seventh and eighth centuries. Key figures include Abu Yazid al-Bistami of Iran (d. 874) and al-

Junayd of Baghdad (d. 910), and the writings of the great Persian or Iranian poet, Jalal ad-Din ar-Rumi (1207 - 1273). It received its definitive theological formulation and thereby its solid place within Islamic orthodoxy by the great Persian or Iranian theologian-mystic, Abu Hamid Muhammad al-Ghazali (1058 - 1111). Sufism focusses on the mystical truth and blessing passed on from Allah to Muhammad and, thence, to either Abu Bakr (the first Caliph) or 'Ali (the fourth Caliph), and, then, in sequence to "spiritual leaders" (*Shaykhs* or *Pirs*) who maintain "lines of transmission" (*silsilah*) and establish "retreat centers" (*khannaqahs* or *tekke*) wherein followers cultivate and follow the mystical "path" (*tariqah*). Some of these "retreat centers" became favored places of pilgrimage after the death of a particularly popular Shaykh or Pir.

The inner, spiritual or esoteric mystical path parallels the outer, external or exoteric legal way (*shari'ah*). By the time that Islam entered India, Sufism had already become a mature, orthodox tradition. Three Sufi "orders" became especially dominant in India: the Chishti Order (founded by Mu'in ad-Din Muhammad Chishti, 1142 - 1246), strong especially around Delhi, the Suhrawardi Order, strong mainly in Sind, and the Firdausi Order, strong in the region of Bihar. The Sufis were important in India as a missionizing force, and the obvious parallels between Sufi "retreat centers," "lines of transmission," and popular traditions of pilgrimage, on the one hand, and Hindu-Buddhist-Jain *ashramas* ("hermitages"), monasteries, and devotional (*bhakti*) groups, on the other, became important points of contact between Islamic traditions and older Indic traditions.

Perso-Arabic-cum-Rajput Hindu

With the coming of the Mughals in the sixteenth century, and especially the reign of the great Akbar, Indo-Islamic culture emerged as one of the truly sparkling phases in the world-history of Islamic civilization as well as within the history of the older Indic civilization. Indo-Islamic culture was an intriguing combination of the Perso-Arabic (and

Hellenized) traditions inherited from the cosmopolitan world of the 'Abbasid era together with the Rajput-Hindu traditions of Western and North Central India, largely patterned after Iranian or Persian culture and fashioned by migrant Iranians, Persianized Afghans and Turks and, of course, the many converts to Islam in India from peasant agrarian communities (in Kashmir and Bengal), urban artisan groups (in North Central India and in the spin-off Muslim regional polities in the Deccan) , various trading groups (on the western coast from Gujarat through Karnataka and down into what is now Kerala), and including, last but not least, the fellow-travelling Rajput clans, some of whom converted to Islam but many of whom remained Hindu, in the Rajasthan region.

The state under Akbar's tutelage became an interesting combination of the traditional Muslim notion of kingship and governance, derived mainly from Iranian sources, with its focus on the maintenance of stability, the enforcement of the SharI'ah, and the general moral uplift of the population through the true practice of Islam, together with older pre-Muslim Persian notions of the majesty and grandeur of the king and of the lavish display of royal patronage in cultural productions and grand public works. Akbar also developed a unique administrative system known as the *mansabdar* system, involving a network of administrative military officers in a hierarchical ordering. The position of the military "office-holder" (*mansab-dar*) in the hierarchy was determined by how many troops he was able to provide in the event of a battle.

The administrative military officer was paid in cash or given an estate (*jagir*). The officer would collect revenue and be in charge of a large administrative area. Below him were various local chieftains and regional revenue collectors (*zamindar*-s). The country overall was divided into provinces (*suba*-s), local districts (*sarkar*-s) and subdistricts (*pargana*-s). Most of the administrative military officers were brought from outside of India, but as many as twenty percent were Hindus (mainly Rajputs and Marathas). Over time elaborate lineage systems of both Muslim and Hindu elites were developed. When the British first established their presence in India, they were quick to see the merits of Akbar's system and to imitate them, especially the overall administrative structure and the symbolic, political value of lavish public displays of power and royal patronage.

On the level of material and political reality, it can be plausibly argued that no great transformations took place during the long centuries of Muslim domination. Muslim rulers accomodated themselves to the larger Hindu culture, if only because they were greatly outnumbered overall and very much in need of Hindu support. Hindus were early along designated "protected peoples" (*dhimmis*), and during some periods of Muslim rule—for example, during the reign of Akbar—the "head tax" (*jizya*) for "protected peoples" was waived. For a time under the Emperor Akbar, an open-minded and tolerant attitude towards other religious traditions, including the Hindu, became prevalent, at least among the court elite. Here is where the intriguing blend of Perso-Islamic and Rajput-Hindu traditions became most manifest. Discussions about religion were regularly held in the Hall of Worship with the Emperor presiding.

Taking part in these discussions were Sunni *ulama* ("learned jurists"), Sufi Shaykhs or Pirs, Hindu *panditas*, Jains, Parsis and even some Catholic priests (Jesuits) from Portugese Goa. Akbar also devised a new, eclectic religion, later known as the "Divine Faith" (Din-i-ilahi), a sort of broad-based monotheistic faith that included a variety of religious traditions (mainly Islamic and Hindu). The Emperor likewise encouraged the translations of some basic Vedic texts, and the two great epics, the *Mahabharata* and the *Ramayana*, into Persian. He also appointed a Hindi court poet. Akbar's great grandson, Dara Shikoh (1615 - 1659), a follower of one of the Sufi mystical orders, was also a student of Hindu philosophy. His brother, Aurangzeb, however, who came to power as Emperor (ruling from 1658 - 1707) had Dara Shikoh executed in 1659, mainly for political reasons (since Dara Shikoh was a principal claimant to the throne) but with the "religious" excuse that Dara Shikoh had become too influenced by Hindu ideas.

In any case, with the coming of Aurangzeb's leadership, the brief period of accomodation between Islamic, Hindu and other religious traditions came to an abrupt halt, and thereafter Islamic orthodoxy was enforced in court circles. Even during the years of accomodation between Islam and Hindu traditions, however, many of the orthodox *ulama* ("learned jurists") were opposed to any close connections between Islamic and Hindu traditions. Even many of the Sufi Shaykhs or Pirs were keen to maintain a distance between Islamic belief and practice and Hindu belief and practice. Shaikh Ahmad Sirhindi (1564 - 1624), for example, a Sufi of the Naqshbandi Order, troubled that the Muslim mystical doctrine of the "unity of existence" (*tauhid-i-wujudi*) might get confused with Hindu notions of monism, argued that the authentic mystic experience is simply "unity of experience" (*tauhid-i-shuhudi,* a subjective sense of the presence of God) and not the "unity of existence" (an objective claim that the mystic and God are one), thereby preserving the absolute transcendence of God and the need for revelation.

In a similar fashion, Shah Wali-Ullah (1703 - 1762), also a Sufi of the Naqshbandi Order, during the decline of the Mughal dynasty and before the coming of the British, argued for a clear separation between Islamic and Hindu traditions both spiritually as well as politically. Later in the nineteenth and twentieth centuries, the thought of Shah Wali-Ullah would be used by proponents of Muslim separatism in Pakistan and India. It appears to be the case overall, then, that any compromise or accomodation between Islamic and Hindu traditions on the learned level during the centuries of Muslim domination hardly went beyond very small elite in court circles. Generally speaking, with regard to learned or "great tradition" Islamic and Hindu traditions, there has been little more than bare co-existence over the centuries.

Mutual hostility and deep suspicion among the respective elites have been the order of the day almost from the beginning of the encounter between the two civilizations, and the hostility and suspicion continued not only until the time of Partition in 1947 but is even now, nearly fifty years after Partition, still a potent factor between the Hindu and Muslim communities in India as well as throughout the South Asian area. From the theoretical or theological perspective of the respective elites, of course, the basic reason for the deep suspicion is not difficult to identify. The Muslim belief in one transcendent God who has definitively revealed himself in a cognitively specific revelation (the Qur'an) and who demands absolute submission among all believers who make up one universal community in which all believers are equal is nearly the exact antithesis of the pluralist, plastic, hierarchical and polymorphous spirituality characteristic of Indic (Hindu-Buddhist-Jain) civilization prior to the appearance of Islamic civilization.

It is impossible to imagine from a purely theoretical point of view two more contradictory moral visions or views of the good life than that between the learned Islamic civilization and the learned Indic civilization. Nevertheless, it must also be noted that there were more than a few accomodations and intermixtures of a non-theoretical or practical kind that occurred on the lower peasant agrarian levels and the urban artisan levels. Sufi pilgrimage places were sometimes visited by Hindu pilgrims as were Hindu shrines by Muslim peasants. It was common in Kashmir for Muslims to visit old Buddhist shrines.

This was also the case in Bengal. Muslim peasants in Western India offered vows to Hindu gods for a good harvest, and Muslim women in Bengal offerred *puja* to Sitala, the Hindu goddess of smallpox. There was also a good deal of intermixture among performers and craftsmen in the areas of music, dance, architecture and painting. Moreover, even though Islam accepts the basic equality of all believers and, therefore, in principle rejects the Hindu caste-system, nevertheless, a sort of *ersatz* caste-system has developed among Muslim communities in India, with "*ashrafs*" ("honorable" ones), that is, the ruling descendants of Turks, Afghans and Persians at the top, followed by Muslim Rajputs, followed by "clean" artisan groups and, finally, "unclean" scavenger-groups.

Reactions to Islamic Culture

Regarding developments within the older Indic civilization throughout this Indo-Islamic period, on most levels there was a defensive withdrawal. Buddhist traditions as distinctive and identifiable communities disappeared altogether by the end of the fourteenth century (in the North-West and Kashmir, in the North-East and Bengal and throughout most of the South), partly, as has been mentioned, because of the onslaught of the Turko-Afghan Muslim invaders who found Buddhist monks and monasteries to be easy targets, but partly also because much of Buddhist spirituality, especially of the Mahayana and Tantric variety, was simply absorbed into the larger Hindu framework. Jain traditions somehow survived in certain regional areas such as Gujarat, Rajasthan, northern Maharashtra and Karnataka, partly because of royal favor in certain regional polities and partly because of extensive compromises with the larger Hindu environment.

The basic parameters of the Hindu traditions had been shaped in the preceding pre-Muslim period in terms of the three major kinds or modalities of spirituality: (a) sacrificial ritual (*yajna*) much of which became the simple ritual worship (*puja*) in the home and public temples, (b) ascetic practices or disciplined meditation (the various types of *yoga*) most of which became institutionalized in various monastic orders such as the Dashanamis, and so forth, and (c) devotion (*bhakti*) to a personal god, either in terms of Vaishnava, Shaiva or Shakta devotional groups or in terms of the *pancayatana puja* ("ritual worship of five symbols or deities: Surya, Shiva, Vishnu, Devi and Ganesha) of the Smarta (traditional high-caste and Advaita Vedantin) Hindus. In this Indo-Islamic period, the first two of these three modalities underwent only slight changes, mainly in the direction of greater consolidation and the development of defensive measures against the developing Indo-Islamic civilization. As mentioned earlier, it is undoubtedly in this period that the caste system began to take on its modern, overly rigid structures, and "orthopractical" ritual behavior became minutely codified and pervaded with this emerging "casteism."

Furthermore, in this period Hindus put greater emphasis on vegetarianism, non-violence (*ahimsa*) and the veneration of the cow as a symbol of divine benevolence, all of which notions of ritual purity clearly helped to differentiate the Hindu from the Muslim. Vegetarianism, non-violence and cow-veneration are, of course, much older than the Indo-Islamic period, the first two being traceable to the Indo-Shramanical traditions of the Jains and Buddhists and the latter (cow-veneration) going back even to Vedic times, but it is in this Indo-Islamic period that these old notions and practices became essential in the increasingly defensive self-understanding of Hindus. The great Shivaji (1627 - 1680), for example, mentioned earlier as the warrior hero and organizer of the Maratha tribes in Maharashtra who defended Hindu culture and civilization against Muslim encroachment, suggested that the very definition of Hindu tradition involves veneration of the cow, caste and the protection of the priests.

Regarding ascetic practices or disciplined meditation (*yoga*), already back in the eighth century, as mentioned earlier, the great Vedanta philosopher, Shankara, had organized the various Hindu monastic orders into the ten basic groups (the "ten-named" or Dashanami-s), and Ramanuja and the Shri Vaishnavas (as well as other Vaishnava traditions) developed comparable monastic organizations from the twelfth century onwards. Throughout the Indo-Islamic period these various monastic orders continued to consolidate their traditions and practices. They also developed "militant" orders called *naga*-s ("naked ascetics" in Hindi), arranged in groups or congregations called *akhadas* or *akharas* (meaning in Hindi an "arena" or "place for wrestling" but coming to mean congregations of militant *sadhu*-s or holy men), groups of Yogins trained in martial arts to defend the monastic institutions against the encroachment of Muslim bands or other, hostile Hindu groups.

Mention should also be made of traditions of Shaiva ascetics, called "Yogis," "Nath Yogi-s," "Kanphata Yogi-s," or "Gorakhnathi Yogi-s." They were followers of Tantric *yoga* and *hatha-yoga* ("exertion discipline") and appear to be related to older traditions of both Hindu (Kapalika and Kalamukha Shaiva groups) and Buddhist (Vajrayana or "Diamond Vehicle") Tantric traditions from the preceding Indic period. They are traceable to two founding figures, Matsyendranath and Gorakhnath (in Sanskrit: Gorakshanatha), who lived somewhere between the ninth and twelfth centuries either in the Punjab or far North-West region or in the North-East in the area of Bengal, both of which regions, interestingly, were centers for Tantric traditions. The Nath Yogi-s are called "Kanphata" ("ear-split" in Hindi) because of the practice of cutting the cartilege in the ears in order to hold the large earrings that the cult followers wear.

The focus in these Shaiva ascetic groups is on becoming a "master" (*natha*) or "perfected" Yogin (*siddha*) by making use of magico-religious rituals (including alchemical, occult and erotic ritual performances) and extreme Yogic exertions of posture and breathing. They were largely low-caste groups and paid little attention to caste rules. They became widely prevalent as magic-workers and healers on a popular level in North and Central India between the twelfth and fifteenth centuries, and they seem to have interacted easily with Sufi Shaykhs and Pirs, possibly because of their low caste status and their general indifference to issues of caste.

Of much greater significance for the development of Hindu traditions in the Indo-Islamic period is the remarkable increase in devotional Hindu spirituality or *bhakti*. Here again the antecedents can be traced back many centuries, to the Indo-Shramanical period when hero-cults and local devotional traditions appeared for the first time alongside of the Indo-Brahmanical Vedic system and to such texts as the famous *Bhagavad-gita* in the Indic period which represented the first major theoretical statement about devotion or *bhakti* as a form of *yoga* (*bhakti-yoga*) within an Indo-Brahmanical context (but also clearly under the influence of Indo-Shramanical traditions).

Traditions of *bhakti* developed further with the emergence of the Tamil poet-saints of South India, already discussed earlier, both Vaishnava and Shaiva (called Alvars and Nayanar-s respectively), whose exuberant devotional piety spreads from the Tamil country to Kannada-speaking Karnataka, thence to Marathi-speaking Maharashtra and finally finds its way to the Gujarati-Hindi, Punjabi and Bengali regions of the North-West, North Central and North-East regions. These devotional traditions utilize the local vernacular language rather than Sanskrit, are frequently open to all castes, even low and untouchable groups, avoid excessive ritualism and have for the most part a clear anti-*brahmanical* bias. They represent, in other words, many of the characteristics of the old Indo-Shramanical traditions and indeed may be interpreted as the equivalent of those older traditions in the Indo-Islamic period.

Mention should perhaps also be made to the Lingayats ("wearers of the phallic stone," one of the prime symbols of Lord Shiva) or Virashaivas (devotees of "Shiva the virile one"), a Hindu group, founded by a certain Basavanna in the twelfth century in what is now Karnataka in South India, with its exuberant devotional poetry to Lord Shiva in the regional language of Kannada. Like their Tamil counterparts, Lingayats or Virashaivas also rejected the caste system, eventually coming to be considered in later times a caste-sect.

These older traditions of devotional spirituality became much more intense all across North India, beginning in the fourteenth and fifteenth centuries and reaching a remarkable crescendo in the sixteenth century. This is unquestionably related in important respects to the growing presence of Islamic traditions, especially Sufi devotional mysticism that was spreading rapidly across North India through the medium of the various regional languages, although it is difficult to determine whether Sufi devotional mysticism influenced Hindu *bhakti* or vice versa. It could well be the case that both Sufi devotionalism and Hindu *bhakti* have a natural affinity for one another (possibly traceable ultimately to Indic influences on original Sufi traditions in Central Asia and eastern Iran) and that, therefore, there was simply a broad-based mutual interaction between these traditions in the fifteenth and sixteenth centuries and after.

One might also posit a Weberian elective affinity in the sense that it is hardly an accident that Sufi missionizing was especially effective in areas such as Kashmir, Bengal and those areas of the subcontinent under strong *bhakti* influence, and among low-caste peasants and artisans, areas and groups, in other words, in which the old Indo-Shramanical traditions had been especially prevalent. The devotional songs of Kabir, for example, the poet-saint weaver from the Hindu city of Varanasi, who lived in the late fourteenth or early fifteenth century and who appears to have had some sort of connection with Islam, either in terms of actually having been Muslim or of having been raised in a Hindu family recently converted to Islam, clearly combine Islamic (and probably Sufi) motifs, Hindu *bhakti* as well as Nath Yogi motifs together with a strong critique of the rigidities of both Islamic and Hindu traditions.

According to Hindu traditions, Kabir's guru on the Hindu *bhakti* side was the famed Vaishnava, Ramananda, credited with having brought the Rama cult and the Shri Vaishnava tradition of Ramanuja from the South to North

India. Ramananda settled in the city of Varanasi, supposedly turned away from the high caste orientation of the southern Shri Vaishnavas, developed a rich *bhakti* devotionalism centering on the repetition of the name of Rama, and accepted followers from all walks of life, including low castes, untouchables, women and even Muslims. He taught in the vernacular language (Hindi) and is the supposed founder of the largest Vaishnava ascetic community in North India, the Ramanandi-s, known as Vairagi-s ("renouncers"), who down to the present day have many monasteries in Varanasi, Ayodhya and elsewhere all across North India.

Whether Kabir was really a Muslim originally or whether Ramananda was his guru who taught him to use the vernacular and a *bhakti* devotionalism focussing on the repetition of the name, Rama, are historical issues that have not yet been satisfactorily settled, but the interesting combination of Islamic (Sufi) motifs, Hindu *bhakti* motifs and Nath Yogi references are clearly in the poetry regardless of how these traditions came together in Kabir's own life and training. A somewhat comparable conflation of Hindu, Muslim and Nath Yogi motifs may be found in the spirituality of Guru Nanak (1469 - 1539), the founder of the Sikh religion. Clearly the Sikh tradition's focus on one transcendent God and its rejection of the caste system (in theory if not always in practice) owes much to Islamic ideas, while its incorporation of Hindu devotional songs in its sacred scripture (the Adi Granth, the "Primal Book," or the Guru Granth Sahib, the "Book of the Lord," compiled by Guru Arjan in 1603-04) shows clear influence from the Hindu side. In the final analysis, however, the Sikh tradition is itself a distinct religious tradition that differs from both Islamic and Hindu traditions.

Or again, the untouchable shoemaker, Ravidas (ca., sixteenth century), like Kabir from the city of Varanasi, represents a form of devotional theism that does not quite fit either Hindu or Islamic patterns completely, but owes much to both. Interestingly, all three poet-saints, that is to say, Kabir, Nanak and Ravidas are considered by tradition to be within the same lineage known as the "*sant*" tradition. The term *sant* (a participle from the root *as*, "to be") comes to mean something like a "truly authentic being," or, in other words, a "good or holy person," and the "*sant*-s" are said to be proponents of *bhakti* or "devotion" to the one transcendent God "without attributes" (*nirguna*). God, in other words, cannot be adequately represented in any form or by any particular name. Other forms of emergent *bhakti* are more identifiably Hindu, although they bear clear family resemblances to the composite Indo-Islamic devotionalism so characteristic of this period.

There are, for example, the Hindu poet-saints of Maharashtra, beginning with Jnanadeva and Namdev (ca., thirteenth century), continuing through the work of Eknath (ca., sixteenth century), reaching a high point in the exuberant devotional poetry of the famous Tukaram (1598 - 1649) and coming down to the present, with their intense devotional songs to the various regional forms of Krishna or Vishnu in the regional language of Marathi. In the medium of Hindi in North India, there is Surdas (1483 -1563) and the woman-saint Mirabai (1498 - 1546), both devotees of Krishna. There is, of course, also in Hindi in North India (in and around the city of Varanasi) the famous devotional poetry of Tulsidas (1532 - 1623), author of "The Spiritual Lake of the Acts of Rama," *Ramacaritmanas*, a Hindi version of the famous old Sanskrit epic, *Ramayana*.

Most Hindus who are followers of Rama (and hence also Vaishnavas) are much more familiar with Tulsidas's Hindi version of the *Ramayana* than they are with the older, elitist Sanskrit version. In the North-East region of Bengal, there is the famous Caitanya (1486 - 1533), the great exponent of the Gaudiya Vaishnava tradition (or simply the Bengal Vaishnava tradition), the emotional and expressive devotionalism in the regional language of Bengali (but also utilizing a good deal of Sanskrit as well), focussing on devotion to Krishna and his consort, Radha. Those followers of *bhakti* who believe that God can be named and represented in a specific form, as, for example, Surdas, Mirabai, Tulsidas, *et al.*, are said to belong to the lineage known as "devotion" (*bhakti*) to the one God "with attributes" (*saguna*).

Regarding the overall assessment of the impact of Islam on Indic culture in this period, there have tended to be two seemingly divergent views. On the one hand, there are those who point out the huge gap between the learned Islamic and the learned Indic traditions. On the other hand, there are those who point out the remarkable synthesis that occurs on the practical levels of everyday life. Undoubtedly, there is more than a little truth in both perspectives. The encounter of the Old Indic with the coming of the first phase of the New Indic, though exceedingly painful on many levels, also generated one of the great cultural flowerings in the history of civilization. The program in Indo-Muslim Culture deals with the Islamic cultures and literatures of South Asia, a region that is home to the largest population of Muslims in the world.

The first program of its kind at any Western university, it was established in the late 1960s with generous assistance from the estate of Ozai Durrani, the inventor of Minute Rice, who was an ardent devotee of Urdu mystical poetry and the culture that nurtured it. Professor Annemarie Schimmel, the distinguished scholar of Islamic Studies, was appointed the first Professor of Indo-Muslim Culture in 1970. Studies of Indo-Muslim culture involve interdisciplinary course work spanning several related departments, most notably Sanskrit and Indian Studies, The Study of Religion, History and History of Art and Architecture. Since Indo-Muslim Culture is considered a specialization within the field of Arabic and Islamic Studies, students in the program often take many of their required courses from offerings in this field as well. Literary and religious traditions of South Asia, as well as their cross-relations with Indo-Muslim culture, form an important part of the programme.

Given the wide range of disciplines and subjects, graduate students in Indo-Muslim culture are encouraged to develop, in consultation with their faculty advisor, a program of study that best meets their individual interests. The core element of any program in this field is the study of Urdu language and literature to an advanced level. A wide variety of courses are offered, including several of which focus on literary history and specific literary genres, such as the ghazal. Special emphasis is also given to a solid knowledge of the Persian literary traditions without which it is impossible to understand medieval and contemporary South Asia. Depending on the individual program needs of students, some study of Arabic may also be necessary.

Qualified students may also be able to undertake independent study of Sindhi and Gujarati. Beyond studying languages and literatures, students are encouraged to take a wide range of courses related to the Islamic tradition offered at Harvard. Subjects include Islamic mysticism (Sufism), Islam and the arts, Islamic theology and law, Islamic philosophy, Islamic art and architecture, as well as history of Muslim societies in the Middle East and Central Asia. All students are strongly encouraged to enroll in Religion 1585: Islam in South Asia: Religion, Culture and Identity in South Asian Muslim Societies and Islamic Civilizations 241r: Approaches to Studying Indo-Muslim Culture and South Asian Islam.

In keeping with the common language requirement for all fields in NELC, students are also expected to demonstrate a reading knowledge of French and German. Students prepare four fields for the Ph.D. general examinations; two of these are required: Urdu language and literature and history of Islam in South Asia (Indo-Muslim Culture). The other two fields can be related to any subject within the framework of Islamic and/or South Asian studies and must be determined in consultation with the student's academic advisor.

It is possible for undergraduates to design their individual program in Indo-Muslim studies, involving at least two years of the study of Urdu language. Beyond the language requirement, undergraduates will be expected, with guidance from their advisor, to create a program of study selecting from a range of courses offered within the broader frame work of Islamic Studies and South Asian studies. Courses may be taken through NELC, or related departments, such as Sanskrit and Indian Studies and The Study of Religion. Undergraduates, who are interested in studying Urdu language and literature, without concentrating in Indo-Muslim studies, may be eligible for a language citation in Urdu if they study the language for two years beyond the first year.

9

The Hidden Science in Islam

The Hadith of the Prophet Muhammad (s.l.a.w.s.) shows His eagerness and openness to knowledge no matter who are the "owners" of this knowledge or the effort required to acquire it. He who received the Revelation urged His own people in many Hadiths and Qor'anic verses to devote themselves to the scientific knowledge of the Earth, the living beings and the heavens as well as knowledge of other cultures. As it is revealed, investigating the many fields of knowledge is the only way to reading the Signs (Ayat) of God. In a sense, Islam embraces all the cultures and ethnic groups as a "meta-culture" and a "meta-community", united in their diversity within a common faith and a common eagerness for knowledge. Paradoxically, Islamic civilisation did not particularly prosper in its birth place, instead it has blossomed when Muslims moved to other lands and merged with other cultures and civilisations: i.e. along the Silk Road, North Africa and southern Europe, especially Andalusia. On the other hand, the reader of the Qor'an can only be surprised by the many references to the universe, the heavens and the sun as "signs to those who know".

The rise of Islam was also the rise of Science and Culture – particularly Astronomy which reached a state of the art in terms of accurate observations, mathematical developments and instrumentation. One can only admire the web of astronomers and mathematicians from Baghdad, along the

Silk Road, to China and India: scholars driven by the "eagerness" for technical and mystical approach to knowledge. The Prophet Muhammad Himself travelled along the Silk Road.

When they followed the spirit of the Qor'an and the teaching of the Prophet Muhammad, Muslim scholars revivified the Greek legacy, they embraced and added their own touch to the Persian civilisation as well as Indian and Chinese cultures and technologies, diluting themselves in the reality they encountered. Unfortunately crossing swords for the sake of power and fanatic belief in religious values damaged the Islamic civilisation from outside (during the crusades and the Tatars invasion) and from inside (fratricide wars or hurub at-tawa'if).

Resistance to knowledge and scientific investigation emerged within Muslim groups well before Muslims developed catharsis and resistance to the "modern western" world as a reaction to the crusades and the many colonial aggressions. Securing political power by the rulers meant prohibiting philosophical and scientific investigations. However History has its own subconscious: as a result of the crusades and expulsion from Andalusia, Muslim rejection and resistance to Christianity is now associated with resistance to science and freedom of thought – assumed to be values of the "enemy" – although they are still "Signs of God for those who know".

This is shown nowadays in the difficulty that the Muslim community has to be involved in international research programs in Astronomy for instance (and Science in general) and its resistance to adopt standard international criteria even for the observation of the moon for religious purpose. The question that one might ask is how can a wounded civilization emerge from its wounds and recover its glory in (re)contributing to human knowledge? Recovering its golden role in developing astronomy at the international standard might be part of the process of healing the wounded subconscious of the Muslim community and to restore the damage done to the Islamic values in the name of a belief of which Islam is innocent. Pseudo scientist Muslims and theologians alike who are trying to glorify the Qor'an by making it "the Book of All Sciences" and by developing naive and simplistic emotional views on the Universe (to compete with modern views) are digging the tomb of the Islamic civilisation and throwing dark veils between Islam and scientific progress in one hand and Islam and other religions in the other hand.

Science and the Qur'an

Study of the different religions, whether monotheist or not, shows that every religion has its own cosmogony or representation of the universe on which its transcendent relation to God and nature is based. In the Old Testament, for instance, the chapter of Genesis defines for once the worldview of the Christian cosmogony (whether proven right or wrong by modern science) which has been central not only to the life of the church through centuries but it was certainly at the base of scientific methods and representations developed by the modern Christian world, admittedly or not. There is no such a specific chapter in the Qor'an but the reader can see that the Muslim cosmogony is referred to here and there in many Surats and that it is at the core of the relationship of the believer to God -"The God of the heavens and the Earth" and "The God of those who are in the heavens and those who are on Earth".

All the detailed descriptions of the origin of the universe, its fate and its content are given as "Signs to people of knowledge and faith" to read the work of God and His power and to testify for His Creation. Cosmogony in Islam is not only an attempt to describe the universe; it is also central to human knowledge. It is the path along which an individual develops his/her consciousness as being in the world, awareness of the complexity of the Creation, as well as his/

her consciousness in contributing in human progress: the universe is the 'place' where one witnesses the work of God. The privilege of being "witness" in this world goes through the capacity of being able to investigate the laws of nature and to reveal the hidden complexity of the manifested phenomena, not only through contemplation and prayers.

This is a very special feature of Islam and I think that it is at the basis of the development of Astronomy at the rise of Islam and during all the centuries of its golden era: the rise of modern Astronomy is not a simple revival of Greek or Indian Astronomy by Muslim scholars, but it is bodily connected to the spiritual inspiration that accompanied the rise of Islam. The Qor'an does not provide recipes of physical laws or mathematical solutions, but instead it inspires those who are open to its appeal to experience the process of contemplation / meditation / philosophical argumentation / technical measurement / mathematical proof / calculus / prediction / metaphysical speculation.

For instance the canon texts fix the number and the nature of the prayers, but they do not tell one how to compute technically the times of the prayers during the day and over the year. They also say that the motions of the planets, the moon and the stars are determined with exactitude, but they do not provide the law behind these motions nor how to compute them. However it is up to "those who know" to discover these laws and to develop the methods of how to compute them, as part of the process of honouring His power and the gift He gave us to witness His power. Muslims honoured the revealed message when they followed this line of inspiration and put into practice the transcendental dimension of knowledge. They were the symbol of a mystical state of being expressing itself through the empirical cognitive process of scientific knowledge.

The Exemplar Case of Al-Biruni

In my view, it is clear that in the case of Islam, mysticism has been central not only in promoting the "Love of God"

(Mahabbat Allah) but also in developing a transcendental relationship between the Being of the person and the Being of the world within a harmonious sphere of Faith and knowledge. This has been shown in many examples but I will focus on the case of al-Biruni, for illustration:

Abu Rayhan al-Biruni, born in 973 in Kath (now Kara-Kalpakskaya), was a student of the famous astronomer and mathematician Abu Nasr Mansur. He computed the latitude of Kath at the age of 17 and developed his own method of map projection at the age of 22. Political circumstances and civil wars in the region led him to leave to an unknown place, but he apparently worked with al-Khujandi, in Rayy (Iran), who had built an instrument in a nearby mountain to observe meridian transits of the sun near the solstices.

On 24 of May 997, al-Biruni observed an eclipse of the moon from Kath, and he had arranged with Abu'l-Wafa to observe it in Baghdad, deducing hence the difference in longitude between the two cities by comparing their timings. He wrote his works on the decimal system, the astrolabe, astronomical observations as well as metrology, astrology and history. He was sponsored by the rulers of Khawarazm Ali ibn Ma'mun and Abu'l Abbas Ma'mun, patrons of the Sciences, who allowed him to work with his teacher Abu Nasr Mansur, and to build an instrument to observe solar meridian transits at Jurjaniyya.

He was made a prisoner by the new ruler Mahmud who brought him in his military excursion to India. During this journey, Al-Biruni could make observations which allowed him to determine the latitudes of eleven towns around the Punjab and the borders of Kashmir. In his book "India" (Kitab al Hind) he describes the religion and philosophy of India, its caste system and marriage customs, as well as its systems of writing and numbers, the geography of the country, astronomy, astrology and the calendar. He translated Sanskrit literature into Arabic, and he was well read in original Sanskrit topics such as astrology, religion, grammar, mathematics, medicine, weights and measures. It is worth noting that al-Biruni was more aware of errors than Ptolemy was: Ptolemy had a biased use of observations - without telling the reader, which means for him that reliable observations were those that fitted best with his theory.

However al-Biruni discussed good as well as less reliable observations. He was also aware of rounded errors in calculations. His attitude towards scientific results was then a cornerstone of modern methodology where objectivity and honesty require analysis of errors and bias as the guarantee of the validity of the measurements made. Al-Biruni also measured the radius of the Earth to be about 6339.6 km, a value obtained in the West only in the 16th century. He has also made observations on the velocity of light and compared it to the velocity of sound, anticipating developments of modern physics in the nineteenth century. One of his comments was of great importance for modern cosmogony: he described the Milky Way as "... a collection of countless fragments of the nature of nebulous stars." He corresponded with Ibn Sina (Avicenna) about the nature of heat and light as well as on topics such as philosophy, astronomy and physics. He also corresponded with al-Sizji on the sine theorem.

Al-Biruni was a leading exponent of the experimental method and a great linguist. One of his main contributions to human thought was that he has shown that the development of science is part of a historical process. He showed no prejudice against any religion or race. Instead he could not see a worse sin than that of the Arab conquerors of Khwarazm who destroyed ancient texts. As a Muslim he made the following comment on Christianity which he considered the doctrine of forgiveness: "Upon my life, this is a noble philosophy, but the people of this world are not all philosophers ... And indeed, ever since Constantine the Victorious became a Christian, both sword and whip have been ever employed." This historical statement of Al- Biruni shows the drama experienced by Islam and its complex relation to Christianity.

Present Day Islam

The case of al-Biruni shows how a leading Muslim scholar could develop a rational experimental method and anticipate in setting a modern method in data analysis along with being open to world cultures, faiths and philosophies. His example and many others that we will not discuss here, are living figures of the high spiritual values brought by Islam, far from the dark image depicted by the media and that presents Islam and Muslims as the work of evil. One of the points that particularly attracts my attention as a contemporary Muslim scientist is the dialogue and communication that was going on between the Muslim scholars at that time, despite the poor means of communication, in comparison to modern times where communication is quasiabsent amongst Muslim scientists and intellectuals despite the fast means of communication (i.e. Internet, Telephone, Fax and Air travel).

This is one of the signs of decline of a community, despite all claims about the strength of the Muslim community and the so-called human relationships between Muslims. Certainly this situation does not reflect at all the teaching of the Qor'an and Prophet Muhammad, but the state of a mind that has gone astray. While, in the past, philosophical arguments as well as coordination of astronomical observations from a far distance, and arguments about their accuracy and their interpretation, were part of the life of the Muslim scholars, nowadays it is nearly impossible to witness Muslim scientists sharing these values even within the same country. It is nearly impossible for Muslim scientists to coordinate one single observational project, and my experience in astronomy showed me even more dramatic facts: nowadays there is not one single Muslim country able to predict an eclipse or to compute the rise of the moon crescent with enough accuracy to establish a well defined calendar, or to announce the good news of the beginning of Ramadan in a rational way.

The uncertainty of the observation of the Moon - between Muslim countries - is up to three days while landing robots on other planets of the solar system requires an accuracy of a fraction of a second. We are far from discussing the accuracy of the observations made by Muslim Astronomers centuries ago. What is even more scandalous is not the inaccuracy of the observations but the biased decisions of observations of the moon based on simple political decisions of every Muslim country. A methodological man like al-Biruni would not be pleased to see his data falsified in order to please a political or a theological decision, and nowadays no honest scientist can bear the frustration of such an experience. It is not surprising that this present day anti-creative situation is correlated to a decline of faith and the dominance of ignorance and obscurantism amongst Muslims; avoiding the effort of scientific investigation and turning the Qor'an into a magic book of all solutions and discoveries. This is a pathological situation that is not honouring the history of the Islamic civilization or the teaching of the Qor'an.

Despite the existence of scientific institutions in Muslim countries and their equipment with modern computing facilities, apart from some exceptions, there is an absence of a scientific culture and, as a consequence, there is a general rejection of scientific investigation as a long term investigation process. At their best, Muslim countries "buy" science and technology "clef en main", avoiding any real involvement in scientific research and evacuating hence any scientific debate amongst their own scientists or at the international level. The negative official discourse on the uselessness of fundamental research, for instance, has created a state of despair amongst young intelligent Muslim students who see no prospects in their future. After a past glory, the Muslim community is going through a phase of depression where it is out of touch with its own spiritual values and the universal values of art, literature, science and philosophy developed by its own scholars.

This shows that science and Islam are body and soul: faith belongs to those who seek knowledge, and the signs of God are revealed through inspiration and scientific investigation to those who work for them, as emphasized in the many Surats of the Qor'an. "Iqra'" (learn/read) is the word on which the revelation of Qor'an to Prophet Muhammad has been based, and it does not go without saying that this word has shaped the mind and creativity of Muslim scholars through centuries. The corollary of this fact is that when, in the name of protection of Islam, Muslim rulers started fighting knowledge by humiliating their own scholars, and submitting them to their own power for political and ideological interests, they were actually fighting the spirit of Islam in the name of their dark selfish interests: mystics are far from being interested in wars and political power, and by fighting mysticism Muslim leaders fought actually the core of Islam.

It is out of proportion to discuss here all the causes of the decline of the Islamic civilisation, but one can speculate that when Muslims lost their relation to the transcendent, and replaced it with a horizontal power, they lost faith, and missed the path that was opened to them in meeting the will of God through their own free will. It is not surprising to see the emergence of literalism as a reaction to this depressing situation, while none of the Muslim scholars of the golden era had ever thought of finding in the Qor'an an answer to the scientific problems they were investigating. Instead, they used empirical investigation, armed with engineering and mathematical methods, to measure, explain and argue.

Islam and the International Rules

The present circumstances show us that the Islamic world is trapped between official positions which are not always in favour of scientific development and support to scientists, and, the obscurantist movements, which are opposed to the official representatives of Islam, but with no suggestions other than the return to rigid religious practices and violence (Jihad) to impose restrictions on society and to escape from scientific investigation (Al Jihad al Akbar) which is the path leading to His light. The alternative (third) position which is honouring the golden era of Islam and honouring first of all the appeal to knowledge carried by Prophet Muhammad, in line with modernity and international research, is hardly heard of, when it is not viciously combated, because it requires change of mentalities and identification to the transcendent rather than to any human power pretending to speak in the name of God, be it official or corporatist.

It is the duty and responsibility of the Muslim community to make the decision, and to join international research programmes, in order to recover its place in the universal human development. This effort has to be carried out in all fields of creativity, and the field I am directly concerned with, especially for historical reasons, is Astronomy. Psychologically and from the didactic point of view, it is more positive to start in the area where Muslims have been best renowned for their expertise and methodology. The need for recovering a place in Astronomy is justified not only to join the international efforts in new scientific methods and technologies, but also to solve religious and cultural issues of interest to the Muslim community: i.e. solving the calendar problem, unifying the times of prayer and religious celebrations, and adapting them to the requirements of modern society.

It is clear, from the observation of the love and hate relationships between Islamic countries that the decision will not come from a specific Muslim country, but as a recommendation from Educational and Professional International Institutions, and under their coordination (i.e. the International Astronomical Union). One cannot believe that Muslim countries are still arguing about the methods of observation of the Moon while standard methods of observation, calculus and tables within well controlled errors, have been universally settled by the International Astronomical Union. Not to forget the fact that Astronomy is absent from our education curricula that are themselves crawling under endless chaotic reforms. Not acknowledging international standards and rules in this specific case will increase isolation of the Muslim community from the rest of the international community, and one must say that it is a bad sign for what is going on in the whole process of economic and scientific development

We live in a remarkable time, when deeply hidden spiritual knowledge & practices are now being publicly released. Great Spiritual Traditions around the world are making public much of their formerly secret knowledge, including in recent years the Mayan, Tibetan, Taoist and European Rosicrucian traditions. These world traditions are the caretakers of our birthright: our shared human legacy of accumulated spiritual wisdom. Perhaps the most fundamental — and essential — part of this spiritual knowledge is to know the actual patterns, the energy blueprints, which everything in creation is based on. Everything is based on a specific pattern; knowing that pattern unlocks the ability to make full practical use of it. This is true whether speaking of patterns of higher spiritual realities, psychological and behavior patterns, energetic patterns, or actual structures manifested in the physical world. Only through our knowing these spiritual and energetic patterns can we achieve our full potential: to become conscious, responsible creator beings in the world. In recent times, the term we use to describe these core spiritual, energetic, and physical blueprint patterns is Sacred Geometry.

New Science and Sacred Geometry Patterns

Alongside of the usual mathematical studies of modern science, there exists a thriving sub-culture of advanced scientists studying pure structural patterns as a key to everything from Nuclear Physics to Human Biology. I was surprised to find studies commissioned by Governments, and even by NATO, that analyzed the pure pattern information of natural systems. It became apparent to me that much of modern cutting-edge technology was coming out of these pattern studies. In Nano-technology — the new field in which human beings are now able to create any kind of matter, by creating structures at the molecular level — researchers were unsuccessful in their experiments until they studied the pure geometric patterns identified by the modern genius Buckminster Fuller. In gratitude, they named their early discoveries after him, such as the "Buckyball."

The foundation of all Life and all Creation is this geometric language in nature, which modern science is using to tap the powers of Nature in modern technology. All modern technology is based on the twin variables of SHAPE and MATERIAL; different shapes create different energetic effects, just as different materials offer a full spectrum of different useful energy qualities (energy expresses differently through metal electrical conductors than it does through wood, for example). One key to understand this hidden energy science of Sacred Geometry is: Shape is really a pattern of energy movement frozen in space, a pattern which nature gives a specific power.

As I saw how important this geometric language of nature is for modern science, it became obvious that some spiritual traditions have known parts of this information for thousands of years. Legends of ancient high cultures such as the Egyptian Temple Science indicate how advanced — and how secret — this information was in earlier times. Some patterns were known and used by every one of these traditions, while other patterns seemed to be safeguarded by a single group. For instance, the knowledge of the power of the number 19 was considered critical in Ancient Egypt; today only some groups in esoteric Islam appear to have fully inherited this knowledge. What was truly amazing to me, was how most of the patterns known and used in modern technology were also clearly known and used in ancient cultures. Over a period of 20 years, I was able to create Sacred Geometry courses in which I illustrate the large number of one-to-one matches between patterns used in spiritual traditions, and those used in modern technology.

One little-known example: the same geometric form known and kept very secret by the Greeks over 2500 years ago (because they said it could cause great destruction if misused) is shown in modern declassified military documents to be the *exact same shape used to create the world's first atomic bomb*. Similarly, Sacred Geometry patterns taught in the ancient schools as being related to Alchemy are the same as those found in modern technology to transmute chemical poisons to be harmless, even lethal toxins like Nerve Gas; these same alchemical patterns frozen in matter can destroy pollution, and are even present in your car's catalytic converter. As great as the achievements of modern technology are, they are creating pollution and death in many cases.

Modern science has rediscovered many of the patterns — blueprints of creation — known to the world's great spiritual traditions, but only in materialistic fragments; it desperately needs the holistic understanding and greater context the spiritual traditions have regarding these patterns, in order to create a technology which is healing and life-positive. The practical energy science used in the ancient spiritual traditions could create life-giving effects in a way described today as "magic" or "miraculous"; however, to paraphrase Arthur C. Clarke, 'Magic is what we call any science we do not understand.' This science was based on the knowledge of precise geometric energy blueprints within and behind all things, and the energy functions of these patterns. In Ancient Times, the Initiates of this great knowledge were called *The Masters of the Net'*.

Sacred Geometry Initiation

Modern Physics teaches that the essence of creation is not Matter (despite what you may have learned in school); it is actually a flexible geometric energy grid behind matter, the "Matrix of Space-Time." Matter actually *warps* this background space-time grid; you can find this illustrated metaphorically in many Physics texts, by a picture of a squared grid printed on a rubber sheet, distorted by the weight of a bowling ball on top of it (which represents, for instance, a planet distorting the space time matrix.) This same energetic Matrix of Creation was known in ancient times, when it was called THE NET. Similarly to how it is shown in modern physics texts, this NET of creation was shown as a squared grid, often metaphorically as a physical Net being used to catch birds or fish inside of it. Such illustrations were extremely common in ancient Egypt.

In cultures all over the world, the spiritual knowledge of this energetic NET (the geometric matrix both behind all of creation and within every created being) was one of the highest levels of their Temple Science and Spiritual Initiations. For instance, in India it was referred to as the "Jeweled Net of Indra", and was part of a detailed initiation system which included learning to activate the power potential (Shakti) within geometric forms in the 'Yantra' practice. In Egypt, the Initiates of this knowledge were known directly by the name *The Masters of the Net.* Below is a very short introduction to the appearance of the NET initiation in a series of Western cultures, leading up to the story of how this knowledge has appeared in a new form in Modern Egypt. Each of these cultures has a wealth of knowledge and practices which go beyond the brief descriptions below.

Ancient Egyp

Egyptian spiritual texts and Temple wall illustrations are filled with explicit references to the Net, and to the Initiation process of becoming a Master of these geometric energy patterns. Human Initiates are shown in Temple illustrations learning how to use Nets to "Catch and Cast Magic." The spiritual beings who serve the Initiator of the Egyptian Culture, called the "Baboons of Thoth", are shown casting their Nets into the water to catch fish; the hieroglyphic texts which accompany the illustrations give the true meaning of these Temple teachings. Their hieroglyphic texts refer to uninitiated human beings "caught in the Net" in the spiritual world after their Death, and not capable of free movement, whereas the Initiate understands the Net well enough to be able to use every part of the Net (all the geometric blueprints of Creation) and move freely in the spiritual world.

Thoth himself was shown on the Temple Wall at Karnak in the act of "stretching the cord", which is the act of moving from a spiritual center outwards in order to create forms in the physical 3-dimensions of space; the great hermetic Egyptologist Schwaller de Lubicz labeled this Temple illustration "Thoth, Master of the Net". Chapter 153 of the *Egyptian Book of the Dead* (in Ancient Egypt this text was known by the much more beautiful title *The Book of Coming Forth into the Light*) has a long description of every part of the Net which the Initiate has mastered. Having mastered the Net, the Initiate in the text constantly refers to himself as Osiris, having merged in Resonance with this divine being that has conquered death and knows how to navigate the higher spiritual realms. When the Egyptian high spiritual culture began to decline with foreign invasions, its knowledge went in two prominent directions: to the Jewish culture in Israel, and into the Greek tradition.

Net In the Jewish Kabbalah

One key representation of the NET of creation in the Jewish Kabbalah is called the "231 Gates": this arrays the 22 Flame Letters of the Hebrew Alphabet (each a divine force from the Godhead) around the periphery of a circle or sphere; a line of energy connects each letter with every other letter, creating the NET. This tradition also holds essential knowledge of the Energy Blueprint which creates the human being: the well-known 'Tree of Life'. However there are many layers of the Tree of Life which are not well-known. To give just one very important example, the Kabbalistic text *Sepher Yetzirah* ("The Book of Formation") emphasizes that the 22 letters of the Hebrew alphabet break up into three sets:

a. 3 "Mother Letters"
b. 7 "Double Letters" and
c. 12 "Elemental Letters"

What even most modern Kabbalists do not know, however, is that these numbers represent the actual coding pattern of the human subtle bodies. There are THREE key anchor positions for the human soul (astral body) at the head, heart, and hara (belly area). The human life body (etheric body) anchors at SEVEN positions, and the human physical body at TWELVE specific locations. This coding system — the secrets of which are also part of later medieval alchemical manuscripts — also includes details on the sources of power for these parts of the human subtle body, at the planetary and star levels. With this knowledge, now take a look at the well known Kabbalistic Tree of Life diagram (if you don't know it, a picture of it can easily be found on the internet): it has THREE horizontal lines, SEVEN vertical lines, and TWELVE diagonal lines. Within these sacred geometric patterns there are deep secrets of the spiritual construction — and potential healing — of every human being.

Ancient Greece

In Greece the NET was referred to very directly, as it was in Egypt. There was a famous Greek Gnostic text bearing the title of "The Net." Ancient Greek coins depict Apollo (the Sun Being) sitting on the Foundation Stone of Delphi; beneath him a Net of energy covers the Foundation Stone of this spiritual city. Interestingly, modern esoteric energy research has shown that the Sun does indeed create critical energetic networks and effects on the surface of the Earth. The term "The Net" was also integrated directly into the Greek temple designs. Greek (like Hebrew and other languages) has a system which exchanges every *letter* of the alphabet for a given *number*: the Greeks called this system 'Gematria.' Names thus have a specific vibratory number quality, in addition to the power of the vibrated sounds of the name. In Ancient Egypt the 'REN', the name of the person, was understood to be so important that it was considered to be one of the levels of the human subtle body.

The Egyptians and Greeks knew that the 'Names of Power' carry the true Vibrational Code of the being they name, and can access the power of that being through the Name. Just as similar sounds will resonate together (one tuning fork, struck and brought close to a second tuning fork of the same musical note, will create vibration in the second fork), so similar number qualities will resonate together also. A Greek Temple for example may have the name 'Apollo' translated into a number, and the name "The Net" also translated into a number, and those numbers become then a particular measurement used in designing the Temple. This hidden practice is also related to the power of specific sacred measurement systems — The Egyptian Royal Cubit, the Remen, etc. — used in the ancient world.

New Testament and Holy Grail Traditions

Spiritual references in the New Testament are derived directly from a combination of Jewish and Greek esoteric Initiation teachings. References to the NET can be found in the New Testament, and are also embedded in the later Holy Grail Tradition. Examples include Christ telling his disciples to cast their Nets into the ocean for a miraculous catch of fish; this is the same image as found in the aforementioned Egyptian temple wall illustrations of the Baboons of Thoth casting nets into the water, to catch the "fish" of human souls caught in the 'Net' of the geometric space-time energy matrix. Reference to their being precisely 153 fish caught in the Net is a direct reference to specific Sacred Geometric numbers taught in the Greek mysteries.

Islamic Tradition

Islam has extremely deep Spiritual Initiation teachings, which tragically are rarely represented in the media outside of the Middle East; as in Christianity, it is the intolerant fundamentalist sects which appear most often in the news. Islam actually contains within it many classical secrets from the Middle Eastern traditions, especially Ancient Egypt. One example is that Islam is one of the only world traditions to focus on the Power of the Holy Number 19. The power of the number 19 and its proper use was a fundamental teaching in the Ancient Egyptian Temple Science. One of the primary grids used in Ancient Egypt to lay out designs on the Temple walls was the grid based on 19 vertical divisions; this is known to Egyptologists, but they have no idea of the significance of this fact.

In brief, the number 19 is built into the spiritual blueprint of the human being and all of creation. It is related to an energetic grid surrounding every human being, which contains within it the precise positions and functions for all of the spiritual energy centers in the human being (not only chakras, but a large number of power centers not taught publicly by any tradition even today.) The Egyptian priesthood knew that the Grid of 19 was in reality the background of the human archetypal energy blueprint. They also knew that the correct use of the 19 in design (as 19 design elements, or by building the number into measurement and proportional systems in design) creates a very powerful emanation of beneficial energy; this is the Golden light often referenced in ancient Egyptian texts as essential for spiritual development and for consciousness after death.

European Rosicrucians

The true Rosicrucians have been caretakers and researchers of this ancient knowledge within modern Europe. The most advanced teachings from this tradition can be found in the over 350 volumes of books and collected lectures by

Dr. Rudolf Steiner (1861 — 1925), by far the most advanced Rosicrucian teacher ever to teach publicly. The Rosicrucian work preserves the knowledge of earlier cultures in Egypt, Greece, and Israel and translates them into a clear, concise form which uses our own cultural references rather than that of earlier cultures. It is within these Rosicrucian works from Steiner that one can find advanced information which is intentionally hidden in the earlier traditions; Steiner as a Rosicrucian knew that we are living in a time when the Mysteries need to be made public, as a natural step in human spiritual evolution.

To give just one example of the information revealed in his work: for thousands of years, initiation traditions have used the symbols of the five pointed (pentagram) and six pointed (hexagram) stars in public material to represent certain ideas; however they never taught the public the real energy science behind what these forms actually *are* and what they *do*. Steiner was teaching back in 1907 that the Pentagram actually exists as a key pattern within every human being's Etheric Body of life energy and the Hexagram in 3-Dimensions (commonly referred to today by Leonardo's term 'Star Tetrahedron' is one form of the human Astral Body. The five and six pointed stars (and many other important forms beyond them) were used in Initiation to resonate with higher beings & higher planes, to activate functions within the human subtle bodies, and for powerful spiritual protection.

Hidden Energy Science

Even from this very superficial overview, the Masters of the Net initiation tradition is of obvious importance for our own modern spiritual knowledge and practices. A true "Master of the Net" would not only clearly understand the divine principles and the Sacred Geometry Blueprints of Creation, but could also practically apply their knowledge and create any energy effect needed. The Unified Energy Science understands how any one (or all) of the different qualities of nature can be used to create a desired energy effect.

New Breakthrough in Modern Egypt

Some of the most important new developments in the teaching and practice of the true holistic energy science are now emerging from Egypt. Although still almost unknown in North America, a remarkable Egyptian Architect and Scientist have recently demonstrated the ability to detect, differentiate, manifest, and transmute the living energy qualities which create our world. The Architect is Dr. Ibrahim Karim of Cairo, who has developed an entire holistic science of energy quality which he has trademarked under the name of BioGeometry. His work only began to be made public in Egypt in the 1990's, following an astonishing series of scientific projects where he demonstrated the ability to create energetic effects considered 'theoretically impossible' by orthodox scientists.

Egyptian National Research Centre

Dr. Karim was brought to this advanced research facility run by the Egyptian Government, and challenged to alter the life functions in living organisms using only simple geometric forms. The assembled scientists and medical doctors at the Research Centre were shocked by the successful results. The report on the experiments issued by the Centre's Department of Microbial Chemistry stressed that, "Further experimentation on this type of interaction between the Bio-Geometrical shapes and a variety of microorganisms is a top priority... To me the essence of this type of interaction seems to surpass explanation through our traditional and classical knowledge in basic science."

The experiments were so successful that Dr. Karim was named the head of a special new research project at the Centre, studying the Effects of Geometric Forms on Life Processes.

Egyptian National Hepatitis C Research Project

Hepatitis C is rampant in Egypt and North Africa, leading to the Egyptian government sponsoring medical trials to determine the most effective remedies. Along with groups studying the effects of Interferon and other pharmaceuticals, one research group was given to Dr. Karim to use only BioGeometry geometric patterns with those patients. Dr. Karim gave each participant a special medallion he had developed, which was covered with geometric patterns he calls "BioSignatures"; these are 2-dimensional representations of the actual movements of energy within the human body which create life functions.

The magazine Egypt Today described the results of the Research Project: "Dean of Al Azhar University's faculty of Pharmacy, Taha Khalifa, invited Karim to take part in a National Research Project aimed at testing the available medication for Hepatitis C. Karim created a special aluminum laser-engraved chip which was used by 300 patients over a period of three months. The results were astounding, with the normalization of the liver enzymes of 90 percent of the users in contrast with the usual success range of 20 to 25 percent."

Project leader Dr. Khalifa also announced the successful results with BioGeometry on a national prime-time Egyptian television program. This television show revealed the existence of BioGeometry to the Egyptian public for the first time, and featured numerous patients from the BioGeometry control group of the Hepatitis C research project speaking about their experiences. Many of the patients on the program even brought with them their official medical records, proving that their blood now tested clean of Hepatitis C. That program and other television coverage elevated Dr. Karim to celebrity status in Egypt.

Vibrational Medicine Research

Reuters News Service distributed internationally an article on Dr. Karim's BioGeometry, including interviews with Egyptians who had experienced stunning transformations in their personal health. In one case they reported that: "...a 24-year old engineering student with a low platelet count had some reservations about the healing power of shapes.

But having undergone a $25,000 course of treatment in the United States and having had his spleen removed to no avail, he decided to try Karim's method. 'When I met Ibrahim he put a ring on my finger with a design print on it, then he gave me a medallion. At first I thought it was strange, but after all I'd been through I was prepared to give it a go,' he said. Overnight his platelet count went up to 35,000, and in four more days it soared to 250,000, he said."

Another interviewee in the article reported similar success with an entirely different problem: "Hassan Hafez Amin, 57, a retired marketing consultant with gout, says Karim's methods had worked where others had failed.'I went to Ibrahim with an open mind and he gave me a medallion inscribed with a geometric pattern to wear. In one month my uric acid levels decreased from 9 to 4.8,' he said."

Growing Crops—In Salt Water

Dr. Karim was invited to the Red Sea by Engineer Adel Ammar to see if he could find a way to use salt water for irrigation, rather than Red Sea farmers having to pay the high costs for desalinization. As reported by *Al-Ahram Weekly*, by integrating specific shapes into the water channels and containers Dr. Karim actually succeeded in growing Sweet Potatoes in Salt Water drawn straight from the Red Sea; yet another result which was theoretically impossible until he accomplished it.

Clearing Electro-Magnetic Stress Problems

After a powerful cellphone tower was put in the middle of the Swiss city of Hemberg, residents began to fall ill. Animals and birds were seen to leave the area, and those confined to pens suffered miscarriages; animals raised for food were found to have tumors when slaughtered. The problems got so bad that Swiss evening news programs showed pictures of local residents who had moved their beds down to their root cellars, to try to escape the Radiation effects. Dr. Karim was invited to help, and by using precise Geometric forms and BioGeometry techniques was able to clear the area of electro-stress problems. One Swiss newspaper called Dr. Karim the "Wonder-worker from Egypt."

Dr. Karim was so successful that the Hemberg town council gave Dr. Karim the Key to the City and demanded that the Swiss National Government implement similar BioGeometry corrections throughout the country. This led to Dr. Karim being invited to clear similar problems from the city of Hirschberg Switzerland, while being observed by Swiss government representatives; just as in Hemberg, the project was tremendously successful and was reported in newspapers and Television news programs across Switzerland.

Water Revitalization Research with Dr. Masaro Emoto

Dr. Karim is also good friends with the well-known Japanese Water Crystallization researcher Dr. Emoto. Emoto's HADO laboratory in Switzerland studied the effects of Dr. Karim's BioGeometry shapes and tools in improving water structure. They found perfect structures created in their water samples simply by having one of Dr. Karim's tools (known as a *BioGeometry Cube,* a modified Cube shape covered with specific energy patterns) in the same room as the water. Researchers also commented that Dr. Karim's BioGeometry created more consistent crystallization patterns than virtually anything else they have tested. Dr. Emoto joined Dr. Karim for an international press conference in Cairo, revealing photographs of the powerful structuring effects of BioGeometry patterns on water crystals.

This is only a very short list of Dr. Karim's successful projects: there are many more projects conducted with Government agencies, European Universities, Medical Doctors, etc. which is beyond the scope of this chapter. We should note that Dr. Karim, an Architect by profession and not a Medical Doctor, makes no medical claims for his work for obvious reasons. Instead, as he puts it, 'My job is to carry out an experiment with BioGeometrical shapes, demonstrate a fact, repeat this experiment until it becomes a scientific phenomenon, and allow specialists in every field to start research work.'"

Although still almost unknown in North America, Dr. Karim is having a powerful impact in the Middle East. He has been given his own Arabic language television show, broadcast on satellite throughout the Middle East; its title translates as "God Grant Me More Wisdom"; in it Dr. Karim teaches simple ways to improve one's life and transform the energetic environment around us using BioGeometry. Remarkably, BioGeometry is also now taught at the University level in Egypt for advanced Architecture students. In these courses students are shown how to design according to energetic principles, tie buildings into the Earth's own energy patterns as was done in the Sacred Design of ancient times (so that buildings act as living organs conducting the Earth energy through them, as was done with the Ancient Egyptian Temples), and much more.

Although beyond the scope of this chapter, I should note that the principles, patterns, and methods of his work are of amazing depth and power. I have found that Dr. Karim is willing to publicly teach highly practical, advanced energetic information which is literally not available anywhere else in the world. His system allows one to be able to directly detect, manifest, and transmute powerful energy qualities through the precise use of shapes, angles, proportions, movements, colors, and sounds. His work applies to energy balancing not only buildings, environmental areas, and objects, but also all living beings as well.

- *Sacred Geometry*: This is the foundation of knowledge, because it offers the principles of all creation in their most "packed" format. The Vesica training in Sacred Geometry includes the following sub-topics:
    - *Thoughtforms in the Mind of God*: the true unified origin of all Sacred Geometric Forms and

Principles. This is also connected to the meditative practices which allow us to directly perceive the Sacred Geometry patterns used in higher spiritual realms, and how they affect the physical world.

- *The "Divine Alphabet" of Shape*: Every major energy pattern in the world is like a letter in an alphabet. We can learn to read this Divine Alphabet the same as we learn to read an Earthly language as a child, one letter at a time. This is the true language of Creation, and the foundation for practical work by knowing the functions created by each pattern.
- *The Hidden Energy Science of Sacred Geometry*: The history of the "Masters of the Net" lineage, and the specific principles and practices behind the true Temple Science.
- *Vibrational Medicine*: The use of shape and pattern for healing living beings. This topic expands into the holistic use of all energy qualities in the world (not just shape but also angle, proportion, color, movement etc.) for health and healing.
- *Union of Spirit and Science*: The Sacred Geometric patterns which give power modern science and technology, and the expanded holistic understanding of the same patterns within the World's Great Spiritual Traditions. This is the common basis for both science and spirituality, and overcomes the painful split between these two fields which we find in modern culture.
- *Sacred Design*: The design principles and precise methods which create physical structures with optimal geometric and energetic qualities. This includes the drafting techniques of the last 5000 years of Sacred Architecture, including the "Masters of the Compass" Masonic traditions of different world cultures. Hidden within this design science are the keys to the human transformation of the

Earth to its next stage, a transformation process which the classical Masons called "The Royal Art."

- *Spiritual Initiation:* Every great world tradition teaches its initiates some aspects of Sacred Geometry, because it reveals the true patterns behind the Spiritual Creation of the World. Sacred Geometry is the true guide to understanding Spiritual Realities, Beings, and Forces. This field collects key principles taught in Spiritual Initiation Traditions around the world.
- *Biogeometry*: Hands-on training in the essential principles and practical methods used by Dr. Karim in his successful projects. This is a powerful, comprehensive foundation for a new Holistic Science of Energy. Techniques taught in the training can be applied to greatly benefit humans, animals, plants, locations, and/or buildings: it is truly a holistic science of energy balancing.

  This Vesica Training in BioGeometry is certified with Dr. Karim's Egyptian organization, and students completing Vesica's Foundation and Advanced level courses in Bio-Geometry qualify to attend trainings directly taught by Dr. Karim and his Egyptian experts. This includes the option to train directly with Egyptian senior instructors to become a Certified BioGeometry Practitioner.
- *Earth Studies*: Vesica offers an overview of key discoveries in modern holistic Earth studies, particularly discoveries from Europe which are almost unknown in North America. Includes the German rediscovery of the many varied Earth Energy Grids on the planet, modern Central European methods to heal the Earth, Russian and American discoveries of different Geometric patterns in the Earth Grid, French methods to test the energy qualities present at any location, etc.

- *Sacred Arts*: Development of the human body and soul through sacred movement, painting, music, etc. There are certain spiritual understandings which can only take place through active engagement in these sacred arts. The Vesica Institute includes courses in rare fields such as the European Roscrucian movement art of *Eurythmy*.
- *Vibrational Medicine Research*: Cutting edge principles and methods behind international Vibrational Medicine advances and includes sponsoring courses in the most advanced techniques, such as the highly effective application of precise light frequencies to human energy centers in the German Naturopathic science of *Colorpuncture*.
- *Global Esoteric Studies*: Universal spiritual principles found in multiple world traditions. This is every human being's inheritance of our accumulated spiritual knowledge, preserved by the generations before us. Vesica also offers special trainings in the knowledge of the European Rosicrucian tradition, which has collected the esoteric knowledge of the Western tradition (Egypt, Israel, Greece etc.) and puts it into clear modern concepts. All Vesica trainings leave the student completely independent; we do not ask students to "join" or believe in any particular world tradition, but leave them free to find the specific knowledge and practices which will be essential for their own spiritual journey.
- *Holistic Education Resources*: Materials for both childhood and adult education in the above areas includes extensive resources for home schooling children in Sacred Geometry and holistic sciences.

"Modern science directly implies that the world is organized strictly in accordance with mechanistic principles. There are no purpose principles whatsoever in nature. There are no gods and no designing forces that are rationally detectable. Second, modern science directly implies that there are no inherent moral or ethical laws, no absolute guiding principles for human society. Third, human beings are marvellously complex machines. The individual human becomes an ethical person by means of two primary mechanisms: heredity and environmental influences. Fourth, we must conclude that when we die that is the end of us."

"And they say: "What is there but our life in this world? We shall die and we live, and nothing but time can destroy us." But of that they have no knowledge: they merely conjecture:" The Holy Qur'an, Chapter 45, and Verse 24.

All the recorded information indicates that the evolutionists- or that are unconsciously evolutionists even though they do not name themselves so are in some kind of mental vicious circle. The most important factor that stops them from pondering deeper is their belief in the concept of 'modern science'. They regard modern science as absolute and true religion, and want to impose this view to all humankind. We can summarize this degenerate understanding: The referred people and the system of thought that shape their mentality impose that this 'scientific', in other words 'experimental' knowledge, is the unique guide for mankind. Experimental knowledge is the knowledge that can be proved or disproved through experiment: "Water freezes at 0ºC" is an example for experimental knowledge. You can make an experiment; get some water, cool it down until it freezes and find if it really freezes at 0ºC. In fact making experiments and observations, science is all what men do to learn about the universe they live in.

According to the evolutionists, experimental knowledge is the only guide of mankind. Even the abstract concepts like love, hate or sorrow can be observed through (psychological) experiments. The consequence of this thought is 'not believing in' things which cannot be proved through experiments and observations, or being systematically sceptic. This thought originated first with the 18th century Renaissance, formed the core of 19th century Positivism, and reflects all essential premises of materialism. According to this belief of science, all religious information is considered as unreal, and questionable. For this reason this materialistic understanding which adheres to modern science as the sole guide considers the existence of the Hereafter, and the existence of Allah, as questionable because they can neither be proved nor observed through an 'experiment'.

The evolutionists maintain the view that religion originated when science failed to provide explanations. Taking this as a fact, it is claimed that the ancient civilizations rationalized things which they could not explain through experiments with the "supernatural powers" - God in monotheist religions: "The more the field of experimental knowledge expands, the more the field of religious information lessens". According to the supporters of this belief, the time will come when everything in the Universe will be explained through experimental knowledge and observation, and the humankind will not need religion.

This positivist mentality that regards 'modern science' as the unique guide is very well summarized in its original source in the text of a free-mason lodge:

In every society with insufficient information, vain beliefs will command mankind for sure. These in fact demolish the freedom of soul and lead men to morality of fear and hope. Thinking of a person who behaves with the fear of God and hell, or the hope of heaven for every deed of his; is there any virtue and nobility in his behaviour? When the man ponders deep and attains the quality of discussing and criticising, he will then understand that mentioned fears and hopes are only the results of mystical imagination. In order to be saved from vain beliefs or ignorance, there is need to attain the principles of positive science and wisdom, and data: the prominent command and inclination of masonry.

This is the understanding that forces evolutionists to explain nature without accepting the existence of Allah in any case. If they happen to accept that nature is created and regulated by a Creator, then they would have to accept an explanation that cannot be proved through experimental knowledge. And this will absolutely cause their excommunication from 'modern science' which they take as religion. They will be regarded as a "transgressor" before their colleagues who devote themselves to this 'religion', because they accept knowledge other than experimental knowledge.

Before answering the above question, we should note the difference between 19th century positivism, and the cognition of science in the 20th century. Because, most people has the wrong understanding that the 19th century positivism is exaggerated, however in 20th century the required balance was established. The positivist thought summarized above, in fact, belongs to 19th century and lost its popularity within that century. With the impact of Einstein's Theory of Relativity, it has been comprehended that science is not an absolute guide that explains everything and, can never be. Various science-philosophers, especially Karl Popper, assert that science cannot explain everything and that it has a "field" and there also exists other fields apart from this.

A natural consequence of these arguments is this dull cliche: "Science and religion have their different fields, and should not interfere one another".

The idea behind this commonly used slogan actually still supports this experimental knowledge as "the most important guide". Only, this "most important guide" should not try to explain the fields of "metaphysics" left to religion. (And surely if there is any discovery that is conflicting religious teachings, science should be preferred, and supported.) Definitely there are some political and social consequences of this enlightened semi-positivism of the 20th century. This science-religion balance isolates humanity from religion, because humanity can be explained by "experimental knowledge and observation" and includes all political, economical, legal, and social regulations. There remain only two limited areas for religion which are personal ethics and belief. This thoroughly means the continuity of the New Secular Order established in the 19th century.

Moreover, New Secular Order, by giving this limited area to religion, created a "safety valve". The defenders of the new secular order now have the right and the chance to say "we are not against the true-religious people, in fact we love them." This "true religion" is the religion within the walls of the temple. In short, there is no basic difference between 20th century semi-positivism and 19th century positivism, like there is no basic difference between Auguste Comte and Karl Popper. Both models are in agreement that 'experimental knowledge' is more reliable than religious knowledge, the knowledge communicated by "revelation of Allah" to humankind. In both models 'modern science' is accepted to be the most important guide with the only difference that semi-positivism has made a more realistic evaluation, and left a small field for religion. This small difference provided an important benefit for them with a 'security valve'. But what was wrong with positivism or semi-positivism?

The Real Meaning of Science

To see the reasons why accepting science as the only guide is wrong, first it should be grasped what science is and what science is not. For the ones who support the idea that science is the guide, science is absolute, and independent from all the cultures, all ideologies and beliefs. According to this, science is the universal criteria different than all other sources of knowledge. It is the centre of everything, and everything should be regulated accordingly. The deception is at this point. Contrary to the propagation, there is no such constant and 'universal' science above religion, cultures and ideologies. Science is not a universal guide, contrarily, science is guided. The "paradigm" concept of American science philosopher Thomas Kuhn explains it clearly. According to Kuhn, who is not semi-positivist like Popper, all kind of science is built on a series of some presumptions.

The general theoretical conjectures, rules and technics that are made up by the people in science and their applications constitute "paradigm". Until a new scientific fact comes up, this paradigm will be valid, but later it will definitely collapse. For example Newton's scientific hypothesis is a scientific paradigm. With the rise of Einstein's paradigm that is valid today, Newton's paradigm lost its validity. This means: when a new scientific crisis appears, this paradigm will lose its validity too. The important point is that paradigms cannot be stated as a general law. Paradigm is nothing but conjecture that is accepted to be true for a temporary period of time. The scientists who take science as their guide and their followers accept a certain paradigm as being the absolute truth; hence in fact they take a conjecture as their guide. The Qur'an points out that the unbelievers:

"....follow nothing but conjecture and what their own souls desire!- Even though there has already come to them Guidance from their Lord!" The Holy Qur'an, Chapter 53, Verse 23.

According to Paul Feyerabend who went further than Thomas Kuhn, it is absolutely the result of a subjective preference to consider science as being superior to any other teaching that humankind has put forward. Therefore the government should give up the education policy that regards science as the guide and assumes it is superior to other branches. These final points show us that science is as "subjective" as any other belief or ideology, and that no paradigm can be accepted as the 'absolute'. Therefore, no one has the right to say "this is the truth discovered by science and all beliefs and thoughts should be evaluated in accordance with it".

The deception behind modern science is hidden here: "New Secular Order" has fixed a paradigm in modern science that fits its own ideology and imposes this produced science as "universal guide" to all cultures. This is offering the ideology with a label of science. The concept behind the basis of this paradigm in modern science is; in simple words "atheism". It is designed to explain the universe in a non-religious way and the aim is to create a society totally isolated from religion. The comment of American biologist Robert Shapiro on Michael Behe's book called Darwin's Black Box is a good example for the above mentioned paradigm. The microbiologist Behe has put forward a very concrete explanation for the basis of being alive: Intelligent design. However Shapiro does not accept this fact and explains his "scientific" attitude:

"Michael Behe has done a top notch job of explaining and illuminating one of the most vexing problems in biology: the origin of the complexity that permeates all of the life on the planet. Prof. Behe selects an answer that falls outside of science: the original creation of life by an intelligent designer. Many scientists, me included, will prefer to continue the search for an answer within science. Nonetheless, this book should be on the essential reading list of all those who are interested in the question of where we came from, as it presents the most through and clever presentation of the design argument that I have seen."

It is clear that the science that Shapiro and many other "scientists" rely upon, which is called "modern science", supports that it is absolutely not possible to accept life to be created. Because, this understanding of science has been developed to serve this purpose and to make people reject creation. As stated previously, the powers that established the New Secular Order insist the social-politic system to be anti-religious, and guide modern science to form the basis of this anti-religious socio-politic order.

This means that people take something they formed themselves as their guide; in other words they idolize it. This makes modern science an important idol of the modern age. This understanding has become so intensive, that even it has been accepted that everything should be approved by them. For example there are some "renaissance men" who claim that "Islam is not scientific". Their stand point is that some of the miracles of the Prophets cannot be explained with the rules of nature fixed by science. (As if the things that they call, "the rules of nature" are independent from Allah who creates the miracles.) Moreover, some of them deny the hereafter thinking that it is not "scientific". In spite of these, some naive ones defend and say "No, Islam is in line with science". However, the question is not that whether Islam is in line with science or not, but whether science is in line with Islam. What needs to be approved is science, not Islam.

Guide of Modern Science

We clearly state that we are not against science, in terms of the aim of learning and discovering the universe that people live in, we are against what is called "modern science" which accepts the New Secular Order as the guide. The information above explains that science cannot be a guide but contrarily, every belief and every ideology guides science in various ways. Science is neither a guide, nor an aim within itself, but only a tool - a tool that can be used in favour of an intention. At this step, an interesting point should be mentioned: the identity of the guide of modern science. Definitely the guide of the modern scientific teaching which was established to support the war against religion is the social powers that established the New Secular Order. However, there is also a "spiritual guide" of these social powers. And the real leader of modern science is this spiritual guide.

This is a well-known guide: Satan who has been struggling to isolate humankind from religion, since the beginning of history! In the article called *'The Scientific Way'* by Moiz Varon, one of the "masters" of the Turkish freemasonry lodges, the first time the Satan encouraged men to rebel against Allah was told as the 'the beginning of science and freedom':

"The humankind to become human started with a mysterious word: "NO". First rebel came from the woman. Man agreed and they chose freedom. They ate the "forbidden fruit", they knew they became conscious. They understood their sexes. With snake's words, they learned to differentiate between right and wrong, they became like God. The price of knowing was mortality and the price of freedom was responsibility."

It is possible to see these kinds of statements in masonry magazines between the lines. In another masonic source: "The torch of the Satan enlightens the darkness at the place where you reach" is stated while mentioning the basis of "renaissance" philosophy. According to this, Renaissance, regarded as the touchstone of modern science and secularism, obtains its lights from "the torch of the Satan". Michael Bakunin, one of the leaders of socialism is the person who expresses clearly this inclination in masonic teaching. Being a very senior free-mason, and as he names himself, being a "Satanist" he relied every "revolutionist" teaching including modern science on Satan's spiritual guidance. According to Bakunin, who regards Satan as "the spiritual leader of all revolutionists and the real guide for human freedom", Devil is the biggest rebel and the "saviour" in the struggle against Allah and religion in history. As the Qur'an informs, the Satan really owns the mission to dissociate people from religion.

The Satan has promised to make humankind transgress:

"He said: "Because you have thrown me out of the way! I will lie in wait for them on your straight way: "Then will I assault them from before them and behind them, from their right and their left: Nor will you find, in most of them, gratitude (for your mercies)." The Holy Qur'an, Chapter 7, Verses 16-17.

Modern science which finds its spiritual guidance in Satan, together with the evolution theory, being its most important component, are the biggest "traps" to make humankind transgress. This trap or deception that finds its spiritual guidance in Satan is supported by social powers that plan:

"A plot by day and by night: and order to be ungrateful to Allah and to attribute equals to Him!" The Holy Qur'an,

Chapter 34, Verse 33. If this modern science relies on such a basis, then we should get rid of this deception and achieve a holy understanding of science as soon as possible. Instead of a dogmatic understanding of non-existence of a creator, there should be an understanding that confirms the clear existence of Allah and searches for answers to explain "how the universe is created".

"They said: "Glory to You, of knowledge we have none, save what You Have taught us: "In truth it is You who are perfect in knowledge and wisdom." The Holy Qur'an, Chapter 2, Verse 32. What's more, Kuhn, a relativist, definitely does not accept that the people who put forth a paradigm are either objective or impartial. Kuhn, strongly opposing to the ones who claim that there should be unique, universal and standard criteria for advancement of science (especially to Imre Lakatos) states, "There is no standard higher than the ascent of the relevant community."

Kuhn again states that scientific information, like a language, is the intrinsically common characteristic of a certain group, and nothing more. Again according to Kuhn, there is need to know the common characteristics of the groups who create and use it (scientific knowledge). The important point here is that the concept used as society is indeed the people concerned in science. This is a certain proof that science cannot be accepted with no prejudice. Stating more clearly, Newton's paradigm is not independent from the beliefs and prejudices of the people defending Newton's scientific findings. Conseqently, it is not possible to accept science as objective.

With his book Against Method, Feyerabend who challenges the traditional pattern defends that all theories scientifically accepted as true will be discharged. Feyerabend summarizes this view with two words: "All goes!" Feyerabend expresses his view about the scientific view saying that the idea of science is unrealistic according to the universal and accepted rules. Feyerabend says it is unrealistic because it regards human instincts and the view which develops and reasons of it as too simple. It is to be destroyed because the attitude to keep up the rules is due to the professional improvements in our humanity. Feyerabend says, additionally the reason behind destruction of the idea of science is because the complex physical and historical conditions influencing scientific change being neglected. Feyerabend asserts that this makes science less compatible, but more dogmatic.

Feyerabend agreeing to Kuhn's relativity theory on determining criteria for science states that science has no superiority over other branches. He mentions that Lacatos confronts other fields once he completes the re-construction of modern science as if the structure of modern science is against magic and Aristotelian science. But there is no such argument. Wise approaches are considered to be basic scientific wisdom. However this does not evidence it has any higher wisdom than witches'. Feyerabend defending the view that the government should as well include other teachings in the education system since science has no superiority over other branches, states that people living in free societies own the freedom of deciding what to believe in with their own will. He expresses this with an example: while an American citizen can believe in religion he agrees, the students are not allowed to learn magic instead of science at school. Feyerabend says there is a distinction between state and science but no difference between science and state.

10

Sacred Music and Dance in Islam

In a discussion about music in the world of Islam, it is first important to distinguish that Muslims do not use the term "music" in the same manner employed in the English language and in other Western languages. The Arabic term for "music," *musiqa*, does not apply to all types of artistic vocal and instrumental arrangements of sounds or tones and rhythms; rather, the Muslims term this general cases "*handasah al sawt*," or "the art of sound." *Musiqa*, or "music," applies rather "only to particular genres of sound art and for the most part it has been designated for only those that have a "somewhat questionable or even disreputable status in Islamic culture."*Handasah al sawt*" is a recently coined term used by Muslims to separate their Islamic conception of "music" from that held in the Western and non-Islamic world, which, as we will see, often contrasts in very fundamental and critical ways.

In this chapter, it is my goal to study the influence of the Qur'an and Islamic religious beliefs on the role and realization of sound art in the world of Islam. My first step towards this end will be to look at the various ethical considerations that Muslims have made considering *handasah al sawt*. Next, I will look at how religious beliefs are manifested in the sound art itself. I will make comparisons, furthermore, to Western music where I am able. I believe many similarities exist between *handasah al sawt* and various examples from contemporary Western art music, especially, and also certain forms of jazz. Such comparisons are made in the hope of making the "sound art" of the Islamic world more accessible and undertstandable not only to me but also to readers more familiar with developments in the musical world of the United States and of Europe.

Inadmissibility of Music in Islam

"The attitude toward music [in the world of Islam] has always been ambivalent, as expressed in a series of contradictory feelings and concepts: predilection and mistrust; divine-devilish; exalting-disruptive; admissible-prohibited". Views about the admissibility of music, or sound art, in the world of Islam run the gamut from complete negation to complete acceptance, even of dance. Many Muslims fear the "magical," intoxicating powers of music and prohibit it as a tool of the devil. Other Muslims, however, find music inspiring and entirely spiritual. Most Muslims fall somewhere in between these poles, restricting the practice of *handasah al sawt* to some degree but allowing it in various controlled forms. Like other legal judgements in the Muslim world, judgements about the admissibility of music must be based on the sacred writings or on analogy and not merely on individuals' *a priori* decisions or opinions.

Opponents and advocates of music, thus, base their arguments primarily on the (a.) Qur'an and on (b.) the *hadith* literature:

a. As for the Qur'an, nothing of it deals explicitly with the topic of music, though legalists and religious authorities have recourse to a couple verses that they believe have implications on the role of music. Opponents of music claim that "diverting talk" in verse XXXI: 5, refers to music: "There are some men who buy diverting talk to lead astray from the way of God". Those who approve of music, however, claim verse XXXV: 1, refers to a "beautiful voice": "He increases in His creatures that which He wills," and that verses XXXIX: 17-18 refer to singing: "So give good tidings to my servants who listen to *al-qawl* (the spoken word) and follow the fairest of it".

b. These Qur'anic arguments are somewhat far-fetched, though, with no explicit mention of music. Stronger support for or against music can be found in the *hadith* writings, which describe the traditions of the Prophet Muhammad. One *hadith* that is often used to defend the use of music is the story of two young girls performing song to a drum in Muhammad's wife A'isha's house. When Abu Bakr (later the first Muslim caliph) rebukes the girls for singing, Muhammad responds to "Let them alone". However, this same *hadith* is also used by Muslims to oppose the use of music: Abu Bakr had called the above singing "*mizmar al-shaytan* or reed-pipe of Satan and Ibn Umar had once seen Muhammad plug his ears when he heard the sound of *mizmar*. The *hadith* literature, then, like the Qur'an, fails to come to any definite conclusions regarding the role of music in Islam.

The main reason for Muslim reservations about music is that many believe it is a very powerful intoxicating force, capable of creating extreme excitement in listeners that can potentially cause them to lose control of their reason, diverting them from their devotional life and inviting sinful behavior: "...its maximal effect can send the listener into an emotional, even violent paroxysm.... This quasi-somnambulistic state is considered to be in contradiction to the exigencies of rational religious precepts". Such a state of trance, furthermore, is seen as false ecstacy and "a temptation of the devil that dominates the soul and makes it a slave of passion". These anti-music proponents of Islamic society point to music's lack of mention in the Qur'an as proof of its unimportance in life.

Muslims who have supported the use of music, on the other hand, include certain sects of the mystic Sufi Muslims, who believe that music impels a person to seek the spiritual world: "[Man's] soul, which originates in the world above, remembers its homeland [through music] and yearns to attain the state that would enable it to untie the knots binding it to matter, thereby facilitating mystical union with God". Rather than a temptation of the devil, music and dance are seen instead as manifestations of "infinite, ecstatis love of God." These Muslims argue that "the nature of music's influence on man very much depends on the basic intentions of the listener". Therefore, music is not inherently evil: rather, the listener's interpretation of musical experience can be evil. For this reason, these Sufis prohibit much of music for novices and noninitiates, who have not yet been saved from "the clutch of the carnal soul". Advanced gnostics, however, are permitted all forms of music and dance and find inspiration and divine beauty in them.

Questions as to the admissibility of music, it should be further noted, are not unique to the Islamic tradition: one can also find heated religious debate concerning the role of music in Western history as well. In the middle Ages, so-called Gregorian chant was formulated under strict rules of musical structure called "counterpoint" that had foundations in Catholic religious beliefs, restricting the use of certain musical intervals, like the tritone for example, for their supposed evocation of the devil. In ancient times, also, Plato had mapped out certain musical modes and scales in his *Republic* that were considered illegal for evoking certain undesirable and dangerous kinds of emotions. St. Augustine, furthermore, a Christian ascetic, had spent much focus trying to define the point at which music distracts the listener from reflection of God, at which point music thus becomes sinful.

Religious Manifestation in Islamic Sound Art

Regardless of the admissibility or not of music in the Islamic world, however, Islamic music usually strives to realize and express as much as possible the ideas and beliefs of Islam as set down in the Qur'an. Qur'anic chant, for example, can be seen as the prototype of all Islamic music and the most pervasive genre of Islamic sound art. The point of much music in the Islamic world is, therefore, to express and encapsulate the most important concept of the Qur'an: *tawhid*, or "unity with God." We will look at the various devices that Muslims use to express *tawhid*, but in sum these characteristics can all be described as forms of abstraction: "Since *tawhid* teaches that God cannot be identified with any object or being from nature, He cannot be musically associated with sounds that arouse psychological or kinesthetic correspondences to beings, events, objects, or ideas within nature".

Thus, Islamic music must be nonprogrammatic and must not create events that would evoke or express extra-musical ideas that are associated with human emotions, human problems, or earthly/natural occurrences: "We refer to the saying of the Prophet in which he condemned artists who try to 'ape' the creation of God: in their afterlife they will be ordered to give life to their works and will suffer from their incapacity to do so" (Burckhardt, 1987).

Such abstraction can also be readily perceived in Islamic art—"arabesque" art, for example, which never depicts images of humans, animals, or the natural world, but instead focuses solely on the creation of patterns. The point of abstraction in both Islamic art and music is to avoid focus on worldly concerns, which are of no value and only distracts man from focus on God: "Islamic art corroborates a void with abstract forms... instead of ensnaring the mind and dragging it into some imaginary world, it dissolves mental 'coagulations,' just as the contemplation of a stream of water, or a flame, or of leaves trembling in the wind can detach the consciousness from its inward 'idols.' This void which Islamic art creates by its static, impersonal and anonymous quality enables man to be entirely himself, to repose in his ontological centre" (Burckhardt, 1987; italics added). Rather than be transformed and defined by his own art, in other words, man without images of himself can remain more pure and uninhibited from contemplating God.

A good comparison to Western music that displays a similar "impersonal and anonymous quality" is the music of "bebop," which is a special type of jazz created in the 1950s. Jazz is often perceived as a music of passion and energy, but, as described by 20th-century German composer Louis Andriessen, bebop is a very "cold," or impersonal, style of jazz: "This is very important: you think bebop is hot, but it's cold msuic. You can hear this more clearly listening to Miles Davis than to Dizzy Gillespie. But Charlie Parker most of all: he had an enormous distance from his musical material. I call that classicism, in that it's contradictory to romanticism. Romanticism takes you by the hand and leads you to another world; classicism has a certain distance always from the musical object...."

To continue on the point of abstraction, however, not only does the music of Islam try to detach itself from the world, the musician himself in Islamic music tries to detach himself from his music: "The Moslem artist, by his very islam, his 'surrender' to the Divine Law, is always aware of the fact that it is not he who produces or invents beauty, but that a work of art is beautiful to the degree that it obeys the cosmic order and therefore reflects universal beauty" (Burckhardt, 1987). Again, it is Western Romanticism that had created the notions of "individuality," "genius," and "masterpieces" and had thus placed prime importance on the creator of music and art rather than on the creation itself.

However, this is a relatively recent development in the history of Western music (late 18th century), and such principles had not been the *modus operandi* beforehand in the Classical and Baroque eras and nor are they held in most of modern art music in the West, though they may persist in mainstream styles of music. Rather, detachment of the artist from his/her creation, as described of Islamic culture in the above quote, was and has again become the primary focus of Western creation. For example, let us consider the following quote: "For the Moslem mind, art reminds man of God when it is as impersonal as the laws that govern the movement of the heavenly spheres" (Burckhardt, 1987). An excellent literal interpretation of this quote in Western music are the *Freeman Etudes* of American 20th-century composer John Cage, which are based on no other principle than the alignment of stars on star charts!

The points of stars on the star charts are mapped directly into pitches of music in the composer's attempt to remove/detach himself from his own composition, which fully embodies the aim of abstraction also found in Islamic music. In recent Western musical movements like serialism, furthermore, music is created solely through the realization of predefined mathematical systems with the same aim of removing the composer from the act of composition and defining beauty in abstract, unhuman ways rather than on the emotive a priori decisions of the composer. One realization of abstraction in Islamic music is the absence of descriptive titles. Rather than give titles to musical pieces that evoke worldly images, Muslims mostly entitle their works based on the modes, or scales, that the music is based on (e.g. Hossein 'Omoumi's *Dastgah-e Homayun; dastgah* means modal system and *homayun* is one type of modal system). This is similar to much of serial music in the West, which has generally numeric titles (e.g. Karlheinz Stockhausen's *Klaveirstucke XI*) or titles that evoke simple abstract and non-emotive principles.

Another realization of abstraction in Islamic music is its use of form, which is non-developmental, or static. Often no perceivable beginning or ending exists to the music, or any apparent large-scale changes in between: "Instead of exhibiting a developmental form with steady evolution toward one overall climax and a conclusive ending, the sound art performance of Islamic culture defies its experience as a single unity.... It is a dynamism that activates the human mind with the discovery of beautiful patterns that stimulates the contemplation of a greater cause that leads it from concern for mundane matters and personal problems to a higher reality".

A good example of static, non-developmental form in Western music can be found on the record Free Jazz (1964) by free jazz musician/composer Ornette Coleman, about which has been written the following: "Despite an abundance of motivic interaction, the overall character of Free Jazz must be called static rather than dynamic. Only rarely do emotional climaxes occur, and there is hardly any differentiation of expression. The wealth of musical ideas and the continuous exchange of thoughts take place on an unvarying expressive level.... It may be that Coleman set out to create a statical, homogenous whole...." Another example of "static" Western music is that of today's techno, ambient, or trance electronic music, which often tries to create soundspaces for meditative listening rather than to create a musical narrative that must be heard from beginning to end, such as in the music of one of its important founders, Brian Eno.

The example of Ornette Coleman's Free Jazz brings up other similarities with abstractive techniques employed in Islamic music as well. Just as there is "hardly any differentiation of expression" in the Free Jazz composition, so too there is highly limited dynamism in Islamic music. Melodic and rhythmic elaboration is confined to small segments of musical scales, often encompassing no more than four or five tones (al Faruqi, 1986). Intervals of more than a third rarely occur, motivic materials are usually very short in content, and changes in dynamic level (loud vs. soft) are very minimal if at all present (al Faruqi, 1986). And just as "a wealth of musical ideas" exists in Coleman's Free Jazz piece, so too Islamic music is often very ornate and intricate: "Patterns can more effectively attract the attention and concentration of the listener if they are sufficiently involved and complex".

Muslims create intricacy with extremely melismatic melodic lines and ornamental rhythmic figures, extensive use of trills and slides from one pitch to another, durational ornaments such as constant shifts of accent and tempo changes, and also in dividing the octave into more than twelve tones so as to include several microtones in between them. The extreme nature of this intricacy is used to steal focus from any single line of development and thus to strengthen the abstract and nondevelopmental form of the music. The lack of single themes and their elaboration and the lack of fixed meter "explains why foreign listeners unfamiliar with this music sometimes regard [Islamic music] as formless improvisation". Free Jazz has met with similar criticism.

Other techniques that Muslims use to realize abstraction and thus *tawhid* are extensive use of repetition and the creation of infinite patterns. From single notes, to motives, to whole sections of music, outstanding usage of repetition is characteristic to Islamic music. This repetition is used to evoke a sense of the eternal and thus the divine: "Extensive use of repetitions is not the result of a poverty of musical ideas... instead it is a structural feature necessary for the creation of infinite patterns. Repetition denies individualization, but also contributes to the never-ending quality that the aesthetic expression of *tawhid* should manifest".

Examples of extensive use of repetition are also abundant in modern Western art music, especially in a movement known as "minimalism" that employs "minimal" use of musical materials in repetitive ways that change very little (note: limited dynamism, as in Islamic music) and try to thereby recapture the essence and meaning of musical materials in Western music: composer like Louis Andriessen, Steve Reich, Philip Glass, and Terry Riley to name a few. 20th-century French composer Olivier Messiaen, furthermore, was especially intrigued with the creation of "infinite patterns," as in his piece entitled *The Crystal Liturgy,* in which mechanisms of repetitions would take nearly two hours to get back to its starting state. Messiaen had a "concern with time beyond time—with the presence of the eternal in the transitory" (Messiaen, 1979), which is derived from his strong Catholic beliefs and focus on God, much in the way the Islamic ideal of *tawhid* influences Islamic music.

In sum, most Muslim musicians employ various techniques of abstraction to instill a fundamental sense of *tawhid* in their music, or "sound art" (*handasah al sawt*). Though the Western world does not explicitly refer to *tawhid* or to "unity with God" in their music, furthermore, similar abstractions can be seen to operate in much of Western music as well, outside of Romanticism and wherever its influence continues. Religion does play an important role on music throughout Western history, however, and both Islam and the Catholic Church have idependently debated music's very admissibility in light of their worship of God. The heart of man has been so constituted by the Almighty that, like a flint, it contains a hidden fire which is evoked by music and harmony, and renders man beside himself with ecstasy.

These harmonies are echoes of that higher world of beauty which we call the world of spirits; they remind man of his relationship to that world, and produce in him an emotion so deep and strange that he himself is powerless to explain it. The effect of music and dancing is deeper in proportion as the natures on which they act are simple and prone to emotion; they fan into a flame whatever love is already dormant in the heart, whether it be earthly and sensual, or divine and spiritual. Accordingly there has been much dispute among theologians as to the lawfulness of music and dancing regarded as religious exercises. One sect, the Zahirites, holding that God is altogether incommensurable with man, deny the possibility of man's really feeling love to God, and say that be can only love those of his own species.

If he does feel what he thinks is love to his Creator they say it is a mere projection, or shadow cast by his own fantasy, or a reflection of love to the creature; music and dancing, according to them, have only to do with creature love, and are therefore unlawful as religious exercises. If we ask them what is the meaning of that "love to God" which is enjoined by the religious law, they reply that it means obedience and worship. At present we content ourselves with saying that music and dancing do not put into the heart what is not there already, but only fan into flame dormant emotions. Therefore if a man has in his heart that loves to God which the Law enjoins, it is perfectly lawful, nay, laudable in him to take part in exercises which promote it. On the other hand, if his heart is full of sensual desires, music and dancing will only increase them, and are therefore unlawful for him. While, if he listens to them merely as a matter of amusement, they are neither lawful nor unlawful, but indifferent.

For the mere fact that they are pleasant does not make them unlawful, any, more than the pleasure of listening to the singing of birds or looking at green grass and running water is unlawful. The innocent character of music and dancing, regarded merely as a pastime, is also corroborated by an authentic tradition which we have from the Lady Ayesha, who narrates: "One festival-day some negroes, were performing in a mosque. The Prophet said to me, 'Do you wish to see them?' Accordingly he lifted me up with his own blessed hand, and I looked on so long that he said more than once, 'Haven't you had enough'?" Another tradition from the Lady Ayesha is as follows: "One festival-day, two girls came to my house and began to play and sing. The Prophet came in and lay down on the couch, turning his face away. Presently Abu Bakr entered, and, seeing the girls playing, exclaimed, 'What the pipe of Satan in the Prophet's house!' Whereupon the Prophet turned and said, 'Let them alone, Abu Bakr, for this is a festival-day.'"

Passing over the cases where music and dancing rouse into a flame evil desires already dormant in the heart, we come to those cases where they are quite lawful. Such are those of the pilgrims who celebrate the glories of the House of God at Mecca in song, and thus incite others to go on pilgrimage, and of minstrels whose music and songs stir up martial ardour in the breasts of their auditors and incite them to fight against the infidels. Similarly, mournful music which excites sorrow for sin and failure in the religious life is lawful; of this nature was the music of David. But dirges which increase sorrow for the dead are not lawful, for it is written in the Koran, "Despair not over what you have lost." On the other hand, joyful music at weddings and feasts and on such occasions as a circumcision or the return from a journey is lawful.

We come now to the purely religious use of music and dancing: such is that of the Sufis, who by this means stir up in themselves greater love towards God, and, by means of music, often obtain spiritual visions and ecstasies, their heart becoming in this condition as clean as silver in the flame of a furnace, and attaining a degree of purity which could never be attained by any amount of mere outward austerities. The Sufi then becomes so keenly aware of his relationship to the spiritual world that he loses all consciousness of this world, and often falls down senseless.

It is not, however, lawful for the aspirant to Sufism to take part in this mystical dancing without the permission of his "Pir," or spiritual director. It is related of the Sheikh Abu'l Qasim Girgani that, when one of his disciples requested leave to take part in such a dance, he said, "Keep a strict fast for three days; then let them cook for you tempting dishes; if, then, you still prefer the 'dance,' you may take part in it." The disciple, however, whose heart is not thoroughly purged from earthly desires, though he may have obtained some glimpse of the mystics' path, should be forbidden by his director to take part in such dances, as they will do him more harm than good.

Those who deny the reality of the ecstasies and other spiritual experiences of the Sufis merely betray their own narrow-mindedness and shallow insight. Some allowance, however, must be made for them, for it is as difficult to believe in the reality of states of which one has no personal experience as it is for a blind man to understand the pleasure of looking at green, grass and running water, or for a child to comprehend the pleasure of exercising sovereignty. A wise man, though he himself may have no experience of those states, will not therefore deny their reality, for what folly can be greater than his who denies the reality of a thing merely because he himself has not experienced it! Of such people it is written in the Koran, "Those who have not the guidance will say, 'This is a manifest imposture.'"

As regards the erotic poetry which is recited in Sufi gatherings, and to which people sometimes make objection, we must remember that, when in such poetry mention is made of separation from or union with the beloved, the Sufi, who is an adept in the love of God, applies such expressions to separation from or union with Him. Similarly, "dark locks" are taken to, signify the darkness of unbelief; "the brightness of the face," the light of faith, and drunkenness the Sufi's ecstasy. Take, for instance, the verse:

Thou may'st measure out thousands of measures of wine,
But, till thou drink it, no joy is thine.

By this the writer means that the true delights, of religion cannot be reached by way of formal instruction, but by felt attraction and desire. A man may converse much and write volumes concerning love, faith, piety, and so forth, and blacken paper to any extent, but till he himself possesses these attributes all this will do him no good. Thus, those who find fault with the Sufis for being powerfully affected, even to, ecstasy, by these and similar verses, are merely shallow and uncharitable. Even camels are sometimes so powerfully affected by the Arab-songs of their drivers that they will run rapidly, bearing heavy burdens, till they fall down in a state of exhaustion.

The Sufi hearer, however, is in danger of blasphemy if he applies some of the verses which he hears to God. For instance, if he hears such a verse as "Thou art changed from thy former inclination," he must not apply it to God, who cannot change, but to himself and his own variations of mood. God is like the sun, which is always shining, but sometimes for us His light is eclipsed by some object which intervenes between us and Him. Regarding some adepts it is related that they attain to such a degree of ecstasy that they lose themselves in God. Such was the case with Sheikh Abu'l Hassan Nuri, who, on hearing a certain verse, fell into an ecstatic condition, and, coming into a field full of stalks of newly cut sugar-canes, ran about till his feet were wounded and bleeding, and, not long afterwards, expired. In such cases some have supposed that there occurs an actual descent of Deity into humanity, but this would be as great a mistake as that of one who, having for the first time seen his reflection in a mirror, should suppose that, somehow or other, he had become incorporated with the mirror, or that the red-and-white hues which the mirror reflects were qualities inherent in it.

The states of ecstasy into which the Sufis fall vary according to the emotions which predominate in them—love, fear, desire, repentance, etc. These states, as we have mentioned above, are often the result not only of hearing verses of the Koran, but erotic poetry. Some have objected to the reciting of poetry, as well as of the Koran, on these occasions; but it should be remembered that all the verses of the Koran are not adapted to stir the emotions—such, for instance, as that which commands that a man should leave his mother the sixth part of his property and his sister the half, or that which orders that a widow must wait four months after the death of her husband before becoming espoused to another man. The natures which can be thrown in to religious ecstasy by the recital of such verses are peculiarly sensitive and very rare.

Another reason for the use of poetry as well as of the Koran on these occasions is that people are so familiar with the Koran, many even knowing it by heart, that the effect of it has been dulled by constant repetition. One cannot be always quoting new verses of the Koran as one can of poetry.

Once, when some wild Arabs were hearing the Koran for the first time and were strongly moved by it, Abu-Bakr said to them, "We were once like you, but our hearts have grown hard," meaning that the Koran loses some of its effect on those familiar with it. For the same reason the Caliph Omar used to command the pilgrims to Mecca to leave it quickly, "For," he said, "I fear if you grow too familiar with the Holy City the awe of it will depart from your hearts."

There is, moreover, something pertaining to the light and frivolous, at least in the eyes of the common people, in the use of singing and musical instruments, such as the pipe and drum, and it is not befitting that the majesty of the Koran should be, even temporarily, associated with these things. It is related of the Prophet that once, when he entered the house of Rabia, the daughter of Mauz, some singing-girls who, were there began extemporising in his honour. He abruptly bade them cease, as the praise of the Prophet was too sacred a theme to be treated in that way. There is also some danger, if verses of the Koran are exclusively used, that, the hearers should attach to them some private interpretation of their own, and this is unlawful. On the other hand, no harm attaches to interpreting lines of poetry in various ways, as it is not necessary to apply to a poem the same meaning which the author had.

Other features of these mystic dances are the bodily contortions and tearing of clothes with which they are sometimes accompanied. If these are the result of genuine ecstatic conditions there is nothing to be said against them, but if they are self-conscious and deliberate on the part of those who wish to appear "adepts," then they are merely acts of hypocrisy. In any case the more perfect adept is he who controls himself till he is absolutely obliged to give vent to his feelings. It is related of a certain youth who was a disciple of the Sheikh Junaid that, on hearing singing commence in an assembly of the Sufis, he could not restrain himself, but began to shriek in ecstasy. Junaid said to him, "If you do that again, don't remain in my company." After this the youth used to restrain himself on such occasions, but at last one, day his emotions were so powerfully stirred that, after long and forcible repression of them, he uttered a shriek and died.

To conclude: in holding these assemblies, regard must be had to time and place, and that no spectators come from unworthy motives. Those who participate in them should sit in silence, not looking at one another, but keeping their heads bent, as at prayer, and concentrating their minds on God. Each should watch for whatever may be revealed to his own heart, and not make any movements from mere self-conscious impulse. But if any one of them stands up in a state of genuine ecstasy all the rest should stand up with him, and if any one's turban fall off the others should also lay their turbans down. Although these matters are comparative novelties in Islam and have not been received from the first followers of the Prophet, we must remember that all novelties are not forbidden, but only those which directly contravene the Law. For instance, the "Tarawih," or night-prayer, was first instituted by the Caliph Omar.

The Prophet said, "Live with each man according to his habits and disposition," therefore it is right to fall in with usages that please people, when non-conformity would vex them. It is true that the Companions were not in the habit of rising on the entrance of the Prophet, as they disliked this practice; but where it has become established, and abstaining from it would cause annoyance, it is better to conform to it. The Arabs have their own customs, and the Persians have theirs, and God knoweth which is best.

"Whosoever knoweth the power of the dance, dwelleth in God" Sacred Dance has nothing to do with a specific dance style or with particular body techniques. The dancer moves in a way that unites his or her Mind, Body and Spirit with a Higher Spiritual Energy. It is not of importance whether we call this energy "God", "The Creator", "The Great Spirit", "Nature", "The Cosmos" or anything else. What is important is that these results in the dancer feeling spiritually uplifted and filled with joy. Dance is clearly one of the earliest forms of worship. Cave art from early prehistoric times onwards bears witness to the power of the dance. The paintings and engravings occur worldwide. In the western part of Arnhem Land in Australia a cave painting shows two men playing instruments to accompany the dance.

A rock shelter at Cogul near Lenda in Catalonia, Spain portrays a group of nine women. They are wearing knee length skirts and are dancing round a small naked male figure. The State of Madhya Pradash in India has abundant rock art depicting dancers and musicians. The caves in Tassili Algeria have paintings of female dancers and the Etruscans in 500 BC depicted dancing in wall frescoes. Certain dances mimic animals or are aimed to ensure that something happens. For example hunters in ancient times are shown in cave paintings dancing wearing animal skins and masks. We can safely assume that this was to ensure good hunting. Dances miming the gathering of the harvest must also be of ancient origin. As time passed, such dances have become folk dance rather than sacred dance. Sacred Dance is often preceded by elaborate secret preparations such as bathing, avoidance of certain foods and drinks and from sexual intercourse. There may be periods of intense prayer and the taking of trance inducing substances.

One of the best documented European sacred dances is that connected to the cult of the Greek god Dionysus. The rituals in his honor included orgies, the sacrifice of animals, copious wine-drinking and trance dancing which continued until the dancers collapsed with exhaustion. Judaism had no problem with dance being connected to worship. Psalm 150 for example:- "Praise ye the Lord... Praise him with the timbrel and dance". King David is said to have whirled before the Ark of the Covenant. In the Talmud dancing is described as being the principal function of angels. Dance was part of the service in the early Christian church. It took place in the choir and was led by the bishop. Today there are Christian churches that are reintroducing dance sometimes in a very self-conscious style.

Sacred Dance can be Therapeutic

The Shakers, who were an offshoot of the Quakers, were brought to America from England in 1774 by Ann Lee. A vision had told her that sexual intercourse was the source of mankind's troubles. She established a closed community which practiced self-sufficiency and communal ownership of all possessions. The Shakers had a deep understanding of the aesthetic of simplicity which showed itself in all aspects of their lives. Shaker dances were held in the evening. Men and women entered the hall separately. They marched in on tip-toe and formed two rows facing each other about five feet apart. Men were on the right with the women on the left. The Chief Elder stood in the middle and gave a five minute address. He concluded by saying "Go forth, old men, young men and maidens and worship God with all your might in the dance". Men and women did not intermingle. There were pauses to see if anyone had received "a gift". Then two of the sisters would start whirling like tops with their eyes shut. They continued whirling for about 15 minutes when they stopped suddenly and sat down again.

There are no longer any viable Shaker communities and the dances have died out. A certain number of their hymns, however, continue to be sung in various other churches. An ancient Sacred Dance tradition continues to this day in Turkey, the Middle East and North Africa. The Sufis (who represent the mystical side of Islam) have whirling dances. In Turkey the tradition traces back to Celaleddin Mevlana Rumi who died in 1273. His son organized his followers into the brotherhood of whirling dervishes now known as the Mevlevi. When Ataturk gained political power in the early years of the twentieth century he abolished the dervish orders and turned the monasteries into museums. They were revived in 1957. The significance of the dervish dance is connected to the sun, the moon and the revolving stars. The worshipers wear clothing which has symbolic meaning.

The tall conical felt hats signify the tombstones and therefore the death of the dancers' egos. The white robes represent the shrouds around their egos. The flowing black cloaks symbolize the dancers being trapped in wordly tombs.At the beginning of the ceremony the cloaks are removed to symbolize the worshipers deliverance from the cares and attachments of this world. The dance is accompanied by a reed flute. After a series of rituals the worshipers reach a point where they are all simultaneously whirling with their right hands held palm up to receive the blessings of heaven. They hold their left hands palm down to transfer the blessings to earth. Although non-participants are allowed to view the ceremony the dances remain true Sacred Dances for those taking part and for many of those watching. Dervish music should never be used for secular purposes, especially not to accompany oriental dance. The chants are prayers and should be respected as such.

Today Africa remains rich in the area of traditional Sacred Dance. The Yoruba of Western Nigeria have many traditions of deities dancing. Some are said to be able to dance on one leg. Sango (who is associated with thunder) consulted Orunmila (who is associated with divination and wisdom) as to how he could acquire permanent wealth. Orunmila's advice was for Sango to acquire a splendid costume onto which he should sew as many cuari shells as he possibly could. Cauris were once used as currency and are thus a sign of wealth. People seeing Sango so splendidly dressed would assume that he was wealthy. Orunmila told Sango that he should dance around wearing this outfit. The outcome was that through dancing and asking for alms Sango became very rich.

Sango priests carry axes when in company or on parade. They wear feminine hairstyles, beads around the neck and earrings on festive occasions. The dances for Sango are very fast and athletic. All the deities have their associated dances.

To be unable to dance is to be unable to worship properly. In Ghana I have seen young men dancing in trance and slashing at themselves with razor sharp cutlasses. The ferocious slashing never broke the skin or even left a mark. I have also witnessed Sacred Dances to the deities of the Thunder Pantheon. Here older female cult members wandered among the crowds making suggestive gestures with a wooden phallus. The performance was supposed to be amusing and it was. There were also conjurers on hand changing sand to powdered white chalk.

Anyone could come and watch the dances if they showed the proper respect to the deity. This meant that both men and women had to be bareheaded. The men had to tie their cloths around the waist so that they were bare-chested and women had to tie their cloths under their armpits. Shoes and sandals had to be removed. West African Sacred Dances tend to be danced outdoors at night. The dancers come into the dance area which is usually circular and leave it as they see fit. They may all be dancing the same steps but each dancer expresses them in his or her own way. Everyone dances as a group but has their own "space" within it. The dancer and the choreographer are one and the same person.

Africa stands in grave danger of losing its Sacred Dances due to the dwindling number of people adhering to the traditional religions. Only cult members may dance the Sacred Dances. Members of Christian churches and Followers of Islam have always, not unsurprisingly, been expressly forbidden to take part in any Sacred Dances and the number of converts is increasing. Some Christian churches allow a certain amount of drumming and dancing during services. Both the drumming and dancing have little "life force" or visual and aural interest. Musicians are beginning to create new genuinely African Sacred Songs for the church. If anyone knows of choreographers working to create authentic African contemporary Sacred Dance I would love to hear about it.

The cults need younger members. If they fail to materialize then the Sacred Dances will not evolve within their true context. The dances will either die out or become shadows of themselves as social dances danced by all and sundry simply for pleasure. The music is a subject in itself. If you are interested in African Rhythms you try and get hold of "An Approach to African Rhythm" by Dr Seth Cudjoe published by the Institute of African Studies, University of Ghana, Legon. The Sacred Dances of Bali, Indonesia are a beautiful prayer made manifest. No religious ceremony is complete without music and dance. Wali are Sacred Dances indispensably connected with rituals of the same name. They take place on the first day of a ritual, in the inner courtyard of the temple. Sanghyang Dedari and Sanghyang Jaran are both Sacred Dances.

Their eyes were wide open but they were said to see nothing. At the conclusion of the dance they were brought out of trance by a white-clad priest who sprinkled holy water on them. Sanghyang Jaran is a very spectacular dance. A young man wears a belt attached to which is a horse-like head woven from coconut fronds. This young man was put into trance by a priest .He then ran behaving like a horse into a fire of coconut husks. He stood still for a while before jumping around after he had moved out of the fire the burning husks were raked together before once again the young man rushed into the fire. The third time he did this he actually sat in the embers and rolled around. At some crucial point, not identifiable to those watching, the young dancer was pulled clear and helped out of his trance.

11

The Spirituality of Islamic Art

Islamic art can effectively convey messages about Islamic culture, the peaceful teaching of Islam, and the contribution of the Islamic civilization to the world. Nasr (1987) notes that 'Traditional Islamic art conveys the spirituality and quintessential message of Islam through a timeless language which, precisely because of its timelessness as well as its direct symbolism, is more effective and less problematic than most of the theological explanations of Islam". The term "Islamic" refers not just to a religion, but also to a culture and a civilization. Most of the current literature in the West and the media, especially after the tragic events of September 11,2001, has depicted Islam as a violent, irrational, and fanatical force. Islamic art speaks a universal language of aesthetics and functions that illustrates the spiritual and peaceful message of Islam. This chapter introduces Islamic art and discusses workshops conducted at middle schools in the San Francisco Bay Area as part of my doctoral internship.

Faith and a Way of life

To fully understand the richness of Islamic art, an introduction to Islam as a faith and a way of life is necessary, as it under- scores the values and the expressions found in Islamic art. The whole story starts in a cave outside the city of Mecca, in Arabia, in the year 610 CE. where a 40-year-old man is meditating and looking for answers to questions about life and the universe. A voice comes from nowhere, telling him to "recite [read] in the name of your Lord." The voice was from the archangel Gabriel, the man was Muhammad, and the words were God's words that later became what we know as the *Quran.* The Arabic word "Islam" means to achieve peace—peace with God, peace within oneself, and peace with the creations of God through submission to the will of God and commitment to His guidance. Prophet Muhammad did not consider this a new religion, but a continuation and fulfillment of the same basic message that was revealed by God (Allah, in Arabic) to other prophets before him (Abraham, Moses, Noah, Jesus).

Development Information

During the life of Prophet Muhammad, the first mosque was the house of the Prophet himself, in Medina, the city where he settled after the hijra or hegira (emigration from Mecca to Medina in the year 622 C.E.). This date marked the beginning of the Muslim calendar and era. The Prophet's mosque, its elements and functions, became a model and archetype for later mosques. When the Prophet returned to Mecca taking over the holy sanctuary and declaring his devotion to Islam, he destroyed the idols that were placed in or around the sacred Kaaba (the cubic house built by Abraham and his son Ishmael), because people were worshiping these stone statues. This event marked a tradition regarding the representation of living beings and figurative images in Islam that continues to be interpreted in many different ways.

Islamic Art

Is it the art of people who belong to Islam, or is it art that serves Islam as a religion? Is it art produced during the Islamic civilization? Grabar (1987) defines Islamic art as the art produced by "a culture or civilization in which the majority of the population, or at least the ruling element, profess the faith of Islam". Many scholars have also noted that the artist who actually produced a work of Islamic art may or may not be a Muslim. Islamic art "not only describes the art created specifically in the service of Islam, but it also characterizes secular art produced in lands under Islamic rule or influence, whatever the artist's or the patron's religious affiliation". Nasr (1987) suggests that "without the two fountains and sources of the Qur'an and the Prophetic barakah [blessing] there would be no Islamic art". He defines Islamic art as "the result of the manifestation of Unity upon the plane of multiplicity".

Nasr has made a clear connection between Islamic art and Islamic spirituality through the Divine Revelation. For the purpose of this chapter, my own approach to defining Islamic art is based on the features and elements of Islamic art, rather than on its religious affiliation, its chronological development, or the land in which it is created. Islamic art contains visual characteristics that make it "Islamic." The three main elements that unify Islamic art across a diverse and large geographical area are: Arabic calligraphy, the use of geometrical patterns, and Arabesque (floral and vegetal motifs).

The Art of Writing in Islamic Art

The use of Arabic calligraphy represents one of the main unifying elements of Islamic art. The term "calligraphy" in Arabic is "handast al-khatt," which can be translated as "the geometry of writing." This association between writing and geometry is established due to the geometric proportioning of the Arabic letters (straight and curved lines). Arabic calligraphy as an art form has survived to date, as can be seen in the work of many contemporary Islamic artists all over the world. In addition to individual calligraphic art pieces, Arabic calligraphy has been used to decorate architectural sites, including sacred and secular places.

Arabic calligraphy in Islamic and Arabic cultures became a highly respected art form and a way to express one's artistic talents. Safadi (1978) writes that: 'The primacy of the word in Islam is reflected in the virtually universal application of calligraphy. Writing is given pride of place on all kinds of objects—objects of everyday use as well as entire wall surfaces, mosque furniture, the interiors and exteriors of mosques, tombs, and al-Kaaba, the most famous sanctuary of Islam."

Arabic calligraphy is closely connected to the Quran, and beautifying it became an art form. The first revelation of the Qur'an regards the pen (Qalam) as a tool to acquire knowledge; it is written that God has taught humans by the pen. "Recite and your Lord is the Most Bounteous, He has taught the use of the pen. Taught man that which he knew not." (Qur'an 96:1-5)

Geometric Proportion of Arabic Letters

The connection between Arabic calligraphy and geometry lies in the geometric principles that play an important role in the proportion of the alphabet. Khatibi and Sijelmassi (1996), note that "the legibility of a text and the beauty of its line require rules of proportion". The rules of proportion are based upon the size of the first letter of the Arabic alphabet, the alif. The alifis a straight and vertical stroke. The Arabic dot, which is the unit of measurement in calligraphy, is the square impression formed by pressing the tip of the calligrapher's reed pen to paper. The height of the a/z/varied from three to 12 dots. The width of the alif was equivalent to one dot.

The Development of Arabic Calligraphy

The Arabic alphabet belongs to a group of Semitic scripts that were developed from the Nabataeans script, which was itself derived from the Aramaic script. Major developments occurred in the writing system of Arabic, including the development of different styles. There are many styles used in Arabic calligraphy, but only six are widely used. These styles include: Kufic, Thuluth, Nasakh, Ta'liq, Deewani, and Riq'a. The Kufic style is noted for its proportional measurements, angularity, and squareness, and as one of the earliest styles to be used to record the Qiir'an. The other five styles are noted for their cursive letters and their use as ornamental scripts. Additionally, other styles were used and developed, including the Tughra', which was used by the Ottoman sultans as their signature.

Zoomorphic calligraphy was also developed in which Arabic letters or words are manipulated and structured into the shape of a human figure, a bird, an animal, or an object. This is also due to the discouragement of figurative images in sacred art and architecture. The use of Arabic calligraphy as an art form and as a major and unifying element in Islamic art and architecture has a symbolic connection to the word of God. The powerful meanings of calligraphic pieces, which contain Quranic verses and prayers, are common in Islamic culture. These pieces are created for either daily use or decoration so that the message is always visible.

Geometrical Patterns in Islamic Art

The use of geometric patterns has been another unifying factor in Islamic art and architecture. Despite the large geographic area that makes up the Islamic world, with its various ethnicities, cultures, environments, languages, and artistic traditions, Islamic art remains united in its use of geometrical patterns. A number of visual features, principles, or characteristic elements are contributing factors to the unity of Islamic art. These principles govern the elements in decorations and ornaments in Islamic art and architecture and are found especially in the use of geometrical patterns.

El-Said and Parman (1976) referred to the use of geometry in Islamic art and architecture as a "unifying concept of composition despite the diversity of materials, forms or styles used". They also traced this unifying concept to all art forms, including "decorative arts, calligraphy, architecture and the composition of music and Arabic poetry". Geometric patterns have several principles and features, including:

1. *Symmetry*: Geometric patterns have a balance and harmony of proportion between their basic structures.
2. *Repetition:* A repeat unit or cell is the base for geometric patterns. This repeat unit can be in the shape of a square or a hexagon.
3. *Scalability*: Geometric patterns can be used in any size and scale. For example, we can see a pattern on an architectural wall tens of feet high, and the same pattern can be seen on a miniature painting a few inches in size.
4. *Adaptability:* Islamic art elements can be employed with many artistic techniques on a variety of media.
5. *Coverage*: Islamic art tends to cover the entire object that is used for the design. Whether the object is a small dish or an architectural wall, Islamic art elements, including geometric patterns, tend to cover the entire object.
6. *Movement:* Patterns in Islamic art and architecture are not static. The interlacing of strands of geometric patterns in complex star configurations and polygons conveys an illusion of never- ending movement.
7. *Frames:* The majority of geometric patterns are framed or placed within a pre-calculated surface or framed object.

Structure and Construction

Geometric patterns vary in their complexity and design, from simple shapes to very complex polygons and stars. They are constructed from basic elements such as triangles, circles, squares, stars, and polygons. Issam El-Said (1993) offered a theory that Islamic geometrical patterns are based on the

"Square and Hexagonal Repeat Unit and the Root Two and Root Three System of Proportion." A circle can be divided into four, or multiples of four, equal parts; geometric patterns are derived from the resulting shapes. This is what El-Said refers to as "the Root Two system." The other method, which he calls "the Root Three system," is based on dividing the circle into six, or multiples of six, equal parts. One of the traditional practices in constructing geometric patterns in Islamic art and architecture that has survived throughout the centuries is the art of "Zillij" (pronounced "ze-leej").

This technique is based on cutting recognizable shapes to make up certain geometric patterns. Since this practice is widely used in Morocco, it has been referred to as the art of "Moroccan Ceramics." The Zillij shapes are cut from glazed tile and then arranged like a jigsaw puzzle to form sophisticated patterns that can be seen covering the walls and floors of mosques, homes, and schools.

Interpretations of Geometric Patterns

One of the common misinterpretations of the use of geometry in Islamic art and architecture is that it was forced on the Muslims because of Islam's discouragement of figurative art representing living beings. Abas and Salman (1995) state that Muslims recognized in geometry "the unifying intermediary between the material and the spiritual world". Nasr (1987) notes that, the octagon is a result of a rotated square which represents the four elements of the universe (Water, Earth, Fire, Air). Keith Critchlow (1976) has offered a cosmological analysis of geometrical patterns in Islamic art and architecture. He indicated that from the circle originate the three most fundamental figures in Islamic art.

The first and simplest is the triangle, which originates from the expansion of one circle into three circles, and symbolizes "human consciousness and the three basic biological functions: ingestion, digestion, and excretion". Expanding the circle can give us the other two fundamental shapes of Islamic art, the square and the hexagon: "A square often symbolizes earth and its materiality and a hexagon represents heaven." Salma Damluji interprets El-Said's (1993) research on the methodology of geometric proportioning of patterns in Islamic art and architecture, his designs, and paintings as a "conceptual essence of al Mizan," the "balance" mentioned in the Qur'an: "and the sky He exalted and established the balance" (Qur'an LV)".

Arabesque in Islamic Art

Another distinctive feature of Islamic art is the use of floral, vegetal, and plant forms in a spiral pattern. This has been also called "arabesque," a term that refers to an ornament or style that employs flower, foliage, or fruit to produce an intricate pattern of interlaced lines. The arabesque motifs that are used in Islamic art and architecture underwent various changes and developments from pre-Islamic cultures and civilizations to what they are today. The splitting of stems in arabesque designs produces a series of "counter-poised, leafy, secondary stems which can in tura split again or return to be reintegrated into the main stem".

A Divine Presence

The Qur'an, which has many references to plants, trees, flowers, and the beauty of nature, was also decorated with floral and plant motifs as an appreciation for God's creations. This has also been interpreted as the "Divine Presence", and an indication to Heaven's paradise with its fruit trees, flowers, and plants. Verses from the Qur'an that referred to nature have also inspired the use and the development of floral and vegetal motifs.

Islamic Art Projects and Class Activities

The information provided above was used to structure a series of workshops that included art projects and class activities at the Arab Cultural Center and Aptos Middle School in San Francisco. To introduce the students to the elements and features of Islamic art, six workshops were conducted. The first workshop was an introduction to Islamic art by presenting art samples for appreciation and to enable the students to recognize the elements of Islamic art. In the second workshop, the use of geometric patterns was introduced through art projects and exercises. Foam core boards cut in squares resembling ceramic tiles were used for the exercises. The exercises were based on geometric shapes such as squares, circles, and polygons. This workshop allowed the students to duplicate existing geometric patterns by following step-by-step procedures. It also allowed for their own creativity by providing them with the tools to create their own patterns and colors using grid paper and repeating units.

Arabic calligraphy and an introduction to the Arabic language and its use as an art form in Islamic art was introduced in the third workshop. Examples of calligraphic art pieces were shown to the students, including manuscripts, objects for daily use, and architectural decorations. An art project was assigned to the students in which they create their names using Arabic calligraphy styles. Because all students did not know Arabic, a chart of the Arabic alphabet and the equivalent English sounds and translation was given to the students. In the fourth workshop, arabesque was introduced through tracing and coloring exercises. Examples of ceramic plates with arabesque motifs were shown to the students for appreciation and recognition of floral, vegetal, and leaf scrolls. Round paper plates and samples of arabesque patterns and motifs (in outline formats) were provided for the students for tracing purposes as an introduction to drawing their own motifs and patterns.

Materials, techniques and craftsmanship used in Islamic art were introduced in the fifth workshop. Color and grid paper was used to introduce the students to the art of "Zillij." The art activities involved redesigning and cutting recognizable shapes from a Moroccan wall pattern and then re-arranging the shapes in a geometric pattern. The last workshop concentrated on Islamic architecture by using the mosque as a case study. The interior and exterior elements of the mosque such as the minaret and the dome were introduced in coloring and drawing exercises. This work shop also included examples of Islamic architectural sites and the use of elements introduced in the previous workshops in the decoration and design of these sites.

The workshop earned positive evaluations from both the Arab Cultural Center and Aptos Middle School. After the presentations al Aptos Middle School, a teacher commented that the students "were especially interested in the history of this beautiful art form." The projects helped all the students in their art appreciation and also in understanding the mathematics behind the geometric patterns and other elements in Islamic Art. The art teacher noted that the students immediately "noticed the symmetry, repetition, and scaling in many of the designs."

Consistency and Variety

Islamic art has a recognisable aesthetic signature that somehow manages to express itself across an entire range of productions. The 'language' of this art, once established, was readily assimilated by each of the different nations and ethnicities that were brought within the Islamic sphere. Assimilated and built upon, because every region, at every period, produced its own versions of this super-national style. This extraordinary consistency of styles and artistic preferences in the Islamic world clearly derive from a deeper, social consistency.

All Muslims hold to the same basic system of belief, all are familiar with the customary religious observations, and all – despite national and ethnic differences and rivalries – felt themselves to be Muslim first and foremost. This strong sense of identity and continuity tended towards a high degree of social, and artistic, conservatism. As a result, many forms and artistic concepts remained unchanged over the centuries - on the other hand, Islamic art has constantly demonstrated its capacity for the creative reinterpretation of accepted forms. Much of the art of Islam, whether in architecture, ceramics, textiles or books, is the art of decoration – which is to say, of transformation.

The aim, however, is never merely to ornament, but rather to transfigure. Essentially, this is a reflection of the Islamic preoccupation with the transitory nature of being. Substantial structures and objects are made to appear less substantial, materials are de-materialised. The vast edifices of mosques are transformed into lightness and pattern; the decorated pages of a Qur'an can become windows onto the infinite. Perhaps most importantly, the Word, expressed in endless calligraphic variations, always conveys the impression that it is more enduring than the objects on which it is inscribed.

Symmetry and Geometry

Another familiar characteristic of this art, which must also express something fundamental to the Islamic spirit, is its predilection for orderly, symmetrical arrangements in general and for purely geometrical decorative forms in particular. The influence of both religious and philosophical ideas on this aspect of Islamic art was examined earlier, but the abstract, ideational nature of symmetry and geometry clearly fit with the Islamic taste for idealistic otherworldliness. From a purely doctrinal viewpoint, geometrical designs, being free of any symbolic meaning (which is the case in Islamic art), could convey a general aura of spirituality without offending religious sensibilities. In addition, the purity and orderliness of patterns and symmetries could evoke a sense of transcendent beauty which, at best, would free and stimulate the intellect (rather than trap it in the illusions of mere representation).

There is a certain disregard for scale in Islamic art that derives from this perception. Similar kinds of patterning, for instance, might be found on a huge tile panel or on a bijou ornament. This is because decorative effects, in an Islamic context, are never mere embellishments, but always refer to other, idealised states of being. In this view, scale is almost irrelevant. For similar reasons Islamic ornemanistes usually opted for a-centric arrangements in patterning, avoiding obvious focal points – a preference that resonates with the Islamic perception of the Absolute as an influence that is not 'centred' in a divine manifestation (as in Christianity), but whose presence is an even and pervasive force throughout the Creation. A further analogy can be drawn between the patiently created repeats of the 'infinite' pattern (in all its varieties), and the familiar and unvarying customs of Moslem religious observances. In an Islamic context repetition is not tedious; on the contrary, it connects to the world of the spirit.

Whether in a religious setting or not, the work of Muslim artist/craftsmen always manages to convey a certain integrity, even nobility. In fact the distinction between art and craftwork is largely irrelevant in the Islamic world, but even when their works demonstrated surpassing skill and inspiration, the practitioners tended to remain anonymous. This is not surprising; in a culture whose ideal was submission to the will of Allah, it was quite natural to submit creative individuality to a perceived higher notion of beauty.

Earlier Islamic Art

It was seen earlier that the Umayyad's were the first dynasty to rule the newly-established Islamic Empire (from the mid 7th- mid 8th centuries; 41-132 AH). During this early period, which was marked by conquest and consolidation, such art and architecture that was commissioned drew on pre-Islamic traditions (primarily those of Christian Byzantine and Sassanian Persia). Even so, there are clear signs of the emergence of Islamic aesthetic priorities. The main elements of decoration at this time derive from late-classical traditions of stone-carving, floor- and wall-mosaic and wall-painting, but plaster decoration, introduced from the Hellenised East, is also used.

Baghdad, Samarra and Political Fragmentation; 8th - 10th Centuries

The replacement of the Umayyad dynasty by the Abbasid (in 750 CE / 132 AH) saw the removal of the capital eastwards to Baghdad, and later to Samarra. These two great cities were enormously important for the development of Islamic art and culture but, sadly, little has survived of either from the early period. From the fragments of architectural decoration that have been recovered there appears to have been a steady move away from naturalistic treatments, towards more abstract and repetitive forms. The long-established eastern traditions of plaster- and brick-work were adopted as the principle architectural materials in the Islamic East, and were to remain so for the following centuries.

By the early 9th/3rd century, Turks from Central Asia become an ever more dominant political force, and from this time on their tastes exerted a strong influence on Islamic art generally. At the political level, these incursions meant that the Islamic Empire began to fragment into rival factions, with local dynasties establishing themselves in various regions. Islamic art in these turbulent 9th-10th centuries (3rd-4th AH), is represented by local styles, usually based on older precedents, but always bearing the imprint of Islamic tastes and limitations.

Stylistic Maturity; 11th-12th Centuries

As indicated above, the Abbasid Caliphate began to lose political power, and it's Empire to fragment, at the turn of the 10th/4th century. The most serious consequences of this political turmoil, for Islamic culture as a whole, were the accompanying religious controversies and multiplicity of doctrines. In time, in a reverse of the status quo of earlier centuries, Shi'ism became the dominant creed among the various secessionist dynasties, and for a period this interpretation looked set to dominate the Islamic world. But early in the 11th century there began a Sunni revival, which had both religious and cultural aspects. This movement, which saw itself as a restoration of traditionalism, was accompanied by an artistic revival that established many of the enduring forms of Islamic art and architecture – in particular, its canon of decorative art.

The Sunni revival, which began in Baghdad, gradually spread through the Islamic world. As it did so, it became associated with a range of new artistic and architectural forms, which became an identifying mark, a sort of symbolic language. These new stylistic terms were adopted by the Ghaznavids in Khorasan, the Seljuks in Iran, the Zangids in Northern Syria, and the Ayyubids in Egypt. The 'classic' style of Islamic ornament which used distinctive epigraphic, geometric and abstract vegetal elements first came to maturity during this period. This decorative canon was eventually taken up in every part of the Islamic world.

Calligraphy gives a visible form to the revealed word of the Qur'an and is therefore considered the most noble of the arts. It manages to combine a geometric discipline with a dynamic rhythm. Interestingly, none of its many styles, created in different places at different periods, has ever completely fallen into disuse. In the Islamic world it takes the place of iconography, being widely used in the decorative schemes of buildings.

Geometric patterns have always had a particular appeal to Muslim designers and craftsmen. They convey a certain aura of spirituality, or at least otherworldliness, without relating to any specific doctrine. In an Islamic context they are also quite free of any symbolic meaning. Above all they provide craftsmen with the opportunity to demonstrate his skill and subtlety of workmanship, and often to dazzle and intrigue with its sheer complexity.

Vegetal 'Arabesque' compositions are as ubiquitous in Islamic decoration as geometric patterns. It is difficult, without other indications, to determine where or when a particular composition of this genre might have originated. Like geometrical designs, these too are found across the entire range of mediums from book illustration to plasterwork; in ceramics, woodwork, metalwork and ivory-carving, even in carpets and textiles.

Craft-group

As indicated earlier, there was no distinction between 'art' and 'craft' in the medieval Islamic world, just as there was no sharp division between notions of beauty and utility. The idea of the brilliant, lone individual artist was also absent. These are modern concepts. In fact, architectural and artistic productions generally tended to be the work of groups of anonymous craftsmen, whose occupations were usually hereditary and based within guilds or similar craft-groups. However, given that the subject area of 'the decorative arts of Islam' has such an extensive geographical and historical reach, and involved a great variety of craft skills, generalisations of any kind about this broad subject may be misleading. Among such a diverse range of artistic traditions there were bound to be huge variations in working practices, social status, and indeed of expressive intent, in so many and varied creative processes.

By comparison with life in the modern world, medieval Islamic society was highly conservative. We can imagine that working practices, just like the designs and motifs that were used, often persisted for generations with little change. There was no formal training; skills were acquired in the workshops, and were often handed down from father to son. The apprentice/master relationship was usually regularised however, and there is evidence that craft-groups were formed into guilds (which had similarities with the trade-guilds of medieval Europe). It seems also to have been the case that some of these guilds (in some periods at least) were affiliated to religious groups. Details of this kind are naturally difficult to uncover, as they tended to be bound up with the mystique and protectiveness of what were essentially closed professions. It is of more than passing interest though, that these religious connections were usually associated with Sufi fraternities, whose mystical outlook had been imbued with Neoplatonic concepts.

The production of specialised goods, and the particular skills involved, were often localised, but these skills often took artisans far away from their home. Occasionally these movements were less than voluntary. In the turmoil of war craft-skills were generally prized as a form of booty and artisans could be carted off to the victor's base, sometimes en masse. Since the ruling power was usually the greatest patron of arts and architecture, it often happened that new artistic movements were initiated in this way. The dynasty founded by Timurlane was perhaps the most famous example of this effect. It occasionally happened that skilled craftsmen were welcomed as refugees after fleeing invasions and wars. The relative security of Fatimid Egypt attracted many mid-eastern artisans during the turbulent 11th/12th centuries, much to the cultural benefit of Cairo.

The transfer of skills and knowledge as a result of migrations and conquest is of course a time-honoured process. Huge numbers of skilled artisans from various traditions were brought into the Islamic fold as a result of the early conquests, and in the course of time these skills became part of the background of Islamic culture. But there was one craft technology in particular that was acquired in this way that had a profound effect on the course of Islamic civilisation on many levels (including the visual arts). This was the manufacture of paper.

Role of Paper in Islamic Art and Architecture

Paper was a Chinese invention that had spread to Central Asia and Khurasan prior to the Islamic conquests of those regions. As soon as Islamic rule had been established in this eastern end of the Empire the usefulness of this product for bureaucratic and military purposes must have become obvious. The precise history of the uptake of this invention is somewhat hazy, but what is quite certain is that the relative cheapness and ease of production of paper ensured its rapid spread throughout the Islamic world during the 9th and 10th centuries (3rd/4th AH) – and that it transformed societies wherever it appeared. Paper was soon pressed into service by the Baghdad Caliphate, where it greatly facilitated their centralised rule, and Baghdad itself became one of many important centres of paper-making.

As paper became available throughout the Islamic world it was gradually adopted by artists and craftsmen. This usage began, naturally enough, among visual artists of higher status, calligraphers and those involved in the 'arts of the book'. The use of paper was slower among craftsmen at a lower social position (woodworkers, stonemasons, weavers etc,), partly because of the conservatism of their working practices, but also for cost reasons. As it became cheaper and more widely available however, paper became a standard tool in most crafts, and in the process it effected a transformation of the visual arts of Islam. In essence, the adoption of paper into craft-based work-practices introduced a certain separation of the design process from that of manufacture. This was bound to lead to a greater degree of organisation in design right across the board, from architecture through to the humbler crafts of pottery and weaving.

Later this separation of design and making gave rise to a stylistic 'centralisation', such as that exercised by the many Royal studios and workshops that were maintained by the Royal courts. Many dynastic styles were established and maintained in this way. Paper was a common commodity in the Islamic world as early as the 12th century (6thAH) and was already being used by various (usually high-status) artisans to produce preliminary drawings for their work. In the following centuries the use of paper designs was gradually adopted as normal practice. This development undoubtedly fostered stylistic consistency across different mediums and promoted a common currency of style. There are many examples of close similarities between decorative motifs in architecture, book illumination and craft objects.

These is some evidence that the sort of complex patterning and arabesques that are such a characteristic feature of Islamic art first appeared as decorative elements of books (as did calligraphy, of course). As the 'arts of the book' enjoyed the highest status among crafts it seems very likely that these designs would have gradually filtered down to other mediums. It is also clear that once pattern-books and albums of design motifs came into being their repertoire could be applied to a whole range of artefacts, in different settings and at different scales. Designs could be copied, improved upon and, most importantly, they could travel. It would certainly appear that there was, for centuries, a broad awareness and appreciation of the aesthetic aspects of ornament and a lively interaction between different crafts.

The stylistic homogeneity of Islamic art referred to at the beginning of this note may have its foundations in Islamic cultural homogeneity, but its primary medium of transmission was paper. *Islamic Civilization and the Arts* introduces students to various elements of Islamic civilization through a humanities approach. Lessons on art, the mosque, Arabic language and calligraphy, poetry, and music provide students with experience analyzing myriad primary source materials, such as images, audio clips, and sayings of Muhammad, excerpts from the Quran. In each lesson, students learn about the history, principles, and culture of Islam as they pertain to particular forms of art. Hands-on activities encourage students to gain an appreciation for Islamic historical and cultural traditions.

Lesson One, *An Introduction to Islam,* introduces students to the religion of Islam and provides a brief historical background of Islamic civilization to prepare them for the subsequent lessons on Islamic arts. In Part One, students are introduced to a definition of Islam and complete a survey identifying their current perceptions of Islam. Students also read several of Muhammad's sayings and consider what they reveal about the religion and how they might contradict students' initial perceptions. In Part Two, students complete a pre-test to assess their current knowledge of Islam. Through the use of information tables, students create a visual representation of the countries that make up the Islamic world. They then read an informational handout on Islamic civilization as homework. In Part Three, students participate in a class competition, chronologically arranging significant events related to Islamic civilization. They also view several images portraying the Pillars of Islam. To conclude and debrief the lesson, students complete the perceptions survey again and discuss and compare their current responses with those from the first survey. Finally, students compare and contrast Islam with other civilizations and religions.

Lesson Two, *The Role of the Mosque,* introduces students to the mosque through its history and physical features to help them better understand its significance within Islam. The lesson begins with a general discussion about places of worship. Students learn about Islamic worship and the significance, history, and features of the mosque before comparing Islam with Christianity and Judaism. They deepen their understanding through personal association and connection by visiting a local mosque or taking a virtual tour of a mosque. Students reflect on their experience in a short essay. They then learn about the variation among the physical structure of mosques and how that variation reflects the diversity of cultures in which Muslims live. Students view images of mosques from around the world and complete research and presentations on mosques from various regions.

Lesson Three, *Islamic Art,* is an introductory exploration of Islamic art and architecture. Through studying, analyzing, and comparing and contrasting various works of art, students learn about Islamic spirituality and civilization, and their influences on art in other societies. In Part One, students view 11 images relevant to Islamic art and record their initial impressions. These impressions are collected and revisited at the end of the lesson. Students then learn about basic aspects of Islamic art through an informational handout. They view the initial set of images a second time and discuss each one. In Part Two, students apply what they have learned about Islamic art through viewing a second set of images of both Islamic and non-Islamic art. Using what they have learned through handouts and class discussions, small groups study images, write educated descriptions and analyses of each item, and present their findings to the class.

In Part Three, students choose among three art projects to demonstrate what they have learned about Islamic art. In the first project, they reference the Islamic art they have studied and create their own work of art with symbols, motifs, and colors that are of personal significance. In the second project, they take photographs of or sketch objects around their homes or school that remind them of Islamic art and architecture. In the third project, they take photographs of or sketch works of art around their homes or school that reveal information about the civilization in which they live. Students present their projects to the class and, if time allows, to other classes. To debrief this lesson, students revisit the questions from the beginning of the lesson and see how their opinions of Islamic art may or may not have changed. They also discuss what art can reveal about a society and its values.

Lesson Four, *Arabic Language and Calligraphy*, introduces students to Arabic, one of the most widely used languages in the world. By engaging in a range of activities, they will learn about the significance of the Arabic language, particularly its written form, in Islamic history, traditions, and culture. In Part One, students read an informational handout on the Arabic language for homework and answer discussion questions. Then, students engage in a map activity that shows how Arabic has spread throughout the Middle East and beyond. Once students understand the language's prevalence in the world, they learn about the influence Arabic has had on different languages through an activity that focuses on Arabic loanwords used in English. In Part Two, students read and discuss a handout on Arabic script and calligraphy. Upon sharing answers to the handout questions, they view a slide show of art objects that utilize Arabic calligraphy. Applying what they have learned through handouts and class discussions, students' document their thoughts on each item presented. In Part Three, students study excerpts from the Quran in two ways. First, they view Quranic pages that have been written in different calligraphy styles in different time periods and places. In groups, they discuss the similarities and differences among these images. Second, they analyze selected text from the Quran and draw connections to Islamic beliefs.

Lesson Five, *Islamic Poetry*, provides students with the opportunity to gain more knowledge and understanding of Islam through the medium of poetry. In Part One of this lesson, students read and analyze poetry written by poets from around the world and try to determine which is an Islamic poem. They also brainstorm a list of their inferences and conceptions about Islamic poetry. In Part Two, students are introduced to Islamic poetry through an informational handout. Through an analysis of several poems, students consider what poetry reveals about Islamic spirituality. They interpret poems written by some of the most famous and revered Islamic poets throughout the history of Islam. In Part Three, students read Islamic poetry independently and select their favorites to include in an anthology project. Students also compose their own poems expressing what they have learned about Islam. In addition, they write commentaries on each of the poems included in their anthologies. To conclude the lesson, students reflect on what they have learned and compare their initial conceptions in Part One with the knowledge that they acquire by the end of the lesson.

In Lesson Six, *Islamic Music*, students learn to appreciate Islamic music. By listening to and comparing and contrasting music and musical instruments across the

Islamic world, students draw conclusions about how Islamic music has influenced and been influenced by various cultures. In Part One, students listen to a clip of the Muslim call to prayer. They then consider the importance of music in society in general. Through an informational handout and class discussion, students become familiar with the history, role, and characteristics of music in the Islamic world. In Part Two, students are introduced to musical instruments common in Muslim countries and listen to audio clips of each instrument's sound. They explore various types of religious music by reading an informational handout and listening to audio clips of religious and devotional songs. In Part Three, to conclude the lesson and emphasize the diversity and unity of music in the Muslim world, student's research and present group work on regional music. They demonstrate their understanding through a writing assignment comparing and contrasting regional music of the Islamic world.

Oliver Leaman has written yet another challenging and iconoclastic work. Perhaps the most surprising result of this intriguing (and it must be said infuriating) work is that he denies not only that there is such a thing as Islamic art but also that consequently there is no Islamic aesthetic. This might well be disturbing for a reader who has picked up a volume that purports to introduce the notion of Islamic aesthetics! In fact, this book does nothing of the sort; it deconstructs naïve concepts of Islamic art and its appreciation but does not offer an alternative aesthetics. Leaman's key claim (which may seem laudable) is that one ought to move away from essentialising and objectifying disciplines in Islam. Just as philosophy is philosophy, art is art. The adjective 'Islamic' does not qualify anything but merely obscures, occludes and insists that one needs some special training to 'appreciate' it. In a sense this is worrying news for the Islamic art historian. But the real question to consider is whether it is true: is there such a thing as Islamic art? Is there a particular Islamic aesthetics? In order to answer this question, we need to reconsider Leaman's argument and his actual aim in making it, which seems to me to be breaking the closed shop of Islamic art historians and snatching the aesthetic prism away from romantic visions of the 'essential spirituality of Islamic art'.

Leaman begins with setting his sights upon Islamic art historians. He takes them to task for a number of misconceptions. First, by qualifying their objects of inquiry as Islamic they do not take those objects seriously as art. Second, they insist on a particular training in Islamic civilisation to understand what they call Islamic art. Third, and perhaps most importantly, they offer no serious aesthetic theory. These attacks will certainly come as a shock to a number of Islamic art historians who would certainly refuse to admit any of these points. Like Leaman's earlier attack in the early 1980s on historians of Islamic philosophy, this present attack may apply to some practitioners but cannot really be applied to the majority. As before, Leaman's iconoclastic zeal destroys far too much.

Leaman's work is divided into nine chapters which all share a particular theme. The wrong-headed ways in which people approach Islamic art are merely symptomatic of their more general mistaken analyses of the Islamic faith, Islamic thought and Islamic civilisation. Most of these relate to the sin of essentialism in which Islamic studies specialists are seen to be so heavily implicated. He rubbishes the idea that Islamic art is essentially a spiritual, Sufi meditation upon symbolism in Islam, in particular exemplified by the iconic centrality of the Kaba. Over-enthusiastic symbolic interpretation is an esoterist's art; it does not explain but it merely mystifies. Calligraphy is the Islamic art par excellence; another mistake that renders other art-forms somewhat inauthentically 'islamic'.

Two of these mistakes are directly linked to Leaman's earlier work on Islamic philosophy: al-Ghazâlî is accused of having killed off painting, just as he did with philosophy, and Islamic art is seen as a marginal pursuit to the concerns of Islamic civilisation. However, none of these salient and laudable critiques amount to a proper denial of the possibility of Islamic art, let alone its actuality. The second chapter moves on to a popular motif in the study of Islamic art and creativity, namely the postulation that in Islam only God can create and act. If that is the case, the idea that humans can create and fashion artefacts would seem to be a blasphemy. If God alone is *al-khâliq* and *al-munawwir,* then surely there can be no Islamic art? Leaman articulates this nonsensical contradiction to further his argument against essentialist approaches to Islamic art.

Art cannot be reduced to the playful manipulation of existing symbols. Leaman invokes the related theological debate about secondary causality, that is, whether it is only God who acts in the cosmos or whether humans (among others) are real agents possessing ability, will and action. He suggests that much of the essentialist approach is predicated on the simple premiss that the essence of Islam and its theology is Asharite, rejecting secondary causality, affirming an atomistic cosmos and denying true agency and creativity to humanity. Any student of Islamic intellectual history knows that this is a gross generalisation. But the nature of Leaman's exaggerated argument is that it depends upon the construction of an oppositional position that is extremely flimsy and therefore easy to destroy.

The following chapters develop Leaman's argument by considering particular art forms like literature (including a discussion of the miraculous literary quality of the Qur'an), music, gardening, and architecture. Throughout one perceives the pernicious Ash'arite thought lurking in the wings and one cannot help feeling that this present book owes much to Leaman's earlier work on philosophy. The discussion on the nature of the Qur'an is particularly salient because it encapsulates a particular aesthetic vision since the dogma of the scripture is so closely associated with an aesthetic judgement of its inimitability. Leaman concludes the book with two short chapters on the importance of philosophy and the desire to approach art as art and not as a mere cultural artefact or symbol. He is right to argue that philosophy does indeed determine the ways in which we see the cosmos, how we see it and what exactly it is that we see. This is where aesthetics begin to connect with epistemology.

Each Islamic philosophical tradition has a specific doctrine of interpretation that defines three categories of entities: things in themselves, the world in which they dwell and the words that we use to articulate them. Our very act of seeing is both a representation as well as an act of interpretation. Leaman raises an interesting question about whether there can be an Illuminationist, Peripatetic or Sufi aesthetics of representation. But would that in any case entail a consistent, timeless Islamic aesthetics? The very fact that art is respected (or was at least) in Islamic civilisation is recognition of the importance of representation and interpretation. This is a situation quite unlike the disdain for art in a Platonic utopia. Plato famously criticised art for being a doubled inauthentic imitation: at the first level the thing in this world is already a pale imitation of the perfect form in the higher intelligible realm, and at the second level the artist produces an even paler imitation of the thing in his artistic representation.

To invoke his allegory of the cave, it is as if the artist lives within a further cave and is hopelessly remote from reality. Islamic theologians and philosophers did not on the whole have such an austere disregard for things in this world or for the possibilities of beauty here. If anything, Islamic thought can (another gross generalisation yes) be considered to have an optimistic approach to the possibilities of knowing what exists and to recognise that this world and things that exist in this world possess reality as well. Two essentialist slogans (one aesthetic and the other theological albeit with a meaningful message within them) are worth bearing in mind: God is beautiful and loves beauty (as the famous aphorism/tradition has it), and this world is the 'best of all possible worlds'. Can one possibly forsake art when the theologian insists that God does not forsake the world? Would we want to live in such a disenchanted and alienated world?

Leaman's book does raise some interesting questions: is there such a thing as Islamic art? Can Muslims countenance a secular art? Whither the study of philosophy in Islamic culture? Can one produce an aesthetic theory that applies to Islamic civilisation? These are important intellectual matters that ought to exercise Muslim minds. Perhaps because of the nature of the present world situation, Muslims (especially Muslim thinkers) seem to be in such a state of siege that discourses beyond the practicable and the tangible seems to be anathema. But intellectual life sustains and nurtures. The intellectual and cultural products of a civilisation are indispensable aspects of its identity and its sustaining power. It is thus more crucial than ever that Muslims regain the significance of ideas and struggle in the global market of ideas and for this jihad a proper understanding of philosophy (including aesthetics), its historical development and its commitment are more important than ever before. This reviewer has no straightforward answers to offer; all that he can do is to indicate the questions that he thinks are worth pursuing. Such a pursuit of doing well (following the old Zoroastrian saying call it 'thinking, speaking and acting well') increasingly becomes one of the few resources left to our humanity.

'There is No God but God'

From its very inception the Islamic mission was dedicated to a revival and purification of the 'religion of Abraham', that is to say, the Judeo-Christian tradition. It adopted the strict, monotheistic credo of the Old Testament, and was hostile to the paganism that was still flourishing in Arabia. Muhammad's first act, following his acceptance as a religious leader by the townspeople of Mecca, was to destroy the three hundred and sixty idols around the Ka'bah. Up to this time

Mecca had been an important centre of pagan pilgrimage. Like so much else in Islam, this excoriation of idolatrous practices was a clear continuation of the Biblical prophetic tradition - but Islam brought a new understanding of its basic religious principles.

The Islamic rejection of any form of idolatry is bound up with its rejection of any notion of divine intercession. The individual has a direct line to God; ultimately, redemption and damnation are individual matters. The Islamic attitudes towards images and imagery (a subject to which I shall return) have always been concerned with the purity of the human/divine relationship. The worship of idolatrous images, in this view, is therefore both delusory and useless. For other imagery, interpretations vary, but in general, representations that do not seek to create an illusion, or pretence of reality, are acceptable if kept away from any place of prayer.

The Qur'an

The Qur'an, by comparison with the Jewish Book of the Law, has very little to say about images. The Torah makes numerous and quite explicit prohibitions against figurative imagery of any kind. By contrast, the few references to idolatry in the Qur'an are not directed to figuration as such. The Jewish horror of divine representation extends even to the accidental creation of images, and the inadvertent bowing before false gods. This extreme image-phobia led to a culture in which art had a greatly reduced role. This is very obviously not the case in Islam. Islamic concepts, whilst regarding pagan idolatry as an abomination, rarely expressed the same abhorrence of non-religious imagery. In fact, prohibition of iconography was almost unnecessary in this cultural setting - the confession of Muslim faith includes the declaration that 'There is none like unto Him', reflecting the Islamic concept of an absolute and eternal Creator who is, by implication, utterly beyond representation.

In other words, iconoclasm is bred into the very bones of Islam. Non-Muslims have always made much of the supposed Islamic ban on images as a prime determining factor of Islamic art. In reality, representational art was never suppressed, except in the strictly religious field – in any case such a purely negative influence could not in itself account for the many positive aspects of Islamic aestheticism. The Qur'an constantly reiterates the transcendent and inaccessible nature of Allah, with the implication that the Divine Nature can only be experienced through the Divine Word. For this reason there is no equivalent in Mosques of the sort of iconography found in Christian Churches. But its place is often taken by quotations from the Qur'an, which can be quite extensive, and which gave rise to the rich traditions of Islamic calligraphy as an elevated form of architectural decoration.

Various other Qur'anic themes have contributed to Islamic artistic sensibilities, including the perfection of the Creation; 'Thou seest not in the Creation of the All-Merciful any imperfection' (Qur'an 67:3), the divine quality of light; 'Allah is the light of heavens and the earth' (Qur'an 35:24), and a pervasive sense of other-worldly esotericism 'With Him are the keys of the secret things; none knoweth them but He' (Qur'an 6:59). Each of these qualities contributes to the well-known Islamic preoccupation with the dissolution of matter, for the hints of infinity in the patterns of which it is so fond and for the sense of space that it so often seeks. The aim seems always to escape imprisonment within earthly forms. The unwillingness to accept the 'counterfeits' of representation also account for this cultures preferences for abstraction in its decorative schemes.

Traditions (Hadith)

The Revelations that comprise the Holy Qur'an are, of course, the foundation of Islam, but the recorded sayings and deeds of the Prophet, the Hadith, constitute another body of religious texts. The hadith do not have the scriptural authority of the Qur'an, indeed they have varying levels of authenticity, but they are an important secondary source of religious guidance. There are various hadith that refer to artistic creation. The most notable of these records Muhammad as saying that 'No angel will enter a house in which there are images'. Although this has been interpreted as an injunction against figural representation by more puritanical elements, it was almost certainly directed against household idols. Another Hadith warns the maker of images that on the Day of Judgement he will be required to breathe life into his creations, and on failing will be condemned. But this too was primarily concerned with idolatry.

Although the reservations expressed in these hadith about the portrayal of living things obviously derive from the Jewish tradition, the Islamic interpretation makes a new distinction between vegetable and animal subjects, with the former being allowed, even in Mosques, and the latter banned. There is a similar line of demarcation between flat and sculpted surfaces, expressed in a hadith that disapproves of art forms that 'create a shadow'; this is closer to the Jewish original. These concerns are clearly directed towards representations that try to create an illusion of animate reality, an enterprise that might be interpreted as an attempt to imitate Allah, who alone can create life. It is the case, however, that images of plants were used as decoration from the very earliest period of mosque-building.

Islamic Identity and the Image Controversy

The Islamic stance on the use of images for religious purposes was formed at a time when the Christian Church was involved in its own controversy about the subject. Christianity, like Islam, had originally followed Jewish precepts on the matter of images. In the course of time however this influence had receded, but the various Christian's communities and sects had came to adopt very different views on the subject. In fact there were serious arguments within the broader Church for centuries as to whether it was proper, or not, to use images of Christ, the saints and the martyrs as an aid to worship. Naturally, as in all theological matters, the partisans on either side were equally fervent in their beliefs. Islam encountered this controversy, and was obliged to intervene, when it conquered the Christian middle-East.

From an Islamic standpoint, the Christian use of images in their liturgy, together with the dogma of the Holy Trinity and various other articles of their faith, simply proved the extent of Christian departure from pure monotheism. To Muslims they were all anathema. In 721 (102 AH) the Umayyad Caliph Yazid II ordered all images (including those in mosaic) to be removed from the Churches within his domains, and all coins bearing figures of the Christian Emperor to be replaced with de-Christianised versions. In the process, Islamic primacy (and self-righteousness) was asserted and Christian faith and practice backfooted. The effects of this Islamic iconoclast campaign on the Church, both within the conquered territories and in the heartland of the Byzantine Empire, were to be very far reaching. The loss of vast swathes of their territory to the Muslims had already severely shaken Byzantium.

There were many who blamed the Churches wealth and arrogance for invoking this divine punishment, and the long-running dispute concerning the use of images became the focus of a power struggle, and a virtual civil war, within the remaining part of the Empire. The Iconoclast Controversy raged on for well over a century, involving the Emperors themselves, some of whom were partisans for, others against, Icon-worship. Much blood was spilt in this crisis, which saw a constant fluctuation of fortunes between the opposing factions. In the end the Iconophiles won the day in Byzantium. Icons were restored to the Churches in 843 CE (an event that is still celebrated in the Orthodox Church), and their use has continued right up to the present. For the Muslims, of course, the whole episode provided further confirmation (if any were needed) of the grievous errors accompanying Christian belief.

Mizan, Symmetry and Cosmic Equilibrium

Perhaps the most marked and abiding feature of Islam aesthetics lies in its dedication to symmetry principles. The arts of most cultures use symmetries to a varying degree, for various effects – but none place so quite so much emphasis on the constraints of symmetry, or use it so consistently across the entire range of their artistic productions. Clearly, this aesthetic response derives from some deeply-held intuition on the underlying principles of existence. Classical Greek ideas have undoubtedly contributed to this perception, but the motifs of cosmic equilibrium and the general harmony of the Creation also occur in several passages of the Qur'an: 'The sun and the moon to a reckoning, and the stars and the trees bow themselves; and Heaven – He raised it up and set the balance' (Qur'an 55:5).

This notion of a cosmic symmetry, symbolised by the balance-scales (mizan), extends to ideas of eschatological justice and retribution, a most important feature of Islamic religious belief. On the Day of Judgement good works and misdeeds will be weighed to 'an atom's weight' (Qur'an 99). The Mizan is an important and well-known symbol in Islamic theology – some early literalists took the Qur'anic reference to be an actual celestial entity. Interestingly, the term was also used to denote a ground-plan in architecture, and as a technical expression of musical patterns and rhythmic modes. In fact the introduction of symmetry concepts into cosmological speculation has very deep pre-Islamic roots; the scales were an important religious symbol in both Pharaonic Egypt and Zoroastrianism.

Islamic Paradise (al-Djanna)

The Qur'an refers to Paradise in several suras. The picture that is painted is of a luxuriant, sheltered garden full of sensual delights, all of which are essentially beyond human imagination – 'Gardens of Eden that the All-merciful promised His servants in the Unseen' (Qur'an 19:61). In this exalted place the righteous experience the pleasures of the intellect as well as those of the senses. Not surprisingly, the promise of Paradise became a prominent theme in Islamic preaching. It is also a major influence in Islamic art. In Islam the gratification of the senses and the search for perfection are not incompatible with spirituality. On the contrary, earthly beauty is seen as a pale reflection of the transcendent beauty of the Unseen. In this view it naturally follows that magnificent architecture and exquisite objects can put the believer in mind of the heavenly paradise to come.

There are many direct references to Paradise in Islamic art and architecture, in mihrabs and prayer mats for instance, the image of the Garden is frequently symbolised, and carpets designs are often reminiscent of an idealised garden. Similarly, the use of floral and vegetal decorative motifs in an Islamic context is bound to refer to al-Djanna, however faintly. Beyond these more direct references however, the transcendent qualities of the delights of Paradise have exerted a broader influence across many modes of Islamic artistic expression. The high quality of Muslim workmanship in so many fields - in carpets, ceramics, woodwork, the arts of the book and in all the crafts associated with architecture – are well-known, as are its refined standards of taste. The aim seems always to be towards perfection, of style and execution. At their best, the arts of Islam manage to combine the sensual with the spiritual. In this culture, Beauty, represented by colours and forms, and Perfection, as expressed in the in the production of artefacts, always seem ultimately to refer to the numinousness of the divine.

Bibliography

Armstrong, Karen. *Islam: A Short History.* New York: Modern Library, revised ed., 2002.

Ali, Syed Ameer. *The Spirit of Islam: A History of the Evolution and Ideals of Islam,* with *a Life of the Prophet.* London: Chatto & Windus, 1978.

Bloom, Jonathan and Sheila Blair. *Islam: A Thousand Years of Faith and Power.* New Haven, CT: Yale University Press, 2002.

Booth, E. *Aristotelian Aporetic Ontology in Islamic and Christian Thinkers.* Cambridge, 1983.

Bowker, John. *What Muslims Believe.* Oxford, UK: Onewworld, 1999.

Burrell, D. *Freedom and Creation in Three Traditions.* Notre Dame, 1993.

Burrell, D. *Knowing the Unknowable God: Ibn Sina, Maimonides, Aquinas* (Notre Dame: 1986).

Cook, Michael. *The Koran: A Very Short Introduction.* Oxford, UK: Oxford University Press, 2000.

Corbin, H. *History of Islamic Philosophy,* trans. L. Sherrard. London, 1993.

Craig, E. (ed.), *Routledge Encyclopedia of Philosophy.* London, 1998.

Davidson, H.A. *Proofs for Eternity, Creation and the Existence of God in Medieval Islamic and Jewish Philosophy.* Oxford, 1987.

Elias, Jamal J. *Islam.* Upper Saddle River, NJ: Prentice Hall, 1999.

Fakhry, M. *A History of Islamic Philosophy,* 2nd ed. New York, 1983.

Gibb, Hamilton A.R. and J.H. Kramers, eds. *Shorter Encyclopedia of Islam.* Leiden: E.J. Brill, 1997 (reprint ed.).

Hodgson, Marshall G.S. *The Venture of Islam,* 3 Vols. Chicago, IL: University of Chicago Press, 1974.

Keller, Nuh Ha Mim, trans. *Al-Nawawi's Manual of Islam.* Cambridge, UK: The Islamic Texts Society, 1996.

Leaman, O. *An Introduction to Classical Islamic Philosophy.* Cambridge, 2002.

Marmura, M.E. (ed.), *Islamic Theology and Philosophy.* Albany, 1984.

Nasr, Seyyed Hossein. *The Heart of Islam: Enduring Values for Humanity.* San Francisco, CA, Harper San Francisco, 2002.

Newby, Gordon D. *A Concise Encyclopedia of Islam.* Oxford, UK, Oneworld, 2002.

Peters, F.E. *A Reader on Classical Islam.* Princeton, NJ: Princeton University Press, 1994.

Qadir , C.A. *Philosophy and Science in the Islamic World.* London, 1990.

Renard, John, ed. *Windows on the House of Islam: Muslim Sources on Spirituality.* Berkeley, CA: University of California Press, 1998.

Renard, John. *Seven Doors to Islam: Spirituality and the Religious Life of Muslims.* Berkeley, CA: University of California Press, 1996.

Ruthven, Malise. *Islam in the World.* New York: Oxford University Press, 2nd ed., 2000.

Schimmel, Annemarie. *Islam: An Introduction.* Albany, NY: State University of New York Press, 1992.

Schuon, Frithjof. *Islam and the Perennial Philosophy.* London: World of Islam Festival Publ. Co., 1976.

Sharif, M.M. *A History of Muslim Philosophy,* 2 vols. (Wiesbaden: 1963-6).

Stern, S.M. *Medieval Arabic and Hebrew Thought* , ed. F. Zimmermann, London, 1983.

Stern, S.M., Hourani, H. and Brown, V. (eds.), *Islamic Philosophy and the Classical Tradition.* Oxford, 1972.

Waines, David. *An Introduction to Islam.* Cambridge, UK: Cambridge University Press, 1995.

Watt, M.W. Islamic Philosophy and Theology. Edinburgh, 1962, revised ed. 1985.

Watt, William Montgomery. *The Formative Period of Islamic Thought.* Oxford, UK: Oneworld,1998.

Watt, William Montgomery. *What is Islam?* London: Longman, 1970.

Williams, John Alden, ed. *The Word of Islam.* Austin, TX: University of Texas Press, 1994.

Wolfson, H.A. *Studies in the History of Philosophy and Religion,* ed. I. Twersky, G.H. Williams, in 2 vols. Cambridge, MA, 1973, 1977.

Wolfson, H.A. *The Philosophy of the Kalam.* Cambridge, MA, 1976.

Ziai, H. "Islamic Philosophy," in *The Oxford Companion to Philosophy,* ed. T. Honderich. Oxford , 1955.

Index